About the Book

In, "Naked. This is My Story...This is Our Song...", Dr. Masters has, with finesse and conviction, written a basic primer on personal storytelling. With her own mesmerizing story woven throughout, Dr. Masters successfully connects the real with the surreal. Naked is a story within a lesson and a lesson within a story. More than that Naked is life...life bubbling over with success, tragedy, pain, renewal, failure, transformation, and redemption. It is a guttural look at what it means to be a human being...both contemptible and beyond contempt.

Naked is the true story of Leslie Masters, a 45 year old physician, single mother of three, soccer mom, cheer and gymnastics coach, cosmetic medicine expert, entrepreneur, small business owner, imperfect, spiritual human being. As she tells her story in the first person singular, Dr. Masters lures the reader onto the mindboggling and at times bewitching trail of recovery and discovery.

From DEA officers in her office to mice in her kitchen, Dr. Masters' artistry in storytelling will make you laugh, make you cry and introduce you to emotions you have not known before. With the benevolence and compassion of a trusted friend she holds out her hand and both invites and emboldens the reader to tell the one story that only they can tell... their own story. Dr. Masters reaches deep within the wisdom of the ages and from Plato to Jesus, Buddha to Einstein and Sigmund Freud to Bill Wilson, Dr. Masters helps us transform teachings into "right here, right now" applications.

What makes this book special is that it is wretched, raucous, raw and real. Dr. Masters shows with brutal honesty, courage and sophistication just what "telling your story" is all about. Leslie is bright, articulate, and funny...and what she becomes to the reader is a treasured intimate friend. Before the final page has been turned, Dr. Masters has become Leslie...a flawed, broken, faulty, incomplete member of humanity. The result is a captivating work that is relevant, and even necessary, in the world that we all live in today. Fueled by the power of truth, this is a story that needs to be heard.

NAKED

This is My Story...
This is Our Song...

Leslie Masters, MD

authorHOUSE®

AuthorHouse™
1663 Liberty Drive
Bloomington, IN 47403
www.authorhouse.com
Phone: 1-800-839-8640

First published by AuthorHouse 5/28/2010

ISBN: 978-1-4520-1578-1 (e)
ISBN: 978-1-4520-1576-7 (sc)
ISBN: 978-1-4520-1577-4 (hc)

Library of Congress Control Number: 2010927291

Printed in the United States of America
Bloomington, Indiana

This book is printed on acid-free paper.

To Olivia, Georgia and Sam…
Moment by present moment you prove that love is
manifest in the very core of my being and that it is,
as are the three of you, inseparable from me.
…you nourish me each day with your innocent wisdom.

Acknowledgements:

Mike McCarthy - for cherishing, with me, the grandiosity in all of our dreams large or small and for trudging, with me, on this path to happy destiny. The most ardent "thank you" could never be enough.

Marian McCarthy - for guidance and content editing, your wisdom and experience have been priceless gifts in this process.

Nancy Poole - for all photographic art work, thank you for your willingness to experiment with your media and "tell my story with your artistry".

Contents

Part III: Hitting The Bottom

Part IV: Facing the Facts

Part V: Practicing The Art

Prologue

They say there are no myths associated with the world we live in today. The entire history of the world is rich with magnificent, stirring, sumptuous, elaborate myth and yet they say there is no longer myth that we learn from or live by. They say that the myths of old have grown stale and that we no longer know how to interpret them.

Hmmmm? Well let us see, what exactly is "a myth" anyway? See there, we don't even really know what a myth is. Well, a myth is a story within the bounds of a given society. It is a story that a certain culture tells again and again and again about why they do this or why they do that or why they believe this or believe that. Myths are traditional or legendary tales that tend to be about gods or heroes and they explain some practice or rite or phenomena of nature.

Wow! I always thought a myth was an untruth as in, "What Johnny says is pure myth." Well let me teach by telling a little story...

There once was a wonderful King who ruled over a beautiful peaceful kingdom. His life was wonderful and his people loved him. One day, on a foolish dare, he was badly injured. He survived his injuries but was left with lower extremities that did not work. His handicap rendered him incapable of caring out most of his regal duties and he was forced to delegate these to others to carry out for him. The impotence he felt from his impairment was overwhelming and soon the once gregarious King spent most of his time in seclusion. Isolating himself from all but a few knights whom he would command once in a great while to load him into his boat and so he could fish. The good King's life went on in this manner for many years. Over time he became known as the Fisher

King because it was the only time that he would come out of his chambers was when the knights, on his command, would take him fishing.

The Fisher King grew pale and despondent. Now his resources were many and he had time and again sent knights to the far ends of the earth in search of the grail that would cure him. Despite his efforts none had returned with the cure, the grail. And the days and then years passed by and the King grew restless, irritable and discontented. He was angry and resentful, demanding and willful.

One day a young knight name Perceval arrived at the King's castle stating that he would be willing to travel to the ends of the earth once again in search of the grail to cure the King's injury. He beseeched the King's guards to allow him to speak to the King in order to earn his majesties commission and blessing on the very dangerous journey he was willing to take on the behalf of his King. After much discussion and delay, Perceval was allowed in to speak to the King. The young knight had to hold his breath to keep from gasping out loud at the sight of the feeble, disheveled, bitter man. Young Perceval looked into the King's eyes and despite his desire to ask the King a question he did not for it would be improper for a knight to ask questions so he remained quiet. He gained the Kings commission and set off silently to search for the grail, to search for the cure for his King.

Well dear Perceval traveled high and low and encountered adventure after adventure in his travels. He was robbed, he was beaten by thugs and he was tempted by the finest of women, he was offered riches by other kings to abort his mission and live in luxury forever, but he fought off these demons and remained true to his mission. He searched high and low and traveled through kingdom after kingdom but alas returned home to his Kingdom empty handed. Perceval felt defeated and crushed by his failure to find the grail and he trembled and shook as he waited to face his King.

Once again the feeble, disheveled and angry King sat before him and once again he had to stop himself from gasping at the King's appearance. As he had done many years before Perceval looked into the Kings eyes. This time however, he did not hold back, he could not hold back and so he asked the question, "My dear King, what ails you?" The King's eyes opened slightly wider as he peered into the eyes of this young knight that had just so boldly spoken to him. "I have been injured! I need a cure!" He responded angrily. "No my King that is not what I am asking, I am asking what happened, what it was like. I am asking you to tell me your story." Well the King's eyes softened, they grew moist with tears and he responded, "Will you sit with me? I would like to tell you though I know some of it will be painful to remember. No one has ever asked me to share this with them before."

So Perceval sat and listened and he learned and the dear King told the story and he healed. It was little by little but he healed. When Perceval departed he was richer and wiser. When Perceval departed the King had healed. He had healed from the inside out. His injury remained with him but his soul had been healed because someone had reached out a hand in an act of spontaneous compassion and asked him what ailed him…had asked him to tell his story.

So what is the point of this little story? Well first of all it brings home the power of myth. Was it not easier to read the bold print? Stories and myths make our minds dance. They bring our worlds to life. We all love stories, although few of us take time to listen to them or to tell them. Our lives today simply don't permit it. Storytelling and story listening require a pause and few of us have that kind of time. Our lives are BOOM, BOOM, BOOM, check it off, next task.

Second, I tell this story to point out that we no longer live in Kingdoms. We are no longer members of small societies. How could we have myth when a myth is a story told within the bounds of a given culture. Our culture, our society is the entire world. We are no longer members of isolated little societies. We are members of the world wide web for crying out loud! The world is our community. We are all individuals in the world, not members of isolated cultures.

Our myth, our richness lies in our existence as individual beings in a world community. In a community that is the world, there are no "thems", there are no "other" kingdoms. In our "whole world community" there are just a bunch of "us'". The "us" consists of millions of individuals living their own personal stories, one by one. And those personal stories are what make up today's myth. Compiled into one, our stories are our myth, our legend. Our stories are what we will pass on. They are rich with experience, wisdom and honor. They are raucous and rancid with regrets, misfortune and dishonor. Our stories together have all of the components necessary to make up a myth. They have villains and heroes and mentors and tricksters and guardians and allies. They have adventures beyond understanding. They explain why we do what we do or believe what we believe.

Third I tell this tale because, just as we all have a story to tell, we all have a "Fisher King wound". How do we know if we have a "Fisher King wound"? We simply need to ask ourselves if our outsides always match our insides? Does how we act on the outside match how we really feel on the inside? If the answer is no then you, like all of humanity, have a "Fisher King wound".

We all have a need to heal by telling and a need, like Perceval, to learn by listening. We all have a need to receive spontaneous compassion and we all have a need to give spontaneous compassion. A "Fisher King wound" cannot be healed by the greatest of resources, because it cannot be healed from the outside. It can only be healed from the inside. It can only be healed by answering the question. By answering the question, "My friend what ails you?" The "Fisher King wound" heals by having someone else, in an act of spontaneous compassion say, "Will you tell me your story?"

And then you tell your story and find the compunction and grace to do the human thing and ask another person the question and that person asks another person the question and that person asks another.... and one day someone walks up to you again and says, "My friend what ails you? What happened? What was it like? Will you tell me your story?" And the world community, that we are, is connected, again in a web, of ever expanding, unraveling story that becomes the myth of today as it teaches us and defines us and comforts us and emboldens us to reach out again and again and again.

In the pages that follow I will open myself up to you, my community, in a hope greater than hope that some of you will do the same. And just perhaps someday someone will return to me and ask the question, "My friend what ails you?"

This is my story...this is our song...

Part I:
Feeling The Need

1

The (W)Hole

It was a sunny but brisk day in late September. Just about the time the trees start changing color and the Oklahomans pull out the jackets in preparation for colder weather. Her Oncology Clinic was packed as usual with patients fighting the dreaded "C" word...cancer. She sat perched on a high stool at the bustling nurse's station dictating the last patient's progress note. Her RN rounded the corner with the latest update. She grabbed a pen and paper and without pausing dictation jotted down her nurse's latest report. "7 West needs orders on Mr. Swansen, Alice Carmichael is in the ER, one of Dr. Lynch's patients is having a chemo reaction and your next patient is ready in room 3, labs are on the door." Her mind clicked instinctively, re-dictate this note later, chemo reaction patient first then orders to 7 west then labs on door of room 3. The ER could handle Mrs. Carmichael for now. She slid gingerly off the stool with a slight wince and headed to the treatment room.

The patient was flushed, sweaty and with rapid respirations and heart rate, but clinically stable. "50mg of Benadryl IV, 10mg of decadron IV continue hydration and discontinue chemo for 30 minutes then resume and give over 4 hours instead of 2." Typical allergic reaction, a little reassurance, a little TLC and she'll be good to go. The chemo nurses knew the scenario well. What a job she thought, pumping poison into people to try to save their lives.

How the nurses did it day after day had never ceased to amaze her. She scribbled a quick note, wrote down the orders and turned back toward the clinic.

"Dr. Masters," It was Julie the clinic manager, a sweet, caring woman who had always been willing to step between the doctors and outside intrusions. "Dr. Masters there are two DEA agents with badges out front and they say they need to speak to you." Her heart stopped and then resumed beating faster than it ever had before. She feigned a non-concerned nod though she knew the color had just instantaneously drained from her face. "Could you just show them to my office and tell them I will be in shortly." Her mind went wild and every hair on her body stood upright. What do they know? What could they know? Stay calm she said to herself, it could be nothing. Her whole world was swirling. A wave of nausea came and went and then came again. Her hands were clammy, her heart was trying desperately to jump out of her chest and her mind kept repeating, "God help me, God help me."

She picked up the phone and dialed 7 west and like a robot on auto-drive began to talk. "This is Dr. Masters and I have admit orders for Mr. Swansen.

> *Admit: 7 west for Dr. Masters*
> *Diagnosis: metastatic colon cancer with recurrent ascites*
> *Condition: guarded*
> *Vitals: Q2 hours x 2 then Q4 hours*
> *Allergies: none*

She continued to speak but could no longer hear her own voice. The orders seemed to her to just float out of her mouth in slow motion. Why couldn't she hear herself any more. Though she knew that she was speaking she could not hear her own voice. She jotted down the name Donna so she must have asked to whom she was giving orders though she never heard herself say the words. Again she slid off the high stool cautiously and again she winced. She stared blankly down the hall at her office door. She turned and told her nurse to tell room 3 it would be a few minutes. She didn't hear herself say the words but her nurse nodded and she just assumed that she must have spoken them. As her nurse walked

4

away she felt a dread build up from somewhere deep inside her, a dark, wretched dread like she had never felt before.

"Please God, please God," her thoughts kept saying though she no longer believed that He would answer. She didn't even know what God she was talking to. "Not now God, not now God, not now." Her temples pulsed with pain as she gently made her way down the hall. Her thoughts went to Olivia. My God she has been through so much and has been home in Tulsa for exactly one day. Just yesterday the two of them had flown in from Phoenix, victorious after a 9 month long agonizing custody battle that had finally been settled in her favor. Olivia was back at home at last. It had been 9 months of shear torture since Olivia, her then 10 year old daughter, had decided to live in Phoenix with her dad, a decision that lasted about 4 weeks. The 4 week mistake had grown into a 9 month ordeal when her father refused to allow her to return to Tulsa. Night after night she had listened to her anguished 10 year old baby girl beg to come home. Day after day she watched the wheels of the family court system move inch by excruciating inch. "Please God, not now, please," now the begging was hers and the recipient...an unknown God. Her insides felt hollow and vacuous. There was nothing there but an echoing void.

She entered her office to be greeted by two shiny gold badges both in the shape of a star. The man introduced himself as Steve Washborne, an investigator for the Oklahoma State Medical Board and the woman whose name she didn't hear introduced herself as an investigator for the Drug Enforcement Agency. She shook their hands and tried to act cordial and curious, although she knew in her heart why they were there. She listened as they laid out their evidence. "Who is BD?" the man asked. "She is my nanny." She replied. "Why are you writing her so many prescriptions for oxycodone and oxycontin?" They knew. They knew everything. She walked over to her purse and again winced as she bent down to pull from it a prescription bottle for oxycontin. "These are mine," she explained "They are prescribed to me by a pain doctor." "The prescriptions for BD are for her pain from osteoporosis." Her explanation was weak and she knew it but she continued to insist that the fact that they were on the same meds was purely a coincidence. She refused to give in and continued with her feeble explanations. Their eyes were stern and somehow sad. They left after saying, "Dr. Masters we just want the truth. We are only here for the truth."

The remainder of the day was covered by a heavy fog. She tried to hold it all together but realized that she failed when one of her cancer patients asked her what was wrong and if there was anything she could do for her. She loved her patients, every last one of them. And they loved her. She was determined to be the loving, caring rock that so many of them needed. She vowed to be their hope. "No one has a crystal ball," she would insist "we can't see the future so let's just together do what needs to be done today." She cried with them when the news was bad and rejoiced with them when the tests came back good. She prayed with them in desperate moments and held their hands when words were too difficult to utter. She believed with all of her heart that hope had to die last and when, in the end, that hope did die she would sit with them and their loved ones as they took their final breaths. And today, in her own time of need, one of them had reached out her hand of compassion in return.

The short drive home that evening seemed long as her mind whirled. She was alone, caring about everything and about nothing at the same time. Her mind screamed, "Deny, deny, deny," but her heart knew that it was too late for that. She had been writing prescriptions to her nanny and doubling and sometimes tripling her own dose of oxycontin. Her thoughts raced from, "Shit what a cluster-fuck," to "Our Father who art in heaven." Despite the race in her mind she felt nothing. Blank, empty, hollow. From the outside she had it all, a successful career as an Oncologist, three beautiful children, a husband that also worked as a physician, a beautiful home, financial security; on the inside, however, she had severe chronic pain from a crushed pelvis injury, a daily battle of juggling the balls of being a mother, a wife, a physician and a patient. As she struggled to keep those balls in the air one was clearly falling and upon that one all of the others depended...her health. She knew that if she crumbled the rest of the balls would coming crashing down as well and she knew that she was dangerously close to that fall. No one could help her. No one else could be inside her body and endure the pain for her. There was no escape. Her body felt like a tortuous prison. She had been running a race for so long, pretending she could somehow out run the daggers that pulsed from her sacrum and shot out both hips. There would always be this boot heel grinding relentlessly into lower back. It would not stop. No one could help her. The pain would always be hers and hers alone to endure. Pain doctors helped some. Self medicating helped more. She was running the race but the pain was winning. Now the Drug Enforcement Agency of the United States, the Oklahoma Medical Board and her ex-husband in hot pursuit of their ten year old daughter were chasing her as well. They were all aiming to bring her fragile world crashing down.

Despite the chase from the law, the medical board, despite the threat of losing her job, despite the threat of losing custody of her daughter, the only fear that felt real was the sheer terror of having to get off the medicine that made her life tolerable. Memories of pain and terror and no one to help her flooded her soul. A horror filled her being. Recollections of mind boggling pain and a dark tunnel of no relief enveloped her being. Her world was about to crash and all she could see was a very lonely dark place, alone with pain, torment and agony. She needed help. She arrived home to her husband and three children and said nothing. Just as she experienced the physical pain alone, she would endure this emotional pain alone.

A solution for the pain, that was the crucial ingredient to fixing her mess. There had to be someone, something that could help her. If she just didn't hurt she could find a fix for everything else. She put her babies to bed, walked into her bedroom, closed the door and dialed the phone. Her sister lived in Dallas and was married to a doctor specializing in pain management. Her voice was weak and shaky when she spoke. "Laura, I am in trouble. I need help. I am taking way too much pain medicine and I am afraid to stop. I have been self-prescribing and taking way more than my pain doctor is prescribing and the DEA and the Medical Board are after me. They are going to make me stop taking this stuff and I can't. I am so scared. I am going to be left hurting and alone and no one will help me. I don't want to hurt anymore. I don't want to be left alone hurting. Nobody knows. Nobody understands. Nobody can take this away. I don't want to go to that dark place again."She couldn't feel the weight of all the trouble she was in. All she could feel was the fear, the terror of that dark place where she was all alone and hurting.

By 7 am the next morning she was back in her car on her way to Dallas in search for help. She left her husband with the three kids explaining only that she was going to Dallas to find an answer for the pain. She did not tell him of her other troubles. She held them inside. Pain was something she dealt with alone. Her insides were dark and hollow and full, full of fear both emotional and physical. "Our Father who art in heaven..." she continued to try to find God, to find something, someone to help her bear the burdens. She prayed but felt nothing. There was no God there. She prayed to one God and worshipped another. Her God had become oxycontin. Oxycontin gave her relief. She believed in that god. The God of her youth was harder to believe in. She had become too afraid of the pain to believe in that unseeable God. The amazing power that was in that blue and purple place, that had helped her in the early days felt unreal and very far away. She could not get herself to take that leap in to a faith that believed there was comfort anywhere other than in the narcotic relief.

She made one stop at a local hospital to pick up the latest CT scan of her badly injured pelvis and then just drove on. "Our father who art in heaven hallowed be thy name..." she continued to pray to an unknown God as she drove, alone and scared, feeling everything and caring about nothing. The rest of her world was a fog. The pain, her only world was the pain that soared around her and inside her, the one dragon that she could not slay, the one dragon that controlled everything. She had held it off temporarily but it was now coming in for the kill and was about to bring her world down, it was about to claim victory. She did not know if this beast was named "pain" or "fear of pain", but she did know it had become the foe she could not conquer. It wanted all of her and was about to devour her universe. She arrived at the Dallas pain clinic as the DEA arrived at her sister's front door. She looked at the pain specialists and said, "I need help." The DEA agent looked at her sister and said, "She needs help."

She awoke from surgery in a new place. As she lay in the recovery room she felt a sting on her abdomen but something else was different. The world was strange and somehow foreign. There was an unfamiliar peace and stillness. She squinted and looked around. What was it? Where was she? She breathed in, breathed out. There was no dragon in this room. The pain was gone. She laid there and felt her breath go in and out and for the first time in many years the gnawing was gone. The dragon was gone. The chase was over. Her hand reached done to touch the new bulge on her abdomen. The relief was now inside her. A pump had been placed inside her abdomen with a catheter circling beneath her skin, around her waist and into her spinal cord. For her this was the line of life, the magical potion that had at long last slain the mighty dragon. She breathed in and breathed out, intrigued and seduced by a body that did not hurt. She knew she had other dragons yet to slay, but for now the mightiest beast was at bay.

Day after day I see patients in my cosmetic medicine clinic that have made their way to me because they want to *"feel better"*. They rarely say Dr. Masters can you make my waist smaller or my face tighter or my wrinkles smoother or my tummy flatter, they somehow, unconsciously, unknowingly say *"I just want to feel better"*. I can do what it is that I do which is cosmetic surgery but my own inner voice, my own inner being tells me that what they are looking for is something that I cannot give them. It is something that they already have but have, in our chaotic times, forgotten how to find. They have, like me, become too busy, too conditioned, too swept away in the rush of our body politic that they don't know how to see, to look, to seek, to search and most importantly to listen. The times have become a force so powerful that normal everyday life does not act as a sufficient impetus for us to search for something divergent, something disparate, something different. So often it takes a huge wave of reality to crash into us, slam us ruthlessly into the ground, drag us across the sand and slap us into a state of awareness sufficient enough for us to take heed and to say, "stop, enough, something is not working".

The Magical "It"

Our times have left us with the mindset that we should look for a "fix" for every problem or discomfort that comes our way…a one-time, over-and-done remedy. We have been conditioned to look for the "solutions". And so we strive and work and toil and reach for all of the things that our society says we should want. Most often, what society tells us that we should want, is more…more of anything. If we just had more stuff, more money, more power, more lovers, more oxycontin…were prettier, thinner, sexier or famous or ran in the right crowd. We are all waiting to arrive. When I get the right job, when I drive the right car, when I get just one more degree, when I can build my dream home, when I get the kids through school…then I'll be happy, peaceful and content, then the stars will be aligned and life will be grand.

The truth is that this "more of anything" mentality is not really a quest for "more". Rather, it is a desperate scramble to find something, anything that will *change the way we feel*, that will just make us *"feel better"*. Our solutions, simply stated, are *"feelings fixes"*. They are temporary ways to *change how we feel*. The cruel thing is this, they work, they work to *change the way we feel*. *"Feelings fixes"* titillate us with the promise of sweet serenity, lure us in and for a moment make us *feel better*. Like oxycontin theses fixes take away the pain, they make us *feel better*. They do not, however, address the problem. Like stitches in an infected wound, they close the hole but ignore the festering beneath, the aching within. Patch it up and it looks better but the hole remains and the purulence will not be ignored. "More" *fixes feelings*, but just for the moment. "More" is a stopgap remedy dressed as an insatiable temptress. She will dance for us just outside the firelight, spin around, pirouette and convince us to reach for her again and again and again. "More" will, however, never be enough to heal the hole, to make us Whole.

I love the quote by Albert Einstein, "I want to know God's thoughts…the rest are details." It seems so fitting for where we are today. Just gimme the facts man, save the details for someone else. We have become a "bottom-line society". Produce, consume, work, consume, pledge allegiance in the name of progress, consume. An objective glance at our society today is all it would take to tell an outsider where our priorities are, where our values lie, where our faith is placed. We are believers in progress. We are worshippers of technology. I wonder often, did I just get dropped into, somehow indoctrinated into, this world of techno mania and for progress and progress alone I will work, or am I one of the many inventors of this way of life. Did I choose this or did it happen to me? Am I a victim of a society set in motion before I got here or did I voluntarily join this rodeo, hop on my horse and with a few yeehas and yippees encourage myself and my fellow riders to charge ahead. More is always better. It's a free country and there is no one inside my mind except me so I must have chosen this though I keep wanting to let myself off the hook in some way. I hear this little voice in the back of my head screaming my defense: "I was young, impressionable and easily swayed. I didn't know any better! Peer pressure! I was just going to try it out and then the ride started going so fast that I couldn't get off. I'm a victim of mob mentality." When I listen to myself I am momentarily happy that no one asked me to drink a suspicious glass of kool-aid. Scary!

When, we wonder, did we get to this spot where we quit thinking and just started doing. Just start doing whatever it is that we do with no thought, no direction. At some point we jumped into the river of life and have, since that leap, just been willing to flow with the current. Even when the might of the current has slowed and we have been merely swirling in a gentle tide pool we have somehow lost the where-with-all or the motivation or the will or the strength to steer our own vessels. We remain caught up in some real or imagined current of "otherdom". We are no longer willing or able to guide our own ships or to make our own choices. We don't want to change, we just want to *"feel better"*. It is a strange paradox that in a "Me first"/"It's all about me" society we have surrendered our freedom of choice and joined, voluntarily, a system where our values, and therefore our beliefs, have been given to us. "It's all about me" just so long as "you" think I'm cool and "they" think I've got it going on.

The 21st century has brought with it, break-neck speed, multi-tasking and an intolerance of ambiguity. We want solutions and we are fixated on the answers. "Don't tell me about the labor pains. Show me the baby!" should be our new meditative mantra. Results, results, results. Even as we discuss the idea of this *"just wanting to feel better"* most of us have zoomed past the question and are tempted to read the last chapter…"Just show me the baby!"

The Easier, Softer Way

Why, with all of the wisdom accumulated over centuries and centuries; and why, when this feeling of *"just wanting to feel better"* is indeed universal, do we not know how to fix it? There is an answer, but there is no "fix". The key is this, one must truly, in your heart of hearts and in your soul of souls want it. Most people never want the answer bad enough to hear it. Most people never feel the bittersweet desperation necessary to heed it. Most people chose to spend their lives, *their entire lives*, looking for an "easier, softer way".

Typically, the easier, softer way looks something like this…

Yes, that is for me! I'll take the easier, softer way! I'm not proud; I don't need to prove to anyone that I am capable of the difficult, complex, complicated, circuitous route. Just gimme the facts, in as few words as possible, and I'm good. Are there Cliff notes?

Never mind. I know how to do this deal called life. Breathe in. Breathe out. Yeah that's it. I can do this. All I have to do is eat right, no rocket science here; I just need to eat healthier. I'll make a list of all that I need to eat healthier and go grocery shopping and I'll be ready to go. Health, yes, health will make this hole go away. Let's see; yogurt, boneless, skinless chicken breasts, oh hell, I am really ready to do this thing, let's try a little tofu and a sprinkle of wheat germ. Yikes! I need to stop at The Sharper Image and pick up one of those "magic bullet" smoothie makers and a food scale, yes, a food scale. I need one of those cool digital ones. Brookstone. Brookstone will have those. They have yoga mats too. I want one of those. And I need the latest in exercise stuff like that new machine that works so well that I think you only need to do something like 4 sit-ups a day for 3 weeks to get six-pack abs and those extra cool, top secret nobody-knows-how-they-work-we-have-63-patents headphones *that cancel out all noise. I mean if I'm going to eat right then I should probably get some sort of exercise regimen going too. Heck, health is health, and if it's going to "just make me feel better", give me more. Wheeeww! I'm going to need a massage chair to use with the extra cool, top secret nobody-knows-how-they-work-we-have-63-patents headphones. Okay, let's be real, this is definitely not the "easier, softer way". Duh!? I should get some sort of extra credit or something for this plan. Here I come…healthy, svelte, size 4. As soon as I get there I know that I will "feel better".*

You know, I've been thinking, I shouldn't have to be a size 4 to be happy. If "he" could just love me the way that I am then I know this need to "feel better" would go away. That is it, it is not about health or diet or exercise or size 4 or smoothie makers or head phones. It is about being loved for who I am. If he would just love me right then I would start to feel right. I mean, I say "I love you" and he answers…"What is love but a 'second hand emotion'?" Aaaaahhhh! And he wonders why I can't trust! Who could trust a guy with that kind of response? A little love tossed my way and a few behaviors that I can trust and I think this "feeling better" would happen by itself. And then there is sex, whoa! Don't even get me started. After that one night, I was his perfect sexual mate, like no lover he had ever had before, an innocent vixen…and he expects me to do that every night? Rrrright. If I didn't come with a vagina would he even like me? If he would make an effort he would realize that I'm smart and talented and gifted. I am more than big boobs and a tight ass. I have a brain.

That is it! Who needs love or sex or the perfect mate to "feel better"? Not me, I'm going to develop my mind, hone my skills. I may get a degree or write a bestseller or paint a masterpiece. I just haven't lived up to my potential, which is why I have this insatiable need to "just feel better", this feeling of incompleteness. You just wait until that degree is hanging on the wall. It'll be pretty hard to feel incomplete then……

I want, I want, I want. I need, I need, I need. More, more, more. I need more of whatever drug is currently filling my emptiness, whatever drug is currently completing me---food, love, clothes, sex, risk, money, power, fame, drugs, possessions, status, alcohol, stuff. Just keep pouring it in. It helps for a time, and then I'm empty again. My desires are endless. Each desire promises to be the answer. More, more, more. I'm insatiable, like an addict wanting, craving, needing more and more and more. God is there no end? I'm frantic, I'm spinning, I'm dizzy. I'm in a race but there is no finish line. Surely there must be an end. What is the end, the finish line? Death? Is that it? Death is the reason I am doing all of this? Shit! Panic, terror, horror!

And so goes the easier, softer way. The easier, softer way stirs the storm. At times it creates the storm, the storm before the calm. That precious, sacred calm when my soul speaks up and bravely tells my mind that the "fix" is no longer working for me. The anesthesia produced by my "fix" is no longer easing my pain. My mind is quiet now. It is listening. I am ready. I know that there is no easier, softer way. My ego wants to rest. Breathe in. Breathe out. Socrates said, "Wisdom begins in wonder." Centuries later Sam Keen, PhD wondered aloud in *Hymns To An Unknown God*, "How do we winnow our desires, separate the wheat from the chaff, and cultivate the desire for wholeness, for compassion, for a quiet and centered spirit?"

The first thing that jumps out at me in the quote above is "a quiet centered spirit". I want to reply to him, "Are you crazy? You don't know my life." And I am quite certain that I am not the only one with that sort of response. There is just so little in the world today that is quiet. It seems to me that somehow we have decided that quiet is for churches and libraries and if we desire quiet then we need to travel to one of those places. And the same goes for the spirit. There are places that those still interested in that sort of thing go and do whatever those sort do. Our world moves at lightning speed. The pace is unparalleled in history. Communication happens nearly as quickly as we think. In a flash, a text, an IM, a twitter or an email informs us constantly, continually. Life as we know it is so fast and so full that it seems that there is no time much less room for things spiritual. Yet, as they have from the earliest dawns of time, our inner voices whisper softly or screech in desperation, "J'ai soif!" (I thirst!)

The point is that despite the fact that America remains a nation of "believers", with a June 2008 study showing that 92% of Americans believe in God[1], an outside observer could fairly ask, "Exactly what God do you believe in?" A cosmic investigator would likely file a final report looking something like this:

"It appears that their God's name is Louis, Prada or Calvin and that many of them carry bags as symbols of endearment and fondly call Him, Coach. This Coach is a strict, demanding God forcing them to work 60 hour weeks and to bow down before the mighty engine of progress. He has indoctrinated them into believing that more is better, that it matters what kind of car you drive and whose name is stitched into your jeans. It's all a trick to keep them toiling, to keep them working. More is better. He teases them by lining their market shelves with newer, bigger, faster, shinier, better. He blesses them with the magnificent and ever holy dollar and then curses them with a spell that infects them with disease of "More". "More", is the aphrodisiac that keeps them moving keeps them going, keeps them running, keeps them racing. "More" of anything will do...the latest, the greatest, the cutting-edge, the new and improved, anything that sparkles, shines, does tricks, plays music or plays games. He hollers, "Mush, mush! Keep the masses working, keep the machine churning. Progress at all cost." Status, power, machines, technology, markets, media, economics, might... they strive for bigger, faster, stronger. The disease of "More" is what keeps them going. They have been tricked. They are disillusioned, brain washed, blind. He keeps them under the illusion that it's a race. That they must keep running. The ultimate goal is to win. Just win, nobody knows what they will win, they just know that winning is the goal. It is frightening. The religion is pervasive. I see no evidence of freedom, though they are convinced that they are free and boast of it often"

To be human is to ask questions. Why do I exist? What is this thing called life all about? What matters and what doesn't? Is there meaning in life? The "thinkers" throughout time have argued back and forth over this issue. They call it the *summum bonum*, the highest or the chief good or goal. Aristotle, Plato, Descartes, James, Sartre, Marx and many more have weighed in on the subject with conclusions coming mainly down to two...man as a contemplator or man as a lover. But even Plato (after much "contemplation") who tended to favor the idea of man as a thinker had to concede in the *Symposium* that mans fundamental quest is to find a satisfactory object for his love.[2] Although the arguments are long and drawn out, Norman O. Brown writes, "The riddle of history is not in reason but in desire; not in labor but in love."

Ah the "riddle of history", if the answer is love why do we spend so much of our time working for more, more, more. Because it is easier to contemplate, to think, to reason then we don't have to mess with those crazy little things call feelings. It is easier to see eight new-patient consults and do 3 surgeries than it is to reach my hand out in friendship. It is easier to work, to strive, to produce than it is to open ourselves to the vulnerabilities of empathy, compassion and caring.

Reason and work are the easier, softer ways that mislead and misdirect us at every turn. They will never *"just make us feel better."* The easier, softer ways do not work. They will never fill the hole, they cannot light the flame, they cannot make us Whole. The way to meaning and fulfillment and to wholeness is via a tortuous, winding artery that must take us deep into the heart before it brings us back to the surface. "Our most tragic human mistake is that of spending our lives trying to be what we are supposed to be. The second most tragic human mistake is that of, when we tire of being who we are supposed to be, failing to search for what we are."

The (W)Hole

This vessel, this body and this soul, are all that I have been given. I will live this life surrounded by this skin and thinking with this mind and yet what has been given to me I have surrendered to a force outside of me. I have jumped in and let "it" take me. How in the world can I expect to *"just feel better"* when for all practical purposes I have given my primary "feelers", my body and my mind, away to the world outside of me? Again, how did this happen? Was I born this way? I think not. When did this happen? I want to scream, "Has anyone seen that girl? The one I used to be. The girl that hoped and dreamed and idealized and romanticized, you know the one that was innocent and confident and curious, full of life and energy. Energy oh my God the energy! She was so full of energy and spirit, yes, spirit, that intangible something that was infectious and beautiful and kind and loving and desirable. Where and when did she go?" Know the feeling?

Norman O. Brown wrote, "Mankind today is still making history without having any conscious idea of what it really wants or under what conditions it would stop being unhappy and calling that unhappiness progress." We human beings are a restless lot, discontented, even irritable. In search of that magical "It" that will make everything better, that which will fill the hole, make us Whole, complete, content, happy...that which will *"just make us feel better"*. We just keep bustling about preparing to arrive at that ever elusive mirage of spectacular happiness and never ending tranquility.

Brown calls it "unhappiness". Is it truly unhappiness? Perhaps it is more accurate to call it uneasiness or unsettledness. Mystics, Theologians, Psychologists, Philosophers both famous and infamous and "Great Thinkers" both present and past have dug deep into their vocations, their Holy books, their conscious and subconscious and even into their souls searching for a word to describe this incomprehensible feeling. It is a feeling that all humans have felt at one time or another, but one that we have forgotten to name. Ask anyone to tell you what the feeling is and what you will get is people trying to describe the feeling but unable to quite come up with the right word. I don't know what it looks like or what to call it but I know it when I feel it. As I probe deeper and peer down into my own depths I see an anxiousness, a rattled, shifty, unbalanced feeling, a restlessness, an incompleteness. The great thinkers call it a hole, an abyss, a void, an emptiness, a something-is-not-quite-right feeling. Philosopher William James coined the term *zerrissenheit* translated as, "torn-to-pieces-hood." All of these descriptors work, more or less, to put to words something intangible, profoundly personal, yet astoundingly universal; universal not just now but universal throughout the history of mankind. We all *"just want to feel better"*.

The "Experience of Living"

"People say that what we're all seeking is meaning for life. I don't think that is what we are really seeking. I think that what we are seeking is an experience of being alive…so that we actually feel the rapture of being alive." So says renowned thinker Joseph Campbell who devoted his life to studying myth. He studied stories and within the myriad of myths from the earliest dawns of time found again and again the story of that universal quest, that valiant search of all of mankind for a solution to the "torn-to-pieces-hood." Myth after myth, story after story describes the adventure, the meandering, twisting, tortuous journey into ourselves, into "…*the experience of living*…." No expedition, however, is the same. The myths are as numerous as the number of people on this earth, as the number of people that have ever been on this earth. We each have a myth, a story that we are writing with our lives. The *experience of living*" lies within our stories and within our ability to awaken our own personal myths, learn from them, share them with others and bring to life the epics we are writing as we go about embracing or enduring the "experience of being alive"

There is meaning in this crazy world, but it does not come pouring down upon us like a gentle, lovely rain covering our lives with purpose. It doesn't dance and spin and whirl in front of us and say take me I'm yours. It must be found. It must be searched for. We must dig and forage and rummage and want it with all our hearts. We must search and seek and scratch and scour, and we must do it alone. This journey is by requisite a solo one. Others can cheer and support, embolden and encourage, but the steps must be ours and ours alone. No one else could discover what we will find. The treasures are unique and precious. We are the only ones who can uncover these riches and their inestimable value is beyond our wildest dreams. Though the experience of our lives is ours and ours alone, the value in each experience grows exponentially as we forage around, uncover and release it to the world. The path is dark and lonely, scary and even painful, but oh so dear and precious and rich and priceless. The gift we give when we bravely unearth our stories and share them with others is not touchable but like a pebble in a pond will reverberate to the ends of the earth. We each have all we need to set out on the venture. We simply need to know where to start.

We need to know how to embark on this meandering journey into meaning, into ourselves, into the answer of how to *"just feel better"*.

We start where we started…we start with our stories. Before we can fill the hole we must find it and explore it. We must go to the very bottom of the hole, to the very heart of the torn-to-pieces-hood, to the center of the emptiness, to the core of the nothingness in order to create a somethingness, to comprehend a purposefulness and to find meaningfulness. In the midst of the inner void, in the midst of that intangible barren place of inner angst, we will discover an essential truth that is fundamental to personal peace, serenity and joy. We will find that we are not nothing but that we are also not everything. We will find that we are not beasts but we are not gods. In a word we will discover what it means to be human. We will discover that at the core of that perennial Weltschmerz (world-weariness) are not the answers to the age old wonderings of what, why, where, when and how, but rather the tools to teach us how to live with the questions. This journey is one that will flip and turn and backtrack and twist and wind around again and take us to the center of what it means to be a person, what it means to be more than and less than at the same time. It is the discovery of what it is to be both whole and broken, both sober and impaired, both empty and full. It is the discovery of how we *go about living* peacefully in the paradoxes of humanness.

And therein lays the key, *go about living* means we are searching for a *way of life*. It means that we are searching for *a way to live* with the ambiguities, the uncertainties and the unanswerables. It means that in the center of the woundedness, the tragedy and the travesty we are going to learn to live the questions. We are going to unearth a deeply buried truth that teaches us to embrace the *"experience of living"*. We will discover that ancient wisdom is found not only in centuries of treasured myth but also in our own personal myths, our own personal stories. This primordial wisdom is hidden within the stories that each of us writes each and every day as we *go about living*. And hidden this wisdom will remain unless the story is unearthed and shared with another.

The Beginning

It is time to cease and desist in our quest to arrive and begin to take our joy from the wandering and the wondering. And so as every wandering must, our journey needs a place to start. We all start as perfect innocents. I will, however, bet the bank that we, not one of us, popped out of Mama shouting, "Here I am. Perfect and in God's image". We may have been, "perfect and in God's image", but before we were old enough to comprehend the meaning of the statement, "the givens" have gotten us. We enter into this world with a set of "givens". We are beings born into certain circumstances that we have little control over. We don't get to choose where and when we are born or who our parents and ancestors are or what values and beliefs they have acquired in their lifetimes and have chosen to pass on. We don't get to choose that which is inscribed into our DNA—our race, our physical attributes or our natural gifts and talents. So, BOOM, we enter this world and we are already loaded down with all this stuff that we had no say in and then, from that moment on, the world we live in grabs us and shapes us and molds us into "adults" until one day we wake up and say, "whoa pony, let's keep it at a trot". SCREECH, stop right there, go back to the BOOM...this is the stepping off point, this is where we will begin. Our wanderings should begin at the "givens" and proceed forward from there. After all, it is there that our stories began.

No one celebrates the innocence of infancy in a more beautiful, albeit often misunderstood, way than Freud. I think he screws with us (was that a "Freudian slip"?) by his selection of words, but the essence of what he has to say, I think, is lovely and of huge, huge, huge value when it comes to trying to decipher how we get to be how we are. Freud speaks of "infantile sexuality" and "polymorphous perversity" and we all stop right there and label him as mad. Having read and studied a bit of Freud I come away with a huge appreciation and admiration. If I could say anything to him it would be, "Dude, pick some new descriptors. Where did you find those words?" For the sake of this discussion let's just say that Freud had a very special and general definition of sexuality and that basically all he was saying was that infants, oblivious to the serious parts of life, have a unique ability to get pleasure from every part of their bodies. That is to say, infants find a true pleasure from sight, sound, touch, feel, smell, movement; gifts that we are born with but somehow come to under appreciate with time or even to forget about entirely. As we grow, according to Freud and others, this "sexuality" or enjoyment of all that the body has to offer becomes what we call "play". The protestant Theologian Jacob Boehme called "play" the perfect state. Sartre said, "As soon as man apprehends himself as free and wishes to use his freedom...then his activity is play." Herein lies the rub, from the instant we become part of a family, a community, a society we begin to unknowingly give away the freedom that gives life meaning and purpose and we allow ourselves to be morphed, molded and shaped by the world in which we live.

Now, no one is saying let's become kids again and we will all be happy. No one is saying let's regress into some psychoanalytic state of innocence and we will all be happy. What I am saying is that is where I started, that is where my person began and in my story and my story alone is where I will find me. It is where Leslie twisted and turned and was molded and chiseled into the person that she is today. Somewhere on that twisting, turning path sexuality became a dirty word, play became something only children did and purpose was sacrificed for society and the greater good. My autobiography is mine and mine alone. I am authoring my own myth as I "go about living." I have 45 years of story to tell. I have my story memorized. I am the only one that can tell it. I am my story. I own it...more accurately...it owns me.

I was born in Aberdeen, South Dakota in October of 1964. My father was a teacher at the time and my mother a nurse. I was loved and cuddled and cradled. My earliest memories were in the town of Huron, South Dakota where my young family settled when I was about 3. We were a church going Catholic family. I remember the churches well. Ours was The Resurrection, the newer Catholic church on the west side of town. St. Paul's was the other Catholic church in town. It was a more traditional, tall doors, stained glass type church that always left me feeling scared and small. I think it was in church that my little mind first started to ask questions. It was there that my psyche realized that it "had a mind of its own" so to speak. It was there that my "wonderings" started. Why did God care what we wore? Was there something more holy about uncomfortable shoes? To whom was it that God gave the instructions to as to when to sit and when to kneel and when to stand? Where were those instructions written? It seemed to me that if this was the "One True God", as I was being taught, that these instructions should be chiseled in stone somewhere sort of like the Ten Commandments. What was going to happen to all of my friends who went to the Lutheran church down the street? Will they go to heaven too? I thought probably yes but had my doubts about the Lakota Indian kids that lived around the corner. I worried about them a lot. Something deep down inside of me knew that they, like the starving children in Ethiopia that were used to get me to clean my plate, were God's children too and that there was some kind of special plan for them since they weren't able to attend my church of the "One True God". So went my innocent little thoughts. I had my questions but Father Murray and Father Flannery were kind and smart and so were my folks. There is no way they would lead me astray so I believed and I did what they said to do. Father, Son and the Holy Spirit. Amen.

My first real question about what it was that I truly believed came in 7th grade when I was invited to go with friends to a function at their Lutheran church called Awana. I loved Awana. We memorized Bible verses and played games and sang songs and praised God and laughed. I was so good at the memorization part. I knew the books of the Bible frontwards and backwards. I was initially embarrassed when I didn't know how to look up John 3:16 in the Bible. What a strange thing I thought. I have been going to church my whole life and I have never been asked to look up a Bible verse before. Oh well, I supposed the Catholic church was just so organized that they had all of the verses all copied down in our books so we didn't have to waste precious God time looking them up ourselves. The blow came one Thursday night when I came home from school and found Father Murray sitting with my mother. They proceeded to inform me that while what I had learned so far was okay I was no longer going to be able to go to Awana. That *"they" were going to start teaching things that "we" didn't believe in. Oh the blow, crushing. I just couldn't wrap my arms around the idea that anything in the Bible could be wrong. My doubts were raging, my mind was searching but I quietly obeyed. I was angry at the Priest, my parents and even at God. There was something really wrong about all of this…I just knew it. I was suspicious and skeptical about God and church and religion for the first time. But I continued to say my prayers and my "Father, Son and the Holy Spirit. Amen" just in case.*

My life in Huron, South Dakota, population 10,000, was idyllic. My time spent cheerleading for the Huron Tigers and doing gymnastics which in those years was my "true love". The questions of my pre-pubertal youth had largely disappeared into my subconscious my focus on things more tangible. While friends swam in the glory of teenage hormones and freedom from childhood and trivial things far less important than who is "going with" whom and who has started their period and what does so and so think of me, my focus was tunneled. My love of gymnastics and competition. No real goal on the horizon, just love of the game and an urge to improve. My career as a gymnast had been temporarily interrupted by injuries along the way. A broken ankle at 13 and a dislocated elbow at 14 had thwarted my progress. I remember well the evening that I felt my prayers had been answered. I was at a play-off basketball game. The Huron Tigers had been ranked number one all year and the plans to travel the 350 miles to the State Tournament had already been set. This one game was all that stood in our way. My sister, Lisa 16, was cheering and the Huron arena bellowed with thousands of excited fans. Lisa found me in the bleachers and with tears in her eyes broke the news. Our family was moving to Rapid City at the end of the school year. A thrill ran through me but before I could express my delight she continued on obviously looking for an ally to thwart our mutual parental authority and stage a protest. Much to her dismay I was filled with excitement and glee. Rapid City was where the best coaches in the state were and I was thrilled beyond words. For me this was a dream come true. The Huron Tigers went on to lose the game an upset of unparalleled proportion for a small South Dakota town in the dead of winter. My sister's grief tripled and the tears flowed freely. The next week turned ours into a schizophrenic household half excited and have dreading the impending relocation. A simple move on the surface was in all reality quite a big deal. We were known in Huron. The Masters' family. Dad a successful business man ran Dakota Claim service an insurance adjusting firm and Mom, though trained as a nurse, ran the second family business, an Orange Julius store in the Huron Mall. Four daughters, Lisa (16), Leslie (15), Laura (12) and Lavin (9) all active and involved in all that rural South Dakota had to offer. Mom was on the school board and active in the American Cancer Society. We were members at the Huron Country Club and like the picture-perfect little Catholic family we ate brunch there every Sunday. How could we leave this splendor and move away? Despite the gloom of a move and of our team being out of the tournament we busied ourselves and stirred our excitement by dreaming of things to come. Though our team was out the family continued forward with our plans to travel to Rapid City the following week except now we would snow ski and house hunt.

I remained self absorbed, living in my own dreamland with teenage fantasies abounding. The questioning mind silent for now and the "One True God" of my youth just assumed as I went through the paces, "Father, Son and Holy Spirit. Amen" Thus went my "shaping" from zero to 15...but my world was about to change forever, the girl I had grown to be about to disappear into that abyss of circumstance, the God I had questioned could no longer be arbitrary and "out there" somewhere. He would need to come home to me...more accurately...I would need to come home to Him...

2

The Cause, Chance
& Choice

Our stories are full of the *"experience of living"* and it is in the telling of them that we get to embrace the myth that we have lived up to this point. It is in the telling of our stories that they in return will be telling to us. Although we know our stories and have lived our stories, the wisdom that lies within them will forever remain hidden unless we tell them...out loud to another living being. The healing and the treasure lie in the telling. In telling our stories we give a gift to another. I heal be telling. I learn by listening. "Knowledge speaks, but wisdom listens." (Jimi Hendrix).

Our stories begin with our givens. From the moment we enter this world and fill our lungs with that first breath of air our givens have got us. Our givens just are and they start our stories. Our givens are the things we are born with, our DNA, our family, our place and time of birth. Machiavelli identified necessita, fortuna and virtu as the three things that make up our stories. *Cause, chance* and *choice*. We are born with a set of "givens", shit happens and we make decisions.

We are not in control of everything that happens in our world, but we are not without some say in the matter. We get to control OUR OWN actions and reactions, our *choices*. (Note the emphasis on "OUR OWN") Try as we may however, *cause* and *chance* are not ours to control. In sifting through our stories we get the opportunity to sort these out. For me, it goes like this: <u>*Cause.*</u> I was born female, middle class American, Catholic, the second of four daughters. <u>*Chance.*</u> I was critically injured at the age of 15. <u>*Choice.*</u> I made a decision to go to medical school. *Cause, chance* and *choice* have shaped us into the people we are today. *Cause, chance* and *choice* have written our stories up to this very moment in time.

The *"cause, chance* and *choice"* that have already taken place in our lives not only make up the stories we can tell but also make up the people we have become. All of the *"causes"*, *"chances"* and *"choices"* that have occurred have culminated to this very point and time, and direct and dictate how we see and interpret and interact with the world around us. In other words, our stories thus far have shaped us and have left us with ways of comprehending life, viewing life and living life that are uniquely our own. No one else has ever walked through life in exactly the same pair of shoes that each of us, as individuals, is wearing.

By definition, our stories are behind us. We can only tell what has already happened and what has already happened affects us and effects the story we will write in the future.

Daemons

Our pasts are loaded with skeletons in the closets and ghosts underneath the bed. Skeletons and ghosts, those things that stay with us, haunt us, help us, guide us and mislead us. Very often we don't even know what they are, but they are there. They are there in everything we do and say and feel. They are present in our every action and every reaction.

I call them our "daemons". Now, we are not speaking of the evil spirit demons of our current vernacular, but rather of the *daemons* from the Latin and Greek roots meaning: *guardian spirits, geniuses.* Our *daemons ('guardian spirits')* slither out from within us; they don't land on us from the outside; they are born in our experience and make their home in our subconscious. We don't recognize them as *daemons* because they have intercalated their way into our beings and now live in symbiosis with that which is real in us. These *geniuses or guardian spirits* are our coping mechanisms, they are the ways we have learned throughout life to handle being human and flawed and scared and imperfect. They are what Sam Keen would call our "Body Armor"[3]; they are the functional and dysfunctional ways that we have developed to deal with the reality that we live in.

As life proceeds we develop personality traits, (sometimes good ones, sometimes bad ones) that help us navigate the world we live in. These traits evolve as we interact with the rest of humanity. They materialize and become part of us as a result of *cause, chance* and *choice*. They are what is *"genius"* in our design as human beings and they allow us to endure and survive the task of being human.

Our *daemons* are supposed to protect us, to be a shelter, a defense, a safeguard, a harbor, a refuge, a shield; they save us from the ravishes of life.   However, when our *daemons* are used to cover us rather than protect us they become a shroud, a guise, a camouflage, a shade, a facade, a fence, a wall, a mask.   It is then that these great protectors are being used only to hide what is true, authentic and real in us. It is then that our *daemons,* our own personalities, begin to impede our ability to successfully connect, unite and mesh with the rest of the universe.

These 'covering *daemons'* are what we allow others to see, our personas.   Rather than being *guardian spirits* to defend us in difficult times, they become the disguise we don to hide what is pure, substantive and sincere in us. And we hide this pureness not only from others, but also from ourselves.   It is in telling our stories that we begin to dissect these *daemons* and little by little peel away the layers that cover, the layers that cover the angst, that cover the hole and prevent us from being Whole.

My *daemons* define who I have become; they are why I do what I do.   What lies beneath my *daemons* is the answer to who I am, what I am.   I will unveil what lies beneath them when I turn within and begin to write my story.

———————————————

The day was cold and rainy. Typical, really, for South Dakota in March.   Though we weren't packing pompoms or cheerleading sweaters we were excited for the trip to Rapid City, a few days off of school, snow skiing and especially to see with new eyes the town we were soon to call home.   I made my way home from school in the rain, across the field and through a small tree strip into our back yard that was enclosed with a brown picket fence. My older sister Lisa had beat me home was scurrying about loading the family's Jeep Wagoneer in preparation for our trip across the still frozen state. We had 30 minutes to load pick up two other cheerleaders and meet the caravan of Huron Tiger fans that were on their way to the state basketball tournament that our team would not be playing in. My mom and younger sister Laura were traveling in a separate car but with the same caravan, my youngest sister Lavin, fresh out of the hospital after an appendectomy would be staying home with Grandma Grace (my mom's mom). Dad planned to work through the day and drive out alone after the work day was through.

I tossed my orange and black Tigers duffle through the rear window of the Wagoneer and hopped in the driver's seat to roll the window up before everything was soaked by the freezing cold drizzle. I heard the familiar squeak of the rear window start but then nothing. Again and again I pushed the plastic lever that was to close the window but nothing. It had advanced about 3 inches and stopped. Drizzle continued to cover the bags we had tossed into rear. I dropped my head backward thinking what next, what else could go wrong. It was in these times that we turned to the ultimate problem solver of our times...dad.

Much to our dismay another wrench had been thrown into our plan. We would miss the caravan and make the drive to Rapid City on our own, after the window was repaired. We begrudgingly gave the requisite hugs and kisses to Mom and Laura as they loaded the final necessities into their car and prepared to join the group of disheartened Tiger fans on their way to the tournament that would not be. I remember well my last words to my mother, she hugged me and said, "Now you guys be so, so, so careful." My response, "Yeah, yeah, yeah." Lisa and I and Kelly, my fellow sophomore cheerleader, loaded up and headed to pick up our final passenger, Kim, a bouncy, beautiful junior who had moved to Huron just this year and quickly become 'the stunning new cheerleader' at Huron High School and my sisters best friend.

Kim hopped into the front passenger seat waved good bye to her mother who stood in the door way in an effort to avoid the freezing drizzle that continued to fall. Kim promptly passed out Easter chocolates to us all that momentarily soothed the disappointment of our current situation. It was 3:30pm. Our caravan of friends was now two hours ahead of us. We had surrendered to the reality of our latest misfortune and with our bags continuing to absorb the rain that relentlessly blew into the broken rear window we headed to the repair shop. Fate had handed us a minor blow and our plans again had changed, we would get the window repaired and make the 7 hour journey to Rapid City on our own with my Dad still bringing up the rear of the Tiger fans with plans to leave town by 6pm. We laughed, joked and entertained ourselves with the latest teenage gossip while the wagoneer was repaired and by 5pm we were finally ready to hit the highway. Despite the objections from my fellow passengers, I insisted on one last stop at McDonalds on our way out of town, cheeseburger plain, small fries and a coke.

With windshield wipers dancing back and forth we were finally on open road, and in South Dakota that means not another car or building insight just open prairie and miles of desolate highway. Kim handed me another Easter chocolate, it was a little smiling bunny with one ear flopped down and a bouquet of flowers in its hand. My sister drove on as her passengers settled in. I ate my chocolate, laid my head back and closed my eyes. The radio station rattled in and out as we drove out of range of any radio signal.

I awoke to my sister's gasp. I looked out the front window to see miles of open fields rushing by. Time slowed to a crawl. My disorientation cleared as I realized we had slid and were now sliding down the highway sideways. Black-ice. My initial reaction was amazingly calm; whoa we're going to go off the road. Icy roads and sliding vehicles were part of everyday life in South Dakota. As I turned my attention to the highway I realized that this was not going to be just another little spin out. In the distance I could see the first vehicle that we'd seen in miles coming down the road and we were sliding out of control in its lane at 65 miles per hour. Kim and Kelly both slept leaning against their doors on the passenger side of the vehicle. I remember grabbing Kelly's arm to pull her away from the oncoming vehicle and raising my arms up to cradle my head. The vehicle was large and black and as it approached I closed my eyes and the world went dark.

I awoke cold and damp to my sister's voice, "Leslie, Leslie are you okay?" "My leg, my leg hurts" I could hear my voice answer but it seemed disconnected with the rest of me as if it were floating out there somewhere apart from me. Again, my sister spoke, "But are you okay?" The next time I awoke was to the voices of men talking with my sister and trying to get her out of the tangled heap of metal that surrounded me. I was cold, so cold and wanted out too, but in some way wanted no one to touch me. The pain in my leg had numbed in the cold and my mind kept saying just leave me, just leave me to sleep. Again I could hear a voice, it was screaming in terror and fighting someone and yelling no, no, no, stop, stop, please stop. The voice was my own and it would not stop as arms that were not listening pulled me from the wreckage that still contained my friends. I was cold so cold. The third time I woke I was lying flat in what I thought was the back of a pickup truck. I could feel the metal rivets of the uneven bed against my back. Why am I in this truck why did they lay me on this cold jagged metal? I heard a voice say, "She is so broken. She thinks she is laying on an uneven surface. I can't get her to be still." The screaming continued and I wanted it to stop but I couldn't silence my own voice. My tortured howls continued. They wouldn't stop; I couldn't get them to stop. A foggy moment of clarity hit and for a moment the screams stopped. I could see Kelly lying next to me. Tears flowed for the first time and sound ceased. I reached for her and in a voice that was finally my own I heard myself say, "I just want to hold her hand. I will be still if I can hold her hand."

The next thing I can remember is being in a make shift emergency room with people rushing about. I heard someone say "Oh my God there are bones going in every direction." I didn't know if they were talking about me or Kelly but I felt like my foot was missing. It had hurt so badly earlier but now nothing. Somehow I knew we were in Wessington Springs, SD a tiny dirt road town. When I awoke next I was in the Huron emergency room. The screaming had started again. I knew it was me but could not control the voice that wouldn't stop. People kept pressing on my stomach and

I kept saying, "No not there, it is my leg. It's my leg.", but they kept pressing. A nurse was trying to explain to me that she was going to put a tube down into my stomach and that all I needed to do was swallow. She kept saying swallow, swallow but I was choking, I grabbed the tube and pulled it out. She started to cry and I recognized her. I didn't know her name but I knew her and she knew me and she cried the whole time she strapped my arms down and pushed the tube back down my throat. A new scream started but this one wasn't mine. It yelled, "Blood, blood! All I'm getting is blood. Oh my God it is just blood!" The voice was scared; it trembled and cracked between sobs. A man's voice said, "Let's go. We're going right now." He didn't say where but I somehow knew it was to surgery. The scared nurse stayed by me but her sobs continued and got louder and were combined with gasps as Father Murray came up to me and touched my forehead and did the sign of the cross. That was the first time that I realized what was going on. It was my blood and they thought that I was going to die. They think I'm going to die. I wanted to say, "Don't worry, I won't die. Quit crying. It is going to be okay, I promise. I won't leave." I heard the doctor say, "You can see her quickly. We're going to surgery now. She is bleeding badly." A familiar voice answered, "Just go I'll see her when she comes out." The doctor's tone changed and he said, "No, you should see her now. She may not come out." Then I saw my Dad. He touched my hand that was still strapped to the bed and kissed my head. He had tears going down his cheeks and he choked out these words, "I'm here. You're going to be okay baby girl. You're going to be okay." He didn't think I was going to be okay but a strange peace floated inside me. I wasn't screaming. I wasn't scared. I didn't feel pain. Just calmness.

We are born with a set of givens *(cause)*, but events *(chance)*, also shape us bend us, mold us into what we ultimately become—adults with skeletons and ghosts that we do battle with for the rest of our lives. Events can be big or small, catastrophic or serendipitous. They may be huge or seem like the tiniest most insignificant little thing but they shape us. Every Easter I cry. Not because Christ was persecuted and suffered and died and rose again—because they still make that same little chocolate bunny that Kim handed me with a smile on her face. It was the last time I ever saw her. Little things change us. Everything matters. I remember telling a friend who had asked me where I would like to go to dinner the following: "I'm pretty easy going. I like everything. It really doesn't matter to me. I'm not picky. If something matters to me I will tell you, but most things don't matter to me." How naïve! Unbelievable. Where did I ever get the idea that I had any concept of what matters and what doesn't. I have come to believe that it all matters. Everything matters. Everything in my story, in my myth, in my life before this very minute has turned me into the person I am right now. There is value in all of it. Today will become part of the story that I will tell tomorrow.

Our stories are the most real thing about us. Our stories inevitably know us better than we know ourselves. For in them are secrets and untold treasures; and although we have lived them we are unaware of all that is there. When we gather the pieces of our past and place them in order and tell them out loud we create a symphony of our lives. If we tell "a little of this or a little of that" the notes will be shrill, the chorus off-key. Not because the "little of this or a little of that" tale that we tell is unimportant, but rather that when we select little tidbits we give ourselves a pass. We are human, imperfect, flawed and cracked and it is our nature to tell that which comes easy, that which is on the top. Our real nuances, our true *daemons* lie deeper and uncovering them does not always feel good. For me, my chest gets tight and part of me trembles as I open myself and tell my story to you. The remembering is wrenching. The events buried. Until I approached my computer today, I had never told this part of my story. However, the symphony, in all its grandeur, comes not in a single note but in the entire composition. The truth is in the details, it is beneath the *daemons*. As a dear musician friend of mine put it, "I have learned to find myself not just in the notes but also in the pauses between the notes."

"So what," you say, "I can learn more about myself by looking at my story but it probably won't feel good. Thanks a bunch but I have enough discomfort without going searching for more!" Why look? I could probably think of a lot of reasons but two biggies come to mind:

1) We know there must be something more, we have that longing, there is something missing in us, there must be something bigger... we do *"just want to feel better."* Our *choice* is to either go forward, to discover the truth and take our place in the Whole or remain lost in the mindless chaos until we take our last breath and our story has concluded. Our *choice* is to find the palace within us, within our stories, or to continue to live within the dungeon of *daemons* that cover. And the word *"choice"* here is of utmost importance as it (as we shall see later) is the only utensil that we have with which to write our stories.

2.) The life we live and have lived in our past is the one thing that we have been given in this world that connects us intimately to the self deep inside, our fellow creatures and to an ineffable Power that is much bigger than we can ever fathom. Our myths are the heartstrings that hold the past, the present and the future together. Our myths are the heartstrings that connect us to the heartstrings of others. Our stories weave us into the stories being told by countless others and together we become part of the masterpiece that is the Whole.

Willfulness

The things we were born into and the things that have happened and will happen in our lives we have no control over. We cannot exercise our *will* in these areas though we may try. The only tool we have, with which to write our stories today and for all of our tomorrows, is our *choice*. *Cause* and *chance* are out of our control. We cannot *will* these things. We can only *will* our *choices*. The rub is this, the wave of the world has engulfed us in an out of control current called life and our beautiful *daemons* that were intended for good have been in a constant battle with this raging current ever since. Our *daemons* have become automatic reflexes and this autopilot has stolen our freedom to *choose*.

This disappearance of our freedom to *choose* casts us all into the whirl of pretending. Pretending to be able to control and *will* the things that cannot be controlled and *willed (cause and chance)*. We have lost our *choice* and so we trick ourselves into thinking that we can control the *cause* and the *chance*. We delude ourselves into believing that we can *will* the *unwillable*. Our *daemons* have morphed us into what the world says we should be and in our desperation to have some say in the matter we dive head first into a mockery of head-strong foolish *willing.*

Leslie Farber describes in several essays from *The Ways of The Will* how asserting our *will* over things that cannot be *willed* produces an anxiety which he defines as "painful uneasiness of mind over an impending or anticipated ill"… hence the angst, the hole, the torn-to-pieces-hood, the Welschmerz. Farber goes on to call this the "Age of the Disordered *Will*" We have become a society full of *willers, willing* what cannot be *willed.* We can, for example, *will* going to bed but we cannot *will* going to sleep. We can *will* reading but not understanding. We can *will* lust but not love. We can *will* pleasure but not happiness. We can *will* knowledge but not wisdom. When we attempt to *will* what can't be *willed* we enter a vicious cycle quite classic for our times. You see, in *willing* what can not be *willed* we create anxiety, in seeking relief we *will* relief from anxiety—another one of those things that cannot be *willed.* The result, anxiety over anxiety and so goes the classic picture of the "Age of Disordered *Will*". In *willing* what can not be *willed* we lay stake to territory that is not ours. In *willing* what can not be *willed* we are "Playing God". Our new mantra must be, "There is a God. I'm not it".

Our freedom can be retrieved by delving deep within, addressing the *daemons* that have made us into what we are supposed to be and re-capturing the one thing that we can *will*…our *choices.* The angst generated from a world full of people hopelessly caught in the delusion of control has left us in a society of soul sickness, of internal decay, of despondency, of anxiousness. It has left us in a perpetual state of *"just wanting to feel better".* In attempting to control what is not ours to control we destroy the very thing we are seeking. Contentment, peace and true, pure inner joy get besieged by the fear, gloom, grief and heartache of the uncontrollable agitation that comes with our struggle to control something, anything in our lives.

The abduction of our freedom has cast us into a turbulent storm of perpetual struggle and dis-ease. We must tell our stories, learn where we need to pivot and shift and begin applying our *wills* where they were intended to be applied—in our actions and reactions—our *choices.* We must learn to uncover the *willful* daemons, let God be God and be what God made us to be—scratched, dented, needing paint, damaged, defective, FREE beings.

In telling our stories we re-possess the freedom to *choose*. We tackle the *daemons*, expose them, attend to them and engage them in a battle for our liberty and our right to *choose* for ourselves. Our *daemons* have molded us into what we are supposed to be and in doing so have seized our freedom to be who we are. By seizing our ability to make our own *choices* based on who we are, our *daemons* have cast us into an unwinnable battle of the *will*.

I have heard it said, "Do you want to see God laugh?......Tell Him your plans." Oh so true. I mean really, if the world and the people in it would just behave the way I think they should then I would be just fine. Ever hear the saying, "Too many chiefs and not enough Indians"? I love that saying. I say it all the time. Funny thing is I'm always one of the chiefs. I never say it when I am playing the part of the Indian. I am always the chief. The one in charge, I always have a "plan". Once when I was a senior in high school I received an award, it was a plaque that said, "My mind is made up. Don't confuse me with the facts." Think maybe I have a wee bit of a "will" disorder??

So let me give you a "hypothetical" example:

It is spring and love is in the air. Girl doctor runs into boy attorney. Actually, girl doctor re-connects with really hot guy attorney. Hot guy and girl are both really stinging from recent failed and painful relationships. They visit about their similar recent relationship experience and get comfort from visiting about their pain. Hot guy and girl start making up "professional" reasons to get in contact with one another and soon they begin to email back and forth in the guise of a "professional relationship". Little by little the emails become more and more personal and start to be a bit "sporty". Innocent, coquettish conversations continue via the safe medium of electronic transmission. Despite the rather impersonal mode of communication girl starts to feel the youthful flutters of enchantment in her chest every time her blackberry makes that special "ping" which means she has another message from her new found friend, hot guy attorney. Her step becomes lighter and her manner more jovial. Life becomes airy and fresh. She starts to joke with the employees at her clinic, to laugh louder, to smile more. The operating suite no longer rings of the monotonous hum of the infiltration and suction pumps but instead dances with music. Emails turn to late night phone calls where they talk for hours and laugh and flirt and tell each other stories. Girl really likes hot guy and hot guy really likes girl. Hot guy and girl start to spend a lot of time together. They plan fun parties and take trips together. They share secret fears and far away dreams. They tell each other their regrets from the past and hopes for the future.

One day girl is visited by a strange funny looking little man. He explains that he is a thaumaturgical minikin and that he has been sent by the powers of the cosmos to bring her a gift. After greeting him politely, she says, "Come again a thauma what?" The man dutifully replies, "Okay fine. I'm a small magic man but my potion is real and it is for you. You see, this potion will cast a spell on the one person you choose to give it to fall madly in love with you forever and ever." Whoa! She couldn't believe her good fortune and what perfect timing. For the first time in her life she had a man that she loved dearly and now she was certain to get his love in return. She arranged for an early morning coffee with endeared friend the very next day with a plan to quietly pour the potion into his double shot skinny caramel macchiato.

Girl meets hot guy for coffee(America 2009 style). Hot guy drinks his double shot skinny caramel macchiato and just as the small magic man had promised he immediately falls madly and completely in love with girl.

Did they live happily ever after?

From that very day forward girl was tortured and tormented. She grew pale and thin and very weak. Her eyes became hollow and empty. When her beloved would speak to her she would stare at the perfect face she loved so thoroughly but could not hear his words. Though the man she had fallen in love with now loved her in return she would live the rest of her days wondering, "If it were not for the potion, would he love me? Left to his own free will, not my will, would he love me?"

36

You see, our girl had willed something that can't be willed. In doing so she destroyed the very object of her will. Hmmm? Maybe God does know what He is doing after all.[4]

Willing what can't be *willed*. That would qualify as a *daemon* and we all do it. Ugh! I hate that! Truthfully, all of our givens become part of our *daemons,* many good, many bad, most just are that....givens. The stuff that happens to us becomes part of our *daemons* as well. They are part of what has made us see and interpret the world the way we do. We can only view this world through the set of glasses that we have been given by *cause, chance* and *choice.* Our *daemons* have made that world easier to swallow and digest at times. When we decide it is time to see the world and our place in it more clearly, when we decide that there must be something more than a whirling world designed to sweep us involuntarily away in its roaring current, when we decide that it is time to mend our "torn to pieces-hood", rid ourselves of the Welschmerz (world weariness), when our longing to *"just feel better"* is stronger than our fear of confronting what we have become then we are ready to dissect our *daemons*....we are ready to tell our stories. We are ready to own and share our myths. It is then and only then that we will be equipped to step forward with our God given freedom to *choose,* to *choose* freely and to claim our place in the greater Whole.

Worry

We have all in one way or another spent much of our lives worshipping and relying on that which lies outside of us, be that money, power, status, drugs, perfection, approval, acceptance or accomplishment. We have prayed to an unknown, untouchable God but have saved the worshipping for the gods we could see. Faith is always easier when it is something we can see, touch, count or measure. But *"the experience of living"* is like weaving a tapestry over time, it is not a sum of known numbers that has a definite answer. There is no this or that which will make everything grand.

Too often we profess our faith in a Power greater than ourselves but insist on carrying a huge bag of *"worry rocks"* around by ourselves. We hold tight to the mindset of "I can fix it" and that mindset keeps us lost in the heedless anarchy of frivolity. The "I can fix it" mentality insists that we haul around the bag of *"worry rocks"*. We have, by becoming attached to our *daemons,* forgotten how to drop the rocks. We cling to personality traits and ways of coping and interacting so tightly that we blind ourselves to what we can and cannot control, what we do and do not have a say in. We, as imperfect beings, are doomed to return to the traits that have helped us manage in the past. We, as limited beings, are accursed to pick up the rocks of life's struggles from time to time and to give our *daemons* permission to run wild trying to "fix" life, to let ourselves calculate madly pretending that we will somehow come up with that magical sum, that magical answer.

By reaching down deep into our stories, into our *daemons,* into the persons that we have evolved into, we can learn to drop the rocks. We can begin to recognize what is *cause,* what is *chance* and what is *choice* and begin to drop the rocks that are not ours to carry. We can drop the rocks, and even if we inadvertently pick them up again, we can re-drop them, over and over and over until we drop them for good. We can rest peacefully in the knowledge that we as humans are bound to pick up the rocks when we are overwhelmed or over-worried or over-stressed, but we do not have to pack them around with us everywhere we go, we can pause, think and drop them anytime we give ourselves permission. It is okay to need to drop them again and again and again.

So how do we proceed? How do we venture out (or in) and heal the "fisher king wound"? At this point I am going to be bold and take exception to Scott Peck's theory in *The Road Less Traveled* and argue that it is not lack of discipline, laziness or a paucity of psychotherapy that gets us stuck in the world of restless, irritable and discontented rather it is a "stuckness" that results from not knowing where to start. Not knowing how to get out, not knowing what to do. We are not too lazy or undisciplined to get out, we just don't f****g know how! Many of us have spent our lives rebelling from authority of one sort or another. Parents, teachers, preachers, government, religion…all of those things full of "ought's" and "shoulds" and "good girls and boys do this" and "if only you were more…". We don't need someone to tell us that we just need more discipline. Screw that! We need someone to take our hand and look us in the eye and say this is where I've been, this is what I did (yes, I really did that!) and this is how I am today and if you want what I have I will tell you how I got here…I will share my story with you.

Our stories are all we really have to give to each other. Our stories are our experience, strength and hope. Maybe in my story you will see some of yourself. Maybe there is something in my story that will work for you. Maybe in my story you will find similarity, familiarity, a "dejavous-ness". Maybe, just maybe, by seeing my willingness to open up and tell my "stuff" you will find the willingness to do the same. By opening our souls and sharing our stories we join together in an ever compassionate community, each unique and yet the same, imperfect, scratched, dented, human and, yes, Holy. I heal by telling, I learn by listening. As I tell you my story I am healing and I am giving part of myself to you—I am healing the hole and connecting with the larger Whole.

"I'm here Baby Love. I'm here." it was my mother's voice. I couldn't remember what had happened or where I was but I could remember that I had been hurt and that everyone thought I was going to die. I kept thinking, "I didn't die. I knew I wasn't going to die. I didn't die." There were machines all around me and the room hummed. Somehow the machines seemed stacked all around me, blocking my view of the door or pretty much anything else. I tried to wake up but couldn't seem to come out of a hazy bubble that encircled me and the bed I lay in. My mother's voice was always there but I could not see her face. At times I wondered if I had hurt my eyes but I knew I could see. I could see the tubes and tape and the sheets and the machines that I felt were stacked around my bed and I could see pale blue walls.

All my world consisted of was tubes, sheets, machines that hummed and dinged rhythmically and voices and pale blue. It was as if they could see me but I couldn't see them. A lot of fuss was about the one pole. There were lots of poles and bags and tubes I could see but they were blurry and hazy, but the fuss was about the one I couldn't see. It was the blood pole. They put it at the head of my bed and referred to it in whispers but I knew it was there and

I knew it was important. I heard all of the conversations. Most were whispered. I knew that our little town had rallied and that people were lining up to give blood. Glen Carlson at the Texaco station was organizing people to go in shifts and get blood typed and donate. His blood was a match and everyone talked about how much he had donated and that the doctors wouldn't let him give more. They were very afraid of running out of blood. Who else is needing blood I wondered. I somehow knew it wasn't my sister. She was okay; I knew that but did not know how I knew that. The voices must have told me. I also knew that Kelly had hurt her head and that they took her to Sioux Falls but that I was too unstable to send to the "big" hospital in Sioux Falls, a two hour drive. The voices buzzed around me and fussed over me a lot but I don't remember talking back to them. The same voice that I heard tell my dad, "No you should see her now" whispered with my mom a lot. I don't remember most of what it said except for one thing. I remember that same voice saying to my Mom, "Get her the hell out of here." The voices just fussed a lot.

I could feel cuts and open wounds on my chest and face but my arms were busy connecting all of the machines to my body so I couldn't move my hands and touch them. My body was separate from me. I could think and I could hear and I could see a hazy blue surrounding my body, bed and machines but that was all I was. I was not connected to the body. I remember asking to see myself, asking for a mirror. Not sure how I asked because I don't remember ever using my voice. It was not to see what I looked like but to see if I was really there, although I didn't tell anyone else that. I was just this mind spinning around and ears and hazy eyes. Nothing else seemed real. My mother did get a mirror. Her voice told me it was her but I don't recall seeing her. She held the mirror up for me and I knew it upset her and her hand shook. I was right, there was no one there. I had looked into a mirror and I saw nothing. I remember the voices fussing to get a mirror, I remember the little plastic pale green pocket mirror, I remember my mom's hand and her voice, but I do not remember seeing my reflection look back at me.

Aside from the fussing voices and the pole with the blood I

remember two distinct people. *Tim Flanery and John Zwanzigger.*
Tim Flanery was the 17 year old son of Marcia and Dick Flanery.
The Flanery's and the Masters' were the best of friends. The 3
Flanery boys and the 4 Masters' girls had grown up together. My
mother's voice had told me she had to leave for a while and that
Tim was going to sit with me. "Strange choice of replacements," I
thought but that was the only thought. I did not see him come into
my room but I knew he was there because I could hear his voice. It
came from behind the machines. He was supposed to be on my left
side where my mother's voice always sat but his voice stayed behind
the machines on my right. I could tell there was something wrong
in his voice and then it was gone. I could still hear his breathing
and something told me that Tim Flanery was passed out on my
floor. "Someone will find him," I thought and "Guess there will
be no voice on my left for a while." I never thought hard about
why Tim had passed out, then again there was no reflection looking
back when I looked into the mirror.

    John Zwanzigger was also 17. He was my sister's boy friend.
My mother's voice told me the same thing as before. "I have to
leave for just a little bit and John is going to sit with you." Again,
the strangeness of the choice of maternal replacement struck me
but my own voice was not yet talking—I was just thoughts and
hearing and fuzzy seeing. On this day there was a new sound.
Bells. I could hear bells. I voiced no questions aloud; my mind just
recorded the fact that I could hear bells. The first time I remember
my voice speaking was on this day. I asked John, "Why are there
bells ringing?" My question made him uncomfortable and I think
he started to cry. He said, "The bells are for Kim." "Where is she?"
I asked. He started to cry harder. "Oh God! Oh God you don't
know?" he was mortified. He was afraid he would hurt me. I could
hear the panic in his voice and the bells kept ringing. Finally he
said, "Kim is dead. Kim died. The bells are from St. Paul's." That
is all he had to say. Now I knew. My mother had only left my side
for one reason to go to Kim's wake the day before and to go to Kim's
funeral right now. St. Paul's Catholic Church was across the street
and the music I was hearing was the earthling farewell to my friend
with the chocolate bunnies. I closed my eyes. I felt a tear sting my

cut up face. I must be connected with this body I thought, I must be here because I can feel my face stinging. I am here in this broken body and Kim is gone forever. I closed my eyes and I have no other memories of the pale blue room.

Part II:
Gathering The Info

3

The Instincts

History is full of "Thinkers". The great minds that delve into "things" and come up with complex theories of why we do what we do. In a short 200 years "Thinkers" like Hegel, Marx, Nietzche, James, Freud, Jung and Sartre poured onto our humanity countless sociologies, philosophies, psychologies and spiritualities. I love them. I love them all. They mesmerize me and entertain me and make me think, more than that they make me ponder and wonder. They teach me to ask questions, to see things from different perspectives, to dig deeper, to reach higher. What they do not do, however, is tell me how to today, right here, right now, make my life better. They do not tell me or show me how to *"feel better"*.

You see, these great thinkers have theories and the like, but what they do not do is tell me their stories. Theories push me back into the position of the observer. Theories do not allow me to participate. Theories intrigue me, but stories connect me to the whole. Stories draw me in and take hold of my heart and soul. The wisdom in a simple myth will trump a theory every time if its value is measured by the number of human beings it has touched and changed. Stories give birth to theories and bring them to life. Theories give birth to stories as well, but only stories have the ability to add color, to enliven, to infuse life, weave in meaning and intertwine love. Only stories can convey the adventure of being alive. Only stories can link our thinking, and feeling together in a way that connects us to the teller and the whole of humanity. My experience, strength and hope emboldens you and your experience, strength and hope empowers me. In another's story I learn about me and in my story another may find a mirror into his own soul. Stories not only teach me but they also change me. It is still amazing to me to think that I have a story that no one else in this entire universe could tell. We each possess a unique myth, a one of a kind story. We each possess an invaluable gift that we can choose to (or choose not to) give to the rest of humanity. Tell your story. Tell me your story. Listen to my story. What comfort we could give one another if we shared our secrets.

Story telling is this; it is philosophy, psychology, sociology and spirituality for the common folk, for the masses. Above all, it is do-able. We can listen to another's story. We all know how to listen. We can each tell our own story. We have it memorized! Presto! No homework, no cliff notes. The clincher is this, we have to do it. Just thinking about it doesn't cut it. And we have to tell our story to another human being. We can't just sit there and reflect on our past. That is sort of like biting your own teeth. Our best thinking got us to where we are today. More thinking about ourselves with our own brains is likely to simply recycle the same stuff all over again. It doesn't work.

What is also essential here is to REALLY tell our stories. We can't just give a bio, a time-line, a play by play of socially sanctified high points. The important stuff lies deeper at the level of the instinct. Our survival instincts are flight, fight, freeze and f..., ok, let's just call it fertilize. In other words we are born with the innate survival behaviors that ensure we live on. These instincts worked for the cave man and kept him alive to procreate and voila thousands of years later here we are. The instincts must have served him well. He survived to populate the earth. Today our struggle is not so much to keep from literally getting eaten by the saber tooth tiger, but still we need to guard our territory, to protect ourselves, to stand our ground. Our world is threatening and intimidating too. The threats have just been "culturified". We still have to work to put food on the table. The same instincts coded deep into the DNA of our cavemen ancestors have been passed on to us and they still serve the same purpose—they help us survive.

Flight, fight, freeze and *fertilize.* A huge part of our stories lies at the level of these survival instincts and how we have used or mis-used these essential behaviors. Our personal myths are full of characters that we do not recognize until we tell our stories out loud. Each of our stories has a plentitude of the "instinct characters"...*runners, fighters, hiders* and *lovers* (and we will talk about the *lovers* later). Instincts have served us well in trying times. They have also, at times, overcompensated, appeared when they were not needed, gone a little too far, and when this happens, normal everyday instincts undergo a metamorphosis. They change from being simple survival behaviors into what I like to call "instinct characters". Once our instincts have decided to run amuck, once our instincts have gone awry they assume a life all of their own and become actual characters in our myths. Our stories are full of these colorful characters. Our liveliest adventures and most vivid memories are created by these fellows. And although these characters put the comedy and the tragedy in our stories, we are not always proud of the starring role that we played.

Let's see:

1. *The fighters.* They just put it all out there, if the thought or feeling comes to mind...blah...it comes out and they spill it. They are confronters and their words can be venom. Born to wage war, "Hit 'em and move" is their mantra. Piss off a fighter and they will not forget it.
2. *The runners.* These folks ignore the thoughts and feelings all together, they run from them, deny them, refuse to realize that they are even present. Runners are deniers and the world's best procrastinators.
3. *The hiders.* They have thoughts or feelings and they stuff them or file them away somewhere deep inside and pretend that they don't exist. Unfortunately, when defenses are down these well hidden thoughts and feelings come out in a rage, in a flurry of emotion or even more unfortunately, they never come out at all. Hiders are the masters of silent scorn.

The truth is that we all have all of them, we all are all of them. However, we do learn through experience which instincts work best for us (or so we think) and those are the instincts that we start to rely on in lieu of the others. Those are the ones that tend to take on a life of their own and transition into the vibrant figures that make up our stories. Sad to say, but we become predictable.

Hmmm? Let me see…my instincts gone awry…

Let us start with a girl and a boy again. New relationship. The romance and infatuation of a new love is blossoming. Words rarely cross. The other can rarely do anything wrong. All of the little idiosyncrasies are still cute and endearing. It is holiday season and all of the warm fuzzy emotions of the familiar are flowing freely. Plans have been set to spend a first holiday season together as a couple. His kids, her kids, new traditions. A fresh start for two lives that have been torn and tattered by divorce and are looking to rebuild, to maybe start some new traditions that their children will remember and pass on just as they have passed on the traditions that their parents and grandparents gave them. They discuss who is getting what for Christmas, when to open presents, how to do the Santa thing. Different households. Should we all stay at one house Christmas Eve so we can enjoy the Santa surprise together? Like a family, like it was supposed to be before failed marriages and the trials of life shattered the ideal. She has shopped for everyone and placed the presents all under one tree at his house. The tone has been set. It is lovely.

"My office is forgoing the Christmas Party this year. How about yours?" she asks. "We are having one but I don't think I want to go. I'm not sure I want to deal with everyone asking questions about you and me maybe it is just too soon still to deal with what everyone will think." BOOM! BLAH! There it is. It came out and it sits there like a big white elephant in the middle of the room. Dude! I am okay to shop for you and your kids, to plan a "family" Christmas with but you don't want anyone to know.

Whoa! You just gotta wish that thought hadn't come out. Yep, it did, in all of its glory. Now there is absolutely nothing wrong with the thought itself and it obviously needs to be examined further but geez, you think maybe it is one of those thoughts that you should've run by a buddy, a pal, a friend, but nooo, you had to regurgitate it up to the one person who may have a wee bit of trouble empathizing with you. It sort of seems like that thought missed some sort of relay station in the brain that should've funneled it to another situation. I mean really what did you do, eat a bowl of stupid for breakfast?

Obviously trouble is coming and so often don't we just wish we could suck those words back in and think first. The thought, the concern is valid but just because it is in my brain doesn't mean it needs to come out right here, right now. It seems like that old reliable "survival instinct" would have built in an automatic, mandatory pause between thoughts and actions. Sort of like an approval station in the brain that says "you may pass go and you may collect your $200".

Or how about this, an approval station that gives my brain further direction on what to do with any given thought:

1. *Great thought you may proceed to vocalization.*
2. *Needs a different audience please file for later use.*
3. *Beep! Beep! Beep! Bullshit detector activated check yourself Pal.*
4. *Your timing sucks Einstein. Save it for later*
5. *Blah, blah, blah, blah but say it if you want.*

Why isn't that encoded into our damn DNA?

I know, I know, "There is a God; I'm not it."

Although the instincts were designed to help us, often we rely on them too much, and when we do they are transformed into the dreaded, troublesome, sometimes glamorous but always entertaining "instinct characters". We are all *runners, fighters* or *hiders* at one time or another. And when we morph into one of these characters, (and we all do it!) we are at our most colorful. Good, bad or ugly, each of us has been transformed into one or all of these vivid "instinct characters".

It is when that which was intended to help us starts to hurt us that we need to dissect it further. "Great" you say, "I thought you said no homework?" you say. Relax, remember, we each have our own story memorized. We each have a story to recollect and tell, but the hard part is already done. We have already lived the story, the characters have already been born, now we just need to tell the tale. And yep, the "instinct characters" need to be in there!

Let's look at our stories as a beautiful piece of art work, a carving, a piece of ceramic, a sculpture, an exquisite tapestry. It is then that we get to stand back and admire the masterpiece that is our stories, our lives up to this point in time. And if we were to describe to another just the parts of this artwork that we like or just the parts that we do not like then we would not be describing the art in its entirety. Think of it like this, when we apply for a job we give a bio, we hit the peaks and the high points and when we get to know someone well we share a lot of our trials and trying times, the low points or the troughs. In recollecting and telling our stories we need fill in all the space between the high points and the low points. It is in the space between the points that we have done most of our living. It is in the space between the points that our true stories are told and the weaving of the tapestry that is our lives is woven. It is in the space between the points that we find our *instincts gone awry*.

When we look closer at this space, we will see that our art work, like any art work, is not without its fair share of flaws and imperfections. If we look carefully we will see, throughout our past, little cracks and irregularities. Times when then knife didn't slice smoothly, when the glaze didn't spread evenly, when the chisel slipped, when the threads grew thin and colorless. These are the parts of our stories that will teach the most, these are the parts of our stories that we not only need to tell, but that others need to hear.

Paradoxically, it is the flaws in our stories that hold untold value. The cracks are what make our stories inimitable and of incalculable worth. The imperfections prove that we are real, fleshy, earthy, sensual beings. It is in these uneven places between the points that we will see how our natural, innate instincts to survive somehow got a bit cockeyed and came to life as "instinct characters". If we leave these "instinct characters" out of our stories the flaws will be perpetuated. Left unaddressed these *instincts gone awry* will allow the cracks in this priceless piece of art we call our lives to grow wider and deeper. Cracks will turn to nicks and gaps and craters and voids…and yes…to holes.

Fighters, Runners & Hiders

Generally speaking, *fighting* and *running* and *hiding* each leave characteristic cracks, predictable defects.

1. For *fighters*, the stain or the flaw is in the form of resentment. It is unresolved anger at wrongs done to us.
2. For *runners*, denial is the aberration. It is that "if I ignore it, it didn't happen or it will go away."
3. For *hiders,* it is all a masquerade. The blemish is in the pretending.

Regardless of which one we are dealing with however, the root is usually the same...fear. When we react with an instinct behavior it is because we are afraid.

Fighters

We all know *fighters*. We've all been *fighters*. And these characters are a handful. Why? Well, because *fighters* fight. As *fighters*, we believe we have to fight and we take pride in being good *fighters*. As *fighters*, we fight everything and everyone in a glorious battle that we don't even want to win. We are in it for the fight. We have been deluded by this instinct into believing that the only way to save ourselves is to fight. We come out swinging no matter what the occasion. The instinct to fight has gone awry and has become transfigured into an animated chum.... the *fighter* character. He may be a chum but he is no pal. So, although these characters can be entertaining, and sometimes the remembering is even humorous, I caution you now, the *fighter* character always steals from us...he always takes away our *choice*.

Now don't get me wrong, I'm not talking about defending oneself or the kind of fighting that is that normal, natural and healthy exchange of differing opinions. That kind of fighting does not cause "cracks" in our art work. The cracks come from when we use this instinct out of habit and it becomes our natural response to pretty much anything. In normal, healthy fighting the emotion involved is simple anger. For the *fighter* character anger hangs around and doesn't subside. And ultimately it is transformed and the emotion left behind is resentment. Anger comes and goes, resentment sticks around and distorts and colors the way we perceive the world. Resentment brews and simmers and grows and warps our appraisal of the world and the people around us. Resentment takes on a life of its own and ultimately weaves its way into our personalities, convolutes our thinking and pretends to be part of us. It turns us into the "instinct character" of the *fighter*.

So how do we find incidences when we were *fighters*? All we have to do is ask ourselves the simple question, "Who or what do I harbor anger, outrage, annoyance or even hatred toward?" In other words, "Who or what do I have resentment toward?" Asking this question typically brings up a whole range of emotion especially feelings such as, "I was wronged. I was hurt. I was mistreated. I was swindled. I was abused." Those feelings are valid and very often we "deserve" to feel this way. Bad things happen. However, when we let these instances make their home in our beings in the form of resentment we are giving them permission to continue to cause us pain. The cracks caused by deep seated, long held resentments are usually pretty easy to spot not just as we reflect backward into our stories, but they are also pretty easy to spot in our beings each and every day as we "go about living".

An example...

Recently an acquaintance of mine was preparing to take his daughter, who is finishing her junior year in high school, to visit a college campus. He had flown in to Tulsa for the occasion, had rented a car and was staying at an area hotel. Though it was early April and the trees were blooming the local weather stations warned of a cold front and possible snow. Sure enough the day of their trip arrived and we awoke to 6 inches of snow on the ground and it was coming down heavy. The day would have been considered just another day in South Dakota but in Tulsa, Oklahoma had it not been Saturday it would have been considered a "snow-day" with school cancelled. I sent my friend a quick text message offering my vehicle. It said, "Hey the weather is looking bad and it is supposed to keep coming. Maybe you guys should take my vehicle just to be

*safe. They don't clear the roads here like they do in South Dakota."
It was a brand new, four wheel drive, heavy vehicle suitable for
any weather and definitely a safe, capable vehicle for this kind of
day. I have known this person well for a number of years and am
quite familiar with his personality and demeanor. Despite this,
his response surprised me. It was via text message and it said,
"Why would I want to do that?"*

*Whoa! Red flags! Danger Will Robinson, danger! Fighters
fight! I chose to leave the situation alone. My friend subsequently
returned to the airport, exchanged his car for a four wheel drive
vehicle and proceeded on his trip.*

*The point here is not so much what he chose to do as is the fact
that a gesture of kindness was extended his way and he perceived
it for one reason or another as threatening and therefore was not
able to experience "the good". I can only hypothesize as to the
thoughts going through his head but I imagine they were, whether
he realizes it or not, something like this: "She thinks I don't know
how to drive in the snow." Or "She thinks I can't afford to rent
an appropriate vehicle." Or "She thinks I need her help." Or "She
sees me as incapable". In his conditioned defensive posture he was
so busy staying "on guard" that he completely missed the human
kindness.*

He hurt my feelings. Fucking fighters!!

Grudges don't have to be against other people, things or institutions,
they can be directed at ourselves although then we seldom call them
grudges. When they are directed inward they manifest themselves as
an aura of negativity. We walk around expecting the worst, certain
that life is pitted against us. The cup is not only half empty but also has
a hole in it and is leaking fast. Reality in general is not to be trusted.
We are conditioned to being "on guard", ready for the attack at all
times. There must be something more to it we tell ourselves, what is
the catch, what is the angle?

In general, our resentment against ourselves and the rest of the
world repels others, mostly because it is based in an angry refusal to
see things any other way. No one can help us because our instincts

have tricked us into believing that this is just the way it is. Whether we remain passive with a gloomy, pessimistic, colorless outlook; or assertive and continually tell the world how things should be, we create a self-fulfilling prophecy. The world is bad, not to be trusted and other people are against us. We pat ourselves on the back feeling clever, vigilant, observant and cautious when truthfully we, little by little, incident by incident, excommunicate ourselves from that which is the most fulfilling in life…loving connection with the greater whole of humanity and the greater Whole.

It matters not where our battle field lies, it can be the boardroom or the bedroom, the white house or the farm house, the pulpit or the pew. Where ever it may be, we become incapable of playing on the team because our attitude toward the world is as follows:

1. we will control the on goings around us and every one must play along, in the roles and with the opinions, that we want them to have or;
2. we insist that the world is unacceptable and there no point to any of it and we become cynical, contemptuous and scornful.

Either way, this *instinct gone awry* has positioned our *fighter* against the universe and he will run riot, impose his will onto others and when they rebel he will say, "Aha! I knew it! They are all against me!" There is nothing quite like a self-fulfilling prophecy. The mode or the means matter not, a fighter will always attempt to trample over others. The results are typically anger, revenge, rage or repulsion. Nothing good!!!

Despite these destructive cycles fighters somehow manage to function in this world. Taken to its most extreme, however *fighters* become completely separated from reality and hopelessly lost in their instinct to *fight* that has gone mad. Their *fighter character* tells them that everyone is out to get them and eventually this leads to mental illness and paranoia. Paranoids take on an attitude of "it is me against the world" and convince themselves that the whole of humanity is against them. They become deserted on an island of isolation, surrounded by flesh-eating fish. They are locked in bodies that are infected with anger turned resentment turned paranoia.

Fighters hold on to anger, become infected with grudges and begin to view their reality through diseased glasses. The infecting agent is cunning as it enters our being in the guise of an aid, as an instinct designed to help us. What happens in the shadows of our beings, however, is a covert contamination of our view of others and of the outside world. You see, by controlling how we see the outside world resentment takes possession of the only tool we have with which to write our stories…resentment takes possession of our ability to choose. Resentment taints our reading of reality and in doing so limits, directs and dictates our actions and reactions to every situation that we face. It takes away our *choice* of how we wish to act and react. Resentment left unaddressed changes us. It changes us subtly, slowly in miniscule little ways that add up into monumental, global changes in the people we become. Resentment will eventually rot away what is authentic in us and begin to write our stories for us.

Now no one is saying, just let go of it. But how about we simply pull out these instances, tell of them as part of our stories (yes, out loud to another human being!) and then when we put them back into our pasts where they belong we will file them differently. You see, our *fighter* character has refused to file the incident or the occasion into our memory banks and has chosen rather to keep the file active as a grinding, gnawing resentment allowed to tint and taint our view of the world. Our own *fighting* instinct has allowed a wound to fester and grow and has forced us to unwittingly trade the freedom of *choice* for the decay of resentment.

How do we un-do the *fight*, the resentment? Are we, who have become *fighters*, now so hardwired this way that there is little hope? No. We have not always been *fighters*. We learned it. We *fighters* do need, probably more than anyone else, to examine with brutal honesty, the cracks in the art work of our stories. We will remain unable to fully experience the joy of community, of connectedness, of intimacy with another until we clear the distortions that this instinct has woven into our stories, into our lives. It is essential to clean up the rubbish if we are to find what is authentic in ourselves.

As we tell our stories and uncover and expose resentment we have, for a moment in time, a chance to choose differently. We can exercise our God given freedom to choose either to let the resentment fester or to face it, share it and put it where it belongs as a simple event in the stories we have written with our lives thus far…nothing more, nothing less. We can file these events into the complex beings that we have become, as memories, as part of our stories, as something that changed us and shaped us or we can choose to keep it unfiled and to allow the *fighter* to have free reign over our future.

Again, by tinting the glasses with which we view the world, resentment confiscates the one tool we have been given to author our own stories...*our choice*. By exposing resentment, sharing it within the confines of our story and filing it back into our pasts, we are erasing the tint it has placed on our glasses.

Indeed, the *fighter* characters need to be in the stories we tell. Without judgment or blame we need to include them as part of our story, give away the resentment and re-file the memory as an authentic, real part of our story. A story that has thus far been lived, written, is past tense, over and done. We own it, take responsibility for our part in it, educate ourselves with the lessons it has taught us, accept that we can't change it and let it be what it is....part of our story.

Runners

Ah yes, *runners*! *We runners* run, from reality mostly but also from ourselves and from others. Who qualifies as a *runner*? All of us, if we look hard enough at our stories, will find examples of ourselves as *runners*. The proto-types of a *runner* would be the dreamers, the fanciful, the theorizers, the star-gazers. Those of us who tend to idealize and romanticize. I qualify. I am both proud and guilty to announce myself as an incurable romantic. Often I have taken pride in saying, "It's lovely and beautiful. It is how everyone should be." What is wrong with this? Ah hello? We run into major problems when actuality knocks on the door. We dreamers, idealists and escapists tend to focus on "how it should be" and conveniently chose to overlook the "how it is". This purposeful evasion of reality is synonymous with *running*. We chose to deny the actual and to live in an adolescent dream world. The instinct of *running* for the caveman was basically this, run or you are going to get eaten. When brought up to modern day, the *running* is not literally from the saber tooth tiger but rather a *running* from anything our personas or our egos perceive as threatening. Deny, deny, deny. Procrastinate! Say it isn't so! That is it; *runner* characters quite literally tell themselves "It isn't so!" The instinct to run becomes a daemon that requires addressing as this *instinct gone awry* will, just as *fighting* does, steal our freedom and make our choices. The *runner* character chooses to remain in full flight from reality. This means that our *true character* doesn't get to choose. The *runner* steals choice.

It is not difficult to look into our stories and find an event, a vacation, a holiday, a job, a lover that we idealized in our minds, that we romanticized, that we visualized as the Shangri-La. The key word here is visualized, for the *runner* is rarely interested in the real, the tangible, the carnal. The *runner* stays trapped in the ideal. As Sam Keen puts it, "…they are essentially voyeurs. They never get beyond the plastic façade, the attractive surface of the other's persona. Their Eros is aroused more by the image than by the flesh, more by the idea than the actuality of the other."

When I look at my story and see the *runner* in myself I often laugh. To me, a lot of my running is quite humorous in retrospect. Not sure it was so funny in actual time but from a more objective, safe vantage point I shake my head and think "Girl! What were you thinking?"…

I have always prided myself on not really having a "thing", you know, a hang up, a pet peeve. Like I deserve a medal or something for being the easiest going person in the world. As far as I can tell the bed sleeps the same whether it was made that day or not. So if you like it made then go right ahead and make it. No really, it won't bother me a bit, I don't mind. If you don't like it made then don't make it, like I said, it sleeps the same. It doesn't matter to me either way. I am also of the opinion that my coat is just as warm whether I hang it in the closet or toss it on the chair. So sometimes I hang it in the closet and once in a while I'll toss it on the chair or even the ground just to mix things up a little bit. Just the other day I found the cutest spring top, dark green (my favorite color) cotton knit, sleeveless with a little flair at the hip, a bit plunging at the neck line but I figure hey, if it bothers you don't look, right? How easy going is that? Then I go about thinking what a gem I am. Boy am I easy to be around. You don't see me having a fit because the cupboards aren't closed or the dishwasher isn't loaded correctly or the toothpaste tube is all smunched up. Nope none of those "things" really get to me. I may make the bed, I may not. I may hang up my coat, I may not. Boy, living with me is always a surprise! One day I may load the dishwasher with coffee cups on top and plates below and the next I may just squish everything in there and quickly shut the door. And if I'm feeling particularly carefree I may not do the dishes at all. It just depends, I say. On what does it depend? It depends on how I am feeling, on what my mood is, on how hurried or leisurely my schedule is, on how much energy I have, on whether or not the show I want to watch is already on or not, on whether or not I need a clean coffee cup, on who I may have invited over to visit, on whether or not.....

I, I, I, me, me, me, my, my, my.....Okay so maybe my plan doesn't account for anyone else's opinion or want or "thing". I can mold. I can morph. What would you like me to be? Neat and tidy? No problem yo! I can make the bed with military pleats that would make any officer proud. Puff the pillows; pull up the comforter... perfectamundo! Kitchen duty, I got that down too. I know, I know, cups and bowls on top, plates and pans on the bottom. Done! Coat is in the closet, dirty clothes in the hamper. That works for me. See there I am a peach to get along with. No earthly idea why I have been divorced three times. You'd think I had terminal OCD or something when actually I'm pretty laid back and mellow. You what? What do you mean, don't use military pleats because your feet get hot at night? You've got to be joking! You actually want me to organize the forks with the forks and the spoons with the spoons for easier dishwasher unloading? Really? That hanger is yours so I need to choose another? Uuuh, someone wake me up paaaleeez!!! For real? You think this shirt may not be quite perfect for dinner with your boss? Uh hello, I can't control where the man's eyes go. Sounds like you are blaming me for his problem. Nuhuh I'm not responsible for his issues...or yours.

Great! Here I sit innocent little me minding my own business simply excited to wear the first new shirt I have bought in 6 MONTHS! How about trying, "Hey babe, you look great in that shirt, perfect color for you. Maybe you should save that for a romantic dinner for two. You look sexy as hell in that shirt." You

*think maybe that would have been a little softer way to put it? Guys
have no clue. He might just as well have said, "You look like a dirty
little whore. I'd rather have hemorrhoids than let my boss think I
would date any one short of impeccable." After all, it is all about
his image right? Besides if he is worried about his image maybe he
should spit the gum out. I mean, really, who taught him to chew
that way? Switch to mints, pal, the gum is not working for you!! I
think I liked you better in my imagination than in real life. I'm
going back to the fantasy! Make your own damn bed.*

The painful part about being a *runner* is the realization that we are
being chased. The harsh truth of human existence and the reality of
the world we live in are always in hot pursuit. Truth and reality will
eventually catch up to us. Truth and reality will always win this race.
Though I have poked fun at some of the laughable *running* we can do,
truth and reality can be difficult and at times at wrenching. When we
run from the real and live in the make believe world of the ideal we
deny our authentic selfs and we give away our freedom. We reject that
which is imperfect; we throw away our right to be human and flawed.
When we refuse to see our own imperfections we remain aloft in a
fantasy where we cannot possibly know ourselves, we cannot possibly
make free choices and we cannot possibly make ourselves available to
be known by another. In our imaginations we are perfect, grandiose
and faultless and become incapable of even entertaining the idea of
flaws. Our beings are kidnapped and held prisoner by the delusion that
reality should be ideal and this delusion insists on doing the choosing
and thereby perpetuating itself. Again, our freedom to choose is
hijacked by an *instinct gone awry*. We hold others at arms length lest
we see a blemish and have our fantasy fractured. We have no interest
in the warm, fleshy, gnarled, wounded and scarred realness of an actual
human being; we are content to be the comfortable observer of the
unrealistic ideal we have invented. In the extreme, we have become
pornographers…we seek passion without involvement, we are more
content to observe passion from afar.[6] In our make believe world, all
of life is a magical drama played out by actors living the unattainable.
Again we are on an island alone in isolation lost in a grand fantasy that

no other human being could possibly participate in as imperfections are not permitted.

If we *runners* don't fall into the group of grandiose then typically we are in the opposite fantasy where we are less than, worthless, contemptible and ignoble. Oh come on! No one is that bad…which is case and point that the *runner* character is still in a fantasy, although this type of fantasy is torment rather than ecstasy. *Runners* have a tough time just being right sized. They are either too good or too bad. On a scale from one to ten runners are always a zero or a 10 ½, they are never just plain old fives like the rest of us. Nevertheless, even as zeros we remain observers or voyeurs as contact with a real living human being with flesh, bones, scars and stretch marks would shred our nightmare to pieces. It would bring us up to a five and force us to face reality. Remember, *running* from the real is what works for the *runner* even if it means living in a bad dream.

Our art work is indeed cracked by the occasions that we have refused to see reality for what it is and to deal with it head on.

1. Where in our stories have the cracks been caused by a "flight from reality"?
2. Where have we denied our failures, our mistakes and instead turned from them as if they did not happen?
3. Where did we fail to embrace and own our screw-ups?
4. Where did we refuse to admit that we had a problem or that we needed help?
5. Where did we cause pain by inserting the life of another into our twisted, tainted fantasy world and then persecute them when they didn't live up to the unreachable expectations that we set for them, when they didn't know the lines to the masterpiece of "How Life Should Be According To Me"?
6. Where did we harm ourselves and others by holding them at a distance when their hearts needed closeness but ours could not risk the fracture of our illusion?

Yep, these belong in our story. They need to addressed with adult honesty and reconciled with that which is actual and evident. Moving forward from this day, we need to leave the star gazing behind, let go of adolescent day-dreaming and exist in the here and now, imperfect world like everyone else. We need to pull out the occasions when we became *runners*, put them in our stories, tell them to another human being and then re-file them in our memory banks. These incidents were mishaps, flaws, imperfections, flashes of unclear thinking, junctures of instincts gone awry, moments of "humanness", but they stole our freedom of *choice* and therefore need to be in the stories we tell. And then, they can be left there, in our pasts, in the stories we have written thus far.

Hiders

Our caveman ancestors also *hid* from physical danger, that which threatened their very existence. Our *hiding* as contemporary humans is the *hiding* of that which is real in us, from others and from ourselves. You can't hurt me if you don't know me. We *hiders* tend to commit our ills by omission rather than by commission. We *hiders* are "don't rock the boaters" and are therefore an agreeable lot. Our sins of omission tend to be about failing to speak up or speak out, failing to let others in and failing to let ourselves out. Often our answer to anything is whatever it is we think the asker wants the answer to be. We are pleasers, compliers, joiners. Pretenders. The nice boys and girls that everyone likes. We get things done. Follow directions. Do what we are told. Agree. We are...TOO GOOD TO BE TRUE!!!!

We are too good to be true because we are pretending, masquerading. At some point we *hiders* have learned it is safest to keep that which is precious deep inside where it is protected. No one needs to know what is in there except us...the snag is this, eventually the *hider* character gets so good at *hiding* that we hide what is deep down inside even from ourselves. *Hiders* lose track of who we are. On the surface we wear a mask. Since we are not authentic we become agreeable to whomever or whatever we happen to be addressing at the moment. And since we are agreeable to whomever we happen to be around we come off as happy-go-lucky optimists.

Ah but here is the glitch, the *hiding instinct gone awry*, like the *fighting* and the *running*, absconds with the freedom to choose. We hiders, clenching so hard to the illusion of safety that *hiding* provides, surrender our most treasured possession. *Choice.* Hiding has become so safe, such a reliable security blanket, that we become willing to barter away our freedom of *choice* in exchange for the illusion of safety. Albert Einstein described this instance of *instinct gone awry* well when he said, "He who joyfully marches to music in rank and file has already earned my contempt. He has been given a large brain by mistake, since for him the spinal cord would suffice." Hiding steals *choice.*

Hiders skip the essential step into adulthood that requires us to think and decide for ourselves. We skip this step because the instinct to *hide* has, at some point, taken over. The instinct to *hide* has gone awry. We are the most comfortable keeping our true feelings *hidden* and are famous for being what we are supposed to be. We let others *choose* for us and because we never *choose* we are blameless innocents. By latching on to this manner of interaction with our world we don masks and start to pretend so well that we eventually believe our own charade. We can no longer tell the true from the false, we have learned to just go with it. We eventually lose all track of what our own thoughts, feelings and values actually are. We have, for so long, given away our freedom to *choose* them that we no longer know what we value or how we feel. At this point we are not only *hidden* from others but we are also *hidden* from ourselves.

Along with skipping the class on the making decisions for ourselves, we *hiders* also manage to slip right by the course in boundary setting. Boundaries are meant to be something that defines who we are and are not as human beings. *Hiders* build walls, dig tunnels, create camouflages. Hiders use boundaries to keep themselves "in" and to lock others "out". For the *hider* character boundaries do not define they confine. Risking, making a decision or setting a boundary means showing our true colors and as *hiders* we prefer the grey. We just want to blend, at all cost blend, for God's sake blend!

The *hider* characters have a polite pathology about them. Allowing others to *choose* is, after all, kind, thoughtful and gracious, right? Nah, to others, *hiders* are sticky, sweet, plastic and somehow absent. We are incapable of establishing solid, sincere relationships because we have no intention of coming out of *hiding* to participate. *Hiders* start to believe that if we keep the genuine self inside our being we can keep it pristine and pure and safe. In our efforts to protect ourselves we create a slow, tortuous auto-asphyxiation. We leave the "real" deep inside to suffocate, abandoned and forsaken. By not allowing ourselves "out of the box" we, like the *fighters* and *runners*, become isolated and alone without *choice*.

We become unable to seek company even in ourselves as we no longer know who we are. The cruelness of the *hiding* façade is that as *hiders* our pain goes unnoticed. Our isolation is invisible. We have learned to pretend so well that on the outside we appear happy, involved and content. No one knows what remains *hidden* inside. We bow down to God, the church, mom and dad, the government, the boss and what others think. We tend to be the ones that put on a smile, send out happy thoughts and go home and blow our brains out.

Me, I am a hider and sometimes a runner. But mostly I am an excellent hider. The other day I walked into my 16 year daughter's room and she said, "What's up with you? You look tired." I replied, "No, just have a lot on my mind. I have sort of gone into my hole." She answered, "Mom you don't go into holes, you dig tunnels. Just come out, it's not so scary out here." And I thought no one else noticed. I have always consoled myself by saying, "I'm not hurting anyone else. It is just me. This is just how I am. This is how I handle things." Huh? Guess my crack is showing.

It wasn't but a few weeks later that this sweet 16 year old was herself experiencing one of life's trials…the first heartbreak…

After days in her bedroom texting, facebooking and talking with anyone who would listen she emerged and sat down beside me in the living room. She said, "Mom I just want to talk." I tried to listen and I tried to talk with her but every word was met with a hostile reply from her. "I am not going to do that!", "I already did that", "Why won't you tell me what to do?" "You just don't get it!". I felt helpless but I listened and I tried. Finally she began to cry and said, "I can't believe you just sit there and let me be so mean to you. I am just being cruel to you and you just sit there and take it." My response was this…

"It was just a few weeks ago that you pointed out to me that I do not dig holes, I tunnel. Come here, I want to show you what happens when people tunnel." We walked into my room and I showed her a big gash in my wall. "You see that hole in my wall,

you see that stain. Do you know what that is from? It is where I threw my coffee cup against the wall. When people hide like I do eventually they blow. I blew and I hurled my coffee cup against my bedroom wall. I am trying not to tunnel and it is hard to change. I don't ever want you to tunnel.. I would rather have you through insults and unkind words at me than to keep it all inside. I don't want you to be a hider. Get it out baby. That is the healthier way to handle problems. I want you to learn the lessons now and not when you are 45 and still throwing cups at the wall."

And for the moment I was glad that I had not repaired my wall.

The gash in my bedroom wall remains today…it teaches me not to tunnel…

Okay then, let's put all of those *hiding* parts into our stories too. Again, let's recollect the times we have failed to own our essence, when we have given away our God given right to make decisions for ourselves, when we have put up walls instead of boundaries and, you guessed it, put them in our stories, tell them out loud to another human being and leave them there. Leave them in the past where they belong…as memories of when we let the instinct to *hide* go awry and pretended to be something other than ourselves.

I don't know how many days had passed or recall the ride but next thing I remember I was sharing a hospital room with my sister. We were still in the Huron hospital though I knew my parents were working hard to get me transferred to a better equipped hospital. Huron was a small town with a handful of family practice doctors. The night I was hurt was an aberrancy in the Huron emergency room. Staffing the emergency room that night was a surgery resident. A common practice in the rural parts of our country is to get doctors in training to staff rural areas in exchange for forgiveness of their student loans. That is what Dr. Cavanaugh was doing the night I got hurt. He was working to get his student loans forgiven. That was the only reason there was an actual surgeon in the emergency room when they brought me in. Dr. Cavanaugh became an overnight hero in our little town and the love our little town endured as I am told that Dr. Cavanaugh finished his training and returned to the little town that fell in love with him just a few short years later to set up his surgery practice. On his desk today there still sits a frame and in it a picture of a happy 15 year old blonde girl in a Huron Tigers cheerleading uniform.

This room was a dingy yellow color and my bed was the closest to the window. What I remember most about this room is pain. Excruciating, so bad I cannot even scream and I cannot even cry type of pain. Dr. Cavanaugh estimated that it would be another 10 days before I was stable enough to move to Sioux Falls. I had spent 10 days in intensive care and now had been moved to a regular floor bed. Dr. Cavanaugh had saved my life. He repaired tremendous internal injury. A ruptured spleen, a ruptured liver, a torn pancreas and a torn stomach wall. All of which had caused massive internal bleeding that required immediate surgery and 23 units of blood transfused over the subsequent week. What Dr. Cavanaugh had not repaired was the multiple displaced, compound fractures of my hip, leg and pelvis. This was my eleventh day of lying with bones crushed and shattered and unset. I didn't understand why they were letting me hurt so much. I didn't want to move rooms, I didn't want to see my sister, I didn't want my friends to visit; I wanted them to give me medicine and let me die. This is when I became a hider. This is when I learned that the only protection I was going to get from my unfathomable circumstance was inside myself. I learned to hide inside my own head. My instincts were saving me from that which I could not cope.

My orthopedic injuries consisted of the following: two broken thumbs, eight broken ribs, left femur broken in 9 spots, left tibia broken and extending through the skin, left hip fractured, pelvis crushed with 13 fractures. There was no such thing as an orthopedic surgeon in Huron, South Dakota. The bones would have to wait until Dr. Cavanaugh thought I was stable enough for the ambulance ride to Sioux Falls.

So I lived the next 10 days in 1 hour increments. I would count, *hour one, hour two, hour three, relief, repeat. Hour one, right after my shot. It was my favorite hour. This was the catch my breath hour. I could think; I could sleep. Hour two, the pain would start to increase, the anxiety and fear would start to climb. I knew what was coming. "Breathe, concentrate, go somewhere else". It always started in my left hip and pelvis. It felt as if someone was standing on me with the heel of a boot and that they were pushing harder and harder and then they would start to grind it into me. I was breaking in half. It was coming, it was coming. Terror would start, bargaining would start, deal making with God would start. Hour three, this is when Leslie would go away, she would simply vanish. Evanesce, nowhere to be found, no reflection looking back. No one could help her. She was all alone. Two boot heels were pulverizing me now. They were stomping, and so mean and so angry and they just wanted to hurt me more and more and more. "My bones are just powder, just powder." I would tell myself. "You can't crush powder." I was smarter than the boots. "You can't hurt me if I refuse to notice, to care." I would go somewhere that the boots couldn't find me; somewhere so deep that I don't think I could find my way back there now. The worst time was at the end of the third hour because I had to come back to the real world to ask for my shot. One night at one in the morning I was crying hard and the nurses wouldn't come so I flicked my nurse light on and off and on and off. My sister, awakened by the noise, asked what I was doing and then offered to click her light on and off and on and off for a while so I could rest. That is the only thing I remember saying to her or her to me the whole 10 days. I know she was in my room but I don't remember ever seeing her. Shot. Twenty minutes. Breathe, regain control, breathe. Start over, hour one. Three hours. That is how long I had to wait between shots of Demerol. Not sure why but there was no intravenous pain control. I received a shot in my good leg every three hours around the clock. About 5 days into the ordeal my leg was bruised and rock hard and the shots were then given in my arms or my hip or anywhere there was a piece of non-indurated flesh. I had two large tubes coming out of my abdomen that the nurses would come mess with from time to time but I never looked down at them, I didn't want to see. All I knew was that there was a large white dressing that covered my entire abdomen and that it hurt a lot. I also had a large catheter in my left neck where they gave me a yellow fluid that was supposedly my nutrition.*

Lisa had been hurt badly too but her injuries paled compared to mine. She had a bad break in her left arm that was surgically repaired and a hairline fracture of her pelvis. I could hear people come get her each morning for physical therapy and I remember that it hurt her to get up and move. There were a lot of visitors but mostly to see my sister because I didn't want people around me because they would bump my bed and the boot would start in full force. The curtain that separated our beds remained pulled most of the time. My best friend, Marcia Nelson was allowed in to see me one time. I remember her coming up with her mom. I remember telling her that I was wearing the shirt she gave me when I got hurt and that I didn't know where it was now. Marcia had a shirt just like it, grey and pink button-up with ruffles around the neck, and we loved our matching shirts. Curious thing to remember. Guess I still wanted to be a little girl and worry about what little girls worry about. Her mom stood far away from me and only said one thing. She said that Marcia insisted that she come along or she would have to stand in line with all of the other high school kids trying to come see us. I knew our town had come together to support our whole family and that there were hundreds of bouquets of flowers that the nurses had finally started dispersing throughout the hospital to hallways, waiting rooms and other patient rooms. They told me that there were tables on wheels that were full of flowers and balloons that lined the hallways. The doctors didn't want flowers around me but my mom would bring in several rose bowls each day to sit by my bed. Mostly I counted my hours, got comfortable buried deep inside myself and came to realize that deep down inside me there was something or someone else with me that promised to never leave me alone. The third hour terrors still came and the pain never ever, not once stopped but I was not alone with it and whatever Being was with me made the pain separate from that which was me. My body and that which made up the rest of me were no longer connected. Hour one. Hour two. Hour three.

Sometimes hiding does preserve us...

Hey Cinderella...
What's The Story All About?

Approaching adulthood is exhilarating. I have hopefully sewn the oats of the rebellious, renegade years. I've had fun, learned lessons, grown up and a sort of nesting instinct has settled in. Suddenly the idea of a job, marriage, a family, a home of my own sounds nice. The responsibility, routine, predictability that repulsed me just a few years prior is attractive. So I follow the beautiful golden highway of "All grown-up-hood" that my parents and their parents before them lovingly paved.

Planning for "All grown-up-hood" is a little like planning a fabulous vacation – to Italy. I buy a bunch of guidebooks and make wonderful plans. The Coliseum. Michelangelo David. The Gondolas in Venice. I learn some handy phrases in Italian. It's all very exciting.

Months pass, years pass and then one day there is someone shaking me and saying "You are here, you are here. Welcome to Holland." "Holland?!" I say. "What do you mean Holland? I signed up for Italy! I am supposed to be in Italy. I have always been planning on Italy." I look around and sure enough, I am in Holland. At least I am not in a horrible, disgusting, filthy place. I console myself. It is just a different place than I had planned.

So I must go out and buy new guide books. And I must learn a whole new language. And I must prepare to meet a whole new group of people that I would never have met. It is just a different place. It is slower paced than Italy, less flashy than Italy. But after I have spent a little time and adjust and catch my breath, I look around. And I begin to notice that Holland has windmills. And Holland has tulips. Holland even has Rembrandts.

But I see people coming and going from Italy. And they are always talking about how wonderful Italy is and what a nice time they have had in Italy.

And for the rest of my life I will say, "Yes, that's where I was supposed to go. That is what I had planned."

And the pain of not ending up in Italy will never, ever go away because the loss of that dream is a very significant one. But if I spend my life mourning the fact that I didn't get to go to Italy, I may never be free to enjoy the very special, the very lovely things about Holland.[7]

4

Threads

Hello Holland! Boy am I there. When I look back at my story I see the many curves and twists and spirals that my life has taken. These were not part of my plan. I am supposed to be married with 2.7 kids, a handsome husband that adores me, lots of friends and a fulfilling career. This was my Italy. I am in Holland. It is precisely in the examination of and in the telling of my story that I begin to see that somewhere along the way someone gave me a map and told me this was how it was supposed to play out. And for some reason, I just nodded and agreed and accepted that this was THE map, THE plan that I was to follow. I accepted that this was MY map.

And so goes my "Holland". I didn't plan to be where I am today. There has been so much in life that I did not allow for so...in Holland I am and in Holland I will have to stay. The question that remains is what am I going to do in Holland. I do have choices. On paper this is my condition: I am a 44 year old single mother supporting three kids ages 8 to 16. I am a physician working as a cosmetic surgeon though my training and my plan was to be working as an oncologist. I work up to 60 hours a week as a physician and a business owner. My schedule allows for work and kids and not much more.

My left leg is partially paralyzed and I walk with a bit of a limp. In my abdomen there is a pump that delivers pain medicine to my spinal cord to control the chronic pain from a crushed pelvis injury. Without my pump I cannot function without narcotic pain medicine. I am in recovery for addiction to the very substance that allows me to function. Modern medicine has allowed me an option via an electronic, implanted, intrathecal pump that delivers medicine directly to my spinal cord and allows me to keep my head clear and allows me to stay in recovery.

My life is crazy busy and I don't know how to slow it down. I am continually aware that I cannot go at this pace much longer. My physical condition will not allow it. I am lonely and miss the companionship that marriage brings. I have not been successful in this department and that saddens me both for my children and for myself.

This is my Holland. It is not the trip to Italy that I had planned, but I am in Holland and in Holland I must stay. I have found a way to love my Holland, to live in peace and serenity and to experience joy and happiness. My story, my history has taught me much and listening to your stories teaches me even more. I embrace the life, the becoming. My being becoming itself has been an unfathomable journey. As I tell my story to you, parts of my story that I have not told before, my heart spills open and I get to embrace parts of my history that are excruciating and wrenching and blissful and divine all at once. I see instincts gone awry and often I laugh at the comedy of myself struggling to be. The maps drawn for me by others and by me have been crossed out, scribbled on, re-drawn. They are faded and torn and tattered but they remain maps that I continue to clutch as if I will be forever lost without them. The society I have grown up in remains and it will go on with or without me and I continue to grip this creature named "progress" that is going mach five with its hair on fire. I still pretend I can control it all on almost a daily basis but my moments of complete and utter impotency have taught me the art of surrender. It is in these moments that are of great concernment, that I am most keenly aware that I am kindred to all other beings and to the Whole.

We are each the "Hero" in our own stories. We are the "Hero" on the journey of life and what needs to be in our stories here are the **people** and the **society** that gave us the maps of "should have" and "ought to". These people are characters in our stories. They played the parts of mentors, allies, tricksters, guardians and villains, and regardless of the parts they played, they shaped us. They taught us right from wrong, good from bad and gave us a set of standards that we have used to navigate the world we live in. Our **society** and the **people** in it have played parts in the stories that we have lived thus far. So let's look at this "Map" business closer remembering that all of this needs to go in the stories we tell.

Maps

So here I am, somewhere, somehow I picked up this map that I have spent most of my life trying to interpret. Once this map was in my grimy little hands it became the Holy Grail. At every juncture I referred to the map to see where I was supposed to go next, "finish high school and take a right, go 4 years and veer left, you'll go over a hill, the road will swerve right and at the third light turn left, whoops missed that turn, you should've gone right, u-turn, take the E Street exit and accelerate onto the freeway…". Aaaah! Where did I get this map?

Trick question, we have already covered that. The bulk of my map was part of my *givens*. A lot of my map was the where and when I was born, who my parents were, my race, my country, my gifts and talents, my culture and society. They handed me a map that I was "supposed to follow" and I accepted it and pretended it was my own, somehow divinely inspired and prepared especially for me. What I missed in all of this "free map" business is that it wasn't free at all…it took away my freedom.

By trying to follow this map created by others especially for me, I allowed so much of my story to be written by others. Now let's be clear, there was and is nothing that I can do about my givens, they are *cause*. Likewise, there is nothing that I can do about *chance*, shit happens. But somewhere in adulthood I had a *choice* to continue to try to follow the map that was laid out for me. Now don't get me wrong, when I hit this "all-grown-up-hood" I did take responsibility for myself and my own decisions and my own plans, but I couldn't seem to let go of this map that others gave me. It had become seared into me. Then I found myself doing the positively mad thing of trying to interpret my map super-imposed on their map and as it turns out, God thought our maps were pretty funny.

Just as I can't allow others to draw my map or create my story, I can't tell my story in the forward direction. I can only tell it in retrospect. In other words, others cannot plan my life nor can I. I don't get to write it and then live it, I have to live it and then write it. It is in the telling of my story that I see the many occasions that I "made plans", that I tried to write it first and in pursuit of vainglory attempted to live it.

In the Spirituality of Imperfection Ernest Kurtz eloquently points out the following, "The spiritual teachers universally recognized as "great" did not give commandments nor did they impose their way of life on others. They knew that when any "map" was mistaken for the territory; it became more hindrance than help. And so they invited their followers to question the handed-down maps by making available their own maps—their <u>own</u> stories." You see, just as following the maps that others have laid out for me have led me to a point of bondage, have taken away my *choice;* so does another's opinion of or historical recollection of my story fall short.

I can only tell my <u>own</u> story. My story told through the eyes of another is wrought, even when the utmost care is taken to the contrary, with tints, shades and tones of this others view of the world. A person can only see the world through his own media. In other words only I can tell and comprehend, with any semblance of accuracy, my story. Only I know my story well enough to portray it. Only I have access to the true archives.

It is in constructing my story that I first realized how very much I did not know about myself, a thought worth pondering...

We all go around thinking we know ourselves pretty well but not too terribly long ago I began to wonder about this. It all started with my work and what I called... 'Famous last words'...

98% of my patients exclaim, "I have a really high pain tolerance." Yeah right. I mean the way I figure if there is a bell shaped curve for pain tolerance and we all fall on it somewhere. Everyone seems to think they are on the right hand asymptote. If I listen to the patients then one would surmise that the toughest people in the world get liposuction in Tulsa, Oklahoma. I want to say, "If I agreed with you we'd both be wrong," but I don't I just smile and nod. Other famous last words of patients include the following from a medicated patient, "I'm fine. Really I can't even feel the meds yet. I'm okay." These usually come out 30 seconds before they run into the door or hit the floor.

And then there is 'the famous last words' from the "significant others": How about, "I hear you Babe. I'm listening." This is typically followed by, "Oh look a kitty."

How often do I hear myself say, "No honey I'm not mad," and then walk away reciting in my mind, "Leslie, it is illegal to stab someone for being stupid."

In recollecting our stories and preparing to tell them to another we get, usually for the first time, to "see our maps" as they have actually been traversed. They look very different from the original drawn by our families, culture and society and ourselves. We get to look from above as objective observers at the terrain that we have traveled. We get to see where we zigged and zagged and where we chose the harder route and where we made things more difficult than they needed to be. We see where we fell, where we got up, who helped us, who hurt us, who we hurt. How the times, within which we were born and destined our lives, have directed our ways of acting, reacting and interacting. Most importantly we see where we had *choices,* where we had some control in the outcome around us and when the *choices* were not ours to make. And in glorious, vivid technicolor we get to see when we fooled ourselves into thinking we could control things that were completely out of our hands, when we made the incredibly intelligent decision to "play God". When, with instincts running perverse and rampant, with our maps in hand and with society's norms behind us, we tried to control those things and people that we could not control. What typically follows, is us, on a rampage, trying to make ourselves *"just feel better".*

Another little "story"…

  It's a beautiful Friday evening, 5:00pm. Yay! Friday! I think to myself, it's Friday, I don't have kids, he doesn't have kids, we can cook dinner, watch a movie, snuggle on the couch, catch up with one another. Ahhh, exhale. What a grueling week! Yay! Friday! Haven't heard from him all day but for the past year we've looked forward to our "no kids" weekends together. Wonder if he is working late? I've been up to my elbows in fat all day. Four liposuction cases but I am done now. Guess I'll run home and shower. Get myself soft and smooth and smellin' like a peach. Gotta pack a few things for the weekend at his house anyway. Then I'll call and see what he wants me to cook for dinner, stop at the grocery store and head over to his house. A hug and a long, slow deep, wet kiss are in order! I grab the essentials from my office and say the obligatory "have a good weekend" to the staff still remaining and I am gone in a whirlwind of unrestrained urgency. In other words, "I'm outta here!" The briefcase and purse and make-up bag are tossed into the passenger's seat of my truck, the satellite radio cranked up and I am home bound. Yay! Friday! On Fridays traffic is simply something that is obstructing my weekend. I swerve impetuously in and out of cars who obviously don't know who I am or what my life is like or how important these "no kids" weekends are to my sanity, and therefore, to the world as we know it. On Friday afternoons the rules don't apply to me.
  I whip into my driveway and threaten the back wall of my garage with speed at which I enter and come to a halt and flip the truck in park. Bags in tow, I dart to my bedroom. The bags find their resting place in the kitchen and by the time I've reached my room, my shoes, socks and scrub pants have found a cozy spot in the living room to spend their weekend. A quick stop at my computer to get the iTunes library up and blaring. Shower on. Red Wings t-shirt and sports bra find my floor and ahhh hot water on my aching shoulders. Yay! Friday! The triple blade Bic razor goes to work and I lather myself in jasmine vanilla. I'm out, I'm clean, I'm smooth, I'm smelling wonderful. I reach for the blackberry, "Hey Babe,

what's up? Thought about what you'd like for dinner?"He answers (and I quote!), "I hadn't heard from you so I made plans to go watch Jerry race his hot rod.""Oh, okay," I reply acting unfazed by the unforeseen turn of events, "Well have fun. Talk to you tomorrow then."I hang up stunned. I shake my head...and it starts.

Really? You are going to watch a car go fast. Really? Let me say it again. Really? I can feel it coming, the cyclone inside me that says, "Fine, I've got plenty to do without you. I mean shhhooot it is not like I was assuming that you had the same plans that I had. It is a free country. Do what you want, pal." By the "Pal" at the end of that thought I can tell I am going "South" rapidly. Okay, someone call the guys at Neimann Marcus and tell them to lock up the high heeled shoes! When the world doesn't operate according to my plan I do what every healthy, red-blooded, American girl does. I'm going shopping. I leave my house in a cloud of dust. Whether the garage door is still intact I know not. Tonight, I see shoes as proof that God loves us and wants us to be happy. Same goes for purses and bubble bath and comfy pajamas.

My frenzy continues for a good two hours and I return home victorious. Though my will didn't work on another person I found relief exercising it on my spree. Leslie Farber addresses this sort of relief in his essay on "The Will and Hysteria"...Great! I feel better already! : (

Our stories are nothing more than our own personal histories. As we each look at our histories what we see, beyond the givens and the instincts gone awry, beyond the maps given to us by our families and the society we are brought up in, is *the self*, our very essence. *The self* that one moment was not there and the next moment was. We see our individual beings, stripped down to the bare essence, placed at a given time and place in history, prepared to begin the journey of becoming. Our becoming is one of a being becoming itself. As we have seen, that being becoming itself is not left to simply become. It is about to be shaped by givens and instincts and family and society. *Cause, chance* and *choice* are, from *the instant we are born*, about to begin their work.

As soon as we are able to wrap our arms around the idea of the instant we, as individuals, came into being and began the journey of becoming, we need to step back, pause and marvel with awe and trembling at the picture, the Piece of Art, that we have been born into. The beautiful piece of art that is our lives is but a meticulously placed thread in the entirety of the Greater Tapestry. We are beings becoming ourselves in our own private, personal histories, but we are also part of the bigger picture in the history of the universe of Being becoming Itself. According to Hegel, all of History is governed by Reason. Not as in I can reason that I shouldn't put my hand on a hot burner, but as in there is Reason behind all of History. A greater Reason, with a capital "R". In other words, the History of the World is a Rational process, there is Sense to it all. As Hegel himself explains, "The movement of the solar system takes place according to unchangeable laws. These laws are Reason, implicit in the phenomena in question. But neither the sun nor the planets, which revolve around it according to these laws, can be said to have any consciousness of them." In other words, there is Reason behind everything in the Universe though the participants are not always cognizant of the Reason. Nevertheless there is a Reason for it. In religious terms, Providence or that of God controls the happenings of the world. All is not left to chance. "God has a Plan." Hegel preferred to say it, "Reason directs the World". In a masterpiece of thought he goes on to declare that all of History is the playing out of this "Reason" or "Plan". Put simply, a review of the Universal History shows us the "Reason" or the "Plan" working itself out. The Theologies ask us to accept that Providence (that of God) presides over the events of the World and that this Reason or Plan is in fact God. Regardless of personal beliefs, the idea is the same. The alternative to Reason is anarchy and nothingness.

In the same way, we must believe that our own personal history, a microcosm of the Whole of History, is too governed by Reason and Providence. Our own personal history is composed of "Reason" and our lives reviewed gives us glasses into our own beings as they are becoming themselves and oh how different our stories sound when we tell them with peaceful acceptance that Reason or Divine Providence has had, and continues to have, a guiding hand in it all. How different our stories are when we see clearly that, although *choice* is always ours, there is Reason behind the *cause* and *chance*. Not Reason that we always understand, but Reason nonetheless. Just as gravity held us to the earth before, we as human beings, understood it, Reason plays out even when we don't understand it. Telling our stories to another and listening to their stories joins us in the Great Story as together we compose our part in the History of the Whole, as we create and complete our part of the Greater Tapestry.

The Threads of Society

The things we will learn about ourselves go beyond examining, our givens, the occasions where our instincts have gone awry and beyond the "maps" we and others have laid out. The times we live in tends to shape how we live and react to life in subtle but telling ways. The great sexual revolution occurring in Europe no doubt had an influence on Freud and his writings and theories. Similarly, World War II shaped the baby boomers and 9/11 changed forever the X generation. So too do our "times" influence us each individually in quiet, "accepted as normal" ways. Again these outside influences are most evident when examined retrospectively, typically the social happenings, the cultural bends take decades and even centuries to play out.

Technophrenia

That which is the most obvious has been simmering for decades and has now exploded into exponentially—technology. We are a techno world, jump on the rocket or get left behind. Despite the philosophical pros or cons, or the sociological arguments of the detriments of virtual living, Elvis has left the building. There is no stopping the mind boggling explosion of technological "advances" that have invaded and now monopolize our everyday lives. More on this later but suffice it to say we're hooked on our technology and anyone under 90 years old has become accustomed to the technology gods swooping in to take away the mundane, time consuming tasks of everyday life and replacing them with push of the button convenience.

How has technology changed our stories? We can accomplish all we have to do in a day without actually having to talk with another living, breathing human being, all while our "community" has expanded to include the entire world. With the push of a button I can communicate with a person in Thailand, one in Greenland and one in Belgium simultaneously and instantly.

Thus goes the technologic schizophrenia of the 21st century. Our community has expanded yet we are more isolated than ever before. We have become dis-connected from the carnal and therefore from the spiritual, as they only come together. We have eliminated the sensualness of human relations. There is no touch, feel, smell, watch or listen in our communication. We are a read and respond society. We have eliminated the realness and therefore the work of human interactions. Satellites beam communications from one object to the next and, conveniently but tragically, we de-humanize those that we communicate with.

Our quick communications are the new, socially acceptable form of guerilla war-fare. We shoot emails, texts and twitters at unseen others, never certain whether they are friend or foe, never having to address their personhood, their humanness. It is always easier to send live missiles to an enemy we can't see. It doesn't feel like murder if we cannot see the person. Likewise, we can fill up the space below the Christmas tree and load the stockings without seeing one retail clerk with the requisite Santa hat, without hearing one Christmas carol, without saying "Happy Holidays" to one person. How much of this trip to Holland is a result of having "convenienced" ourselves away from the vibrant colors of human interaction, human connection and humanity and toward the grays and neutrals of the convenience, accommodation and ease.

Urgency

Along with our addiction to the convenient comes our next demand---NOW. It is more accurate to say that we "assume" NOW rather than demand it. Meaning the "instancy" of our world has been around long enough and that the demand is no longer necessary. We've come to just assume quick, fast, live. This immediacy of life has, like it or not, changed the way our stories have played out.

Our lives have become filled with pseudo-urgency, even pseudo-emergency. Our days are played out in bullet points. Boom, boom,

boom, boom, done. Next item. Just do it, check it off the list and move on. We skip the blank moments in between the deeds and become consumed with the doing. In doing so, we command the world around us to cooperate, our importunity thrusts itself onto those around us and their importunity pushes back. It has all become a self-perpetuating circle spinning out of control. The powers of supply and demand stretch to accommodate a society besieged with a sense of self imposed haste that they cannot explain and cannot escape. "I need it Now!" is our national motto.

We did not plan for this, our "trip" wasn't supposed to include the hustle bustle. Our "Holland" is the result of a maddening pace that was not on the itinerary and no doubt this has changed the stories we will tell. There is no room for fascination or awe or marvel—they simply take too long.

Confessions from a FedEx junkie...

My name is Leslie and I am a FedEx junkie. I am powerless over overnight mail and it has made my life unmanageable. I stand before you and admit out loud today that I have become addicted to overnight delivery services. I admit that I demand and pay for overnight mail even when I don't need what it is I've ordered for weeks. I like the way it makes me feel. I get a rush from feeling like the word responds to my commands. It makes me feel omnipotent and in control. Overnight mail helps me relax. It sort of takes all of the sharp edges off my world. When I use overnight mail I can loosen up, be myself.

It was Christmas of 2008 that I realized that I had a problem. I tried to quit but I couldn't. Though the Holidays were weeks away I was unable to get myself to stop pushing the overnight mail option on my computer. I spent sleepless nights plotting, planning on how to control my shipping method. I promised myself that I would hit the simple first class mail button but little by little I would work my way back to my drug of choice...overnight mail. I tried switching to 2nd day ground then it would become 2nd day air then overnight with weekday deliveries only but I would always end up back where I started. I was hopelessly addicted to next day deliveries. The shame was overwhelming. I wanted to tell someone, to ask for help but I felt such shame and guilt sure that no one would understand. I vacillated between denial and hopelessness, convinced that there was not another living being that could relate I remained lonely and isolated. As the Holidays came to an end I felt relief and convinced myself that it was just the excitement of the Season that had spiraled me out of control.

By the middle of January my solemn oath to stay away from overnight deliveries was shattered. I got online to order make-up and BOOM! Before I knew it I had pushed the next day delivery button, oblivious to the fact that the delivery cost more than the make-up. I didn't care, I needed that fix. I knew that my tube of mascara had two more weeks of voluptuous long lashes in it but I didn't care. Oh the high of "I want it NOW!" Though I fooled myself for the next 24 hours saying it was just a little slip, my problem really isn't that bad, within a week I was off to the races. One day I ordered some books from Amazon.com and selected the one day air option all the while knowing that I was at the beginning of my current book and there was no possible way I needed or could use those books for at least a week. I told myself that I wouldn't drive after using express mail but inevitably I would hop in my truck and race home to embrace my boxes. I was out of control. The hangovers were horrendous. The let down and the heartbreak of the "morning afters" were indescribable. I tried to blame my family, my friends, the post office, FedEx, UPS and their stupid "go brown" commercials but I knew that it was my own fault. If only Saks and Amazon wouldn't make it so simple. Why did they have to put that option front and center? If it would just take a few more clicks to find that overnight option I would probably have enough time to ward off my craving, my obsession for the "right now".

Hi my name is Leslie; I am an overnight delivery junkie. My last express mail delivery was March 24th, 2009. I have come to believe that a power greater than me can restore me to sanity and I have chosen to turn my will and my life and my computer over to the care of God as I understand Him. I am currently doing a searching and fearless moral inventory of why I "need" immediate gratification and I will share it with God and another human being as soon as I am done. I have had to change my playgrounds and playmates in order to keep myself safe from my mental obsession and physical craving for next day deliveries. Today I take it one day at a time, hitting my knees each morning to ask God for his help to stay away from the FedEx button for just this one day and each night I hit my knees to thank Him for one more day in recovery from the "Right Now!"

The Threads of Other Characters

Both/And

We are indeed a miniscule thread in the Larger Creation, but what we must embrace is that we are miniscule threads together. Some of us are threads, side by side weaving the same tapestry. Others of us are threads that co-mingle and come together and go apart. Still others entwine, intertwine, connect, embrace, enmesh, weave and wind creating our part of the artistic Creation forever connected. How sensuous and romantic it all sounds when written in metaphor, but when we slip back into reality the blatant truth sits before us.

The truth is that, like it or not, as we enter into this "all-grown-up-hood" we tend to "cement" ourselves into a world of "Us" against "Them". In all of our new found maturity, dichotomy becomes the name of the game; with every separation we create being given the label of right or wrong, good or bad. We become joiners and in joining one group we say no to others. As it should be, we search out stability and we find it in community. We find stability and rootedness as we take our place in the society in which we live. In taking our place in that society we become established as an "Us". Since there is and "Us" there must be a "Them" and in every group with which we belong this is the case. As human beings we seek identification of an inner group. In establishing that inner group, we unconsciously create and outer group.

The most obvious "Us" and "Them" is via our national allegiance.

I am an American. This is something that was given to me at birth and as such I am part of this inner group and those not American are part of the outer group as far as nationality is concerned. Sounds simple and innocent enough, but a review of recent world history makes it easy to see how this seemingly innocent identification with a certain group is a powerful force. Our unselfish devotion to the group has, without a doubt, been at the root of some of mankind's' most horrific and ravishing acts. Nazi monstrosities were much more a result of identification with a group, the Nazis', the Aryan race, the Third Reich, than they were aggressive instincts gone mad. An undoubtedly extreme example but OH MY GOD it happened and we do it. We divide ourselves into all sorts of Us/Them disunions. We divide ourselves by nations, religions, genders, races, sexual preferences, educational levels, marital status, social status…. Although the division does give us a sense of belonging to an inner group, it does give us a recognition of community, it also alienates us from the vast majority of the world.

What we need to focus on for the sake of story gathering and storytelling, however, is not our perverse tendency to be taken over by dualism but that, when caught in that dualism, we begin to worship at the altar of "good and evil". We put a good or bad, right or wrong, moral or immoral label on nearly everything. Funny thing is, we all do it, everyone in the world and we all seem to place ourselves into the good, right, moral group. And we *run* or *fight* or *hide* when someone or something attempts to push us into the bad, wrong or immoral group.

This dualism spills beyond the "groups" we chose into our very way of thinking and operating in this world. Duty versus desire, work versus play, science&technology versus religion&art, conscious versus unconscious, intellect versus intuition, quantitative versus instinctive.[8] Where the labels of good are bad are placed depends on who we are and how we view the world. These polarities are part of our personalities and we tend to solidify our alliances in adulthood. The problem with the good and bad labels, although we are often not even conscious of them, is that we are "both/and" beings not "either/or" beings. That is, we are both, good and bad, both right and wrong, both moral and immoral. And because we are "both/and" beings we can never truly embrace ourselves, know ourselves, accept ourselves or forgive ourselves until we relish in and embrace both ends of the dyadic candle.

Through givens and instincts and family and society our personalities have developed and it is in this "all-grown-up-hood" that we align ourselves with whatever it is we see as right and good. We establish an ideal and this becomes our self-image. It becomes the standard that we hold ourselves to. Anything that challenges this idealized self-image threatens our sense of "belonging". It threatens our connection with those that we have become aligned. This threat is perceived as the "them" and the "bad".

This is, however, what we are asking ourselves to do when set out on the great adventure of rediscovering and telling our stories. We are challenging the idealized self-image, the outward personality and we are searching for the self, the "both/and" being. It is a solitary journey. Only I can dive within me, only you can dive within you. Our groups, our connections, our "belonging", our very personalities will have to stay behind. Although the feat sounds simple enough, recollect, recall and tell our stories, many of us will abort the take off the moment we are asked to let loose of the persona, the ego—the personality. We have built a life around the false center of our personalities. "Our greatest addiction of all is to our personality—our routines, roles and rigidities."[9]

Recollecting and telling our stories challenges us to put down the metaphorical "pill" or mask of the persona and discover that mystical, mysterious, profane and, yes, divine being that we have thus far become and will continue to become as we step into the moment after this and continue to weave the reasonable, rational, often incomprehensible thread in the masterpiece that is our lives and the Masterpiece that is our Lives.

Ah the modern day pressures of good and evil...

Long ago and far away, there lived a single mother of three. She and her children lived in a small white house with a quaint red door. The house was on a hill and was made of stone and brick. It had large front windows, a circular drive and a steep pitched roof.

It was the end of November in Oklahoma and that could only mean one thing. You guessed it, Christmas light time.

It was the day after Thanksgiving and her young son's birthday. A "family day". By 8am the cheerful mother had rallied the troops to assist with outdoor Christmas lights. "It'll be fun!" she exclaimed trying in desperation to get her enthusiasm to catch on. "Mom, I really think we should get one of those companies that hangs Christmas lights to help us. Our roof is really steep." her eldest protested. The younger two chimed in with the like. The mother replied, "Now don't you guys go turning all "princess" on me. We can do it. All you need to do is hold the lights and hold the ladder. Besides hiring someone to hang your Christmas lights is pure sacrilege. I hate those perfectly lined houses that look like they belong on a magazine. Those "people" have traded the spirit of the season for "the perfect little image". I don't like it a bit. Not us, nope, we will do it ourselves as a family and kick off the season with some REAL Holiday spirit."

So outdoors they went arms full of boxes of lights and gutter hangers and extension cords. Ladder secured with children at the bottom, the mother climbs upward with strings of lights wrapped around her shoulders. She mounts the roof as her children continue their protests singing in concert, "Mom be careful. Mom come down. Mom this isn't a good idea." As she scales the roof on hands and knees she wonders if maybe there is wisdom in their words. But no, she thinks, I can do this. Her head spins and her stomach flip flops as she looks down. With her heart ticking away at 150 beats per minute she musters the courage to stand and prepares to toss the first string of lights over the peak of the roof. Once this high part is done it'll be a piece of cake she tells herself. The toss is a picture of perfection. In slow motion the string of Christmas lights floats in mid air, end over end. The cord effortlessly unwinds and gently lies itself down flawlessly over the apex of the roof line that lies twelve feet above where the mother stands. As the marvel of the perfectly placed string of lights comes to an end, reality sets in. "God I wish I had connected those lights to the next string." She says out loud to no one but herself as she stares at the male adapter sitting twelve feet above her head. The plan was so perfect if only she had remembered to plug them together. On hands and knees she heads upward. The chorus from below continues in its harmonious protest. The wooden shingles creek as she makes her way up. In a blink a shingle gives way and the ride downward begins. Bump, bump, bump crash. She comes to a rest at the gutter line held on to the roof by only the top of the ladder and three scolding children. In a tangle of Christmas lights, with left elbow pounding with a heart beat all its own, she manages to free herself from the string of lights and descend the ladder with one arm clearly challenged. The choir of "I told you so's!"and "Are you okay's?"bellowed in her ears as she pushed the ladder, that was too heavy for the children to take down, with her uninjured arm and it hit the ground in a crash of thunder like the grand finale of this song of protestation that now seemed to be divinely ordained.

And so goes the Christmas light "look" of 2007. A single string of unplugged in lights laying neatly over the apex of the house and a snarl of wanna be decorations hanging from the gutter. It was definitely a "look" that no other neighbor had. There was no doubt that she had not "hired out" her Christmas decorating. She was not like those "others".

Addendum: In March she finally conceded and did hire someone to go up and remove the solitary string of lights from the apex of the little white house with the quaint red door.

As we embrace ourselves as "both/and" beings we face head on the good and bad labels we have placed on things, on people and on behaviors. These designates must be discarded and herein is the art of storytelling. Again, we are not good or bad, right or wrong, moral or immoral. We are good and bad, right and wrong, moral and immoral. We are perfectly imperfect. The journey of storytelling teaches us to accept and share the perfect imperfections, the flawless flaws. The journey of storytelling heals the dis-ease, comforts the dis-comfort and takes the faux out of the faux pas. Our journeys into our own stories are by necessity solo and soulful ones that require a letting go of all that we are joined. Our journeys require not only a discovery of our stories but also a releasing of the stories we discover to another human being.

It is in the telling of our stories to other "imperfects" and "less thans" that we are re-connected to a Whole that is much greater than we ever imagined.

The trick lies in the disconnecting from the 'fiddling in the margins' of what is real and reconnecting to what really is and can be. It is not a feat for the faint of heart for it will demand of us a mustering of courage that few of us have been asked before. Although it sounds, on the surface, like a simple enough task, a few steps in the inward direction will quickly demonstrate that while it is simple, it is not easy. Many will chose to stay where we are, to stay in the familiar, the safe, the predictable; to stay in the personality rather than search for *the self.* Our *choices* are to stay as we are, to remain the people that we have been told that we are supposed to be, to remain the people shaped by givens, instincts gone awry, molded by a family and a society that were set in motion long before we were here, to remain in the repetition and compulsion of produce and consume and to hold fast to our quest for the "more" that somehow takes the sharp edges off the biting world around us, to cling our most glaring addiction…our own personalities; or to set forth as gypsies of sorts, on a traveling that will be mysterious and mystical, awful and awe-full, luminous and unintelligible, majestic and mundane, magnanimous and suspicious, natural and supernatural; and to return troubadours with lyrical stories that only we can sing. Our lives thus far have been shaped morphed and molded by so much. The familiar is safe and sanctioned. The intimate odyssey on which we are embarking is uncharted, undiscovered, alien and exotic. With fear and trembling we march forward, but march we must.

Courage & Fear

Ah courage…what is it? Really, what is it? It was the infamous Rocky Balboa who said, "It's not about hard you can hit. It's about how hard you can get hit and keep moving forward." There is so much out there that we incorrectly label as courage. We can put our heads down, square our shoulders and "ramrod" our way through about anything. But this is "will" or will power and not truly courage. We all go through trying times. Some of them horrific and we survive, but that is survival. It comes from our natural God given will to survive. It's limbic—flight, fight or freeze. When it comes right down to it, trying times turns us all into *runners, fighters* or *hiders*. Then there are the times that aren't trying but just tough (remember, "Life is difficult"[10]). Most of us can weather the tough times, though some do not. Is this courage? No, this is what is called being "a grown-up". Once we are adults it is no longer courage, at least not as we will discuss it here, once we have transitioned into adulthood it is just LIFE. Finally, there are the individuals that put on parachutes and jump out of airplanes or, to stick with our Rocky example, those that hop into the ring with opponents that are 50 pounds heavier, a foot taller and made of steel and bolts riveted together by titanium! This I would call, among other things, being brave but it is not courageous. Now don't, for a minute, think that there is not value in will power or survival or adulthood or bravery. They are all critical and necessary; they just are not the same as courage.

According to Plato, "Courage is knowing what not to fear." Or as Confucius put it, "Our greatest glory is not in never falling, but in rising every time we fall." Put another way, "It's not about how hard you can hit, it's about how hard you can get hit and keep moving forward." Courage is fearing but proceeding any way. After all, "Who has not sat tense before his own heart's curtain?" No one. Courage is the willingness to open that curtain. Courage is caring enough about ourselves to open the curtain to our hearts. It is opening that curtain just enough to feel the glory of the spot light and to relish in the real just long enough that we should wish to go back for encore after encore of the fleshy, sensual, sacred, carnal and divine. That we may return prepared to forge ahead into a "Holland" that is beyond our wildest dreams, into a "Holland" that is authentic, real and true.

It was a cool but sunny spring day. April 1980. They are moving me to Sioux Falls to have my bones set and I am so scared. My biggest fear for the past few weeks has been that someone will bump my bed and send me reeling in paroxysms of incomprehensible pain and now they are telling me they are going to move me onto a gurney, put me in an ambulance and drive me 120 miles to a new hospital where they will move me again. My fear is impenetrable.

I cannot be comforted. No one knows, no one knows is all my mind keeps repeating. My fears cannot be allayed, I cannot be consoled. These people cannot apprehend. The level of my terror cannot be communicated, it is not human. I cannot cry, I cannot scream, I cannot beg, I cannot. I close my eyes and I vanish into somewhere that is not earth.

I am surrounded by colors of purple and blue. Deep rich colors and these colors are surrounded by deeper shades of blue and eventually it all turns into navy blue. There are specks of white that twist and weave through the brighter colors. My surroundings are blowing and whirling and there is no ground though I am standing and my leg is normal and I have no pain. My hair is whipping gently. This place is peaceful and tranquil but it is not happy for these are not happy times. I am not here to get relief or to be given peace or to feel safe. I am here because I came here and there is no one around me except a veiled Essence that is telling me that it is sorry. In every way it is comforting me and I feel cradled but I know I cannot stay here. I want it to tell me that I don't have to go back but I know it will not tell me this. It is very sad for me. I am so little compared to it. Though I cannot see it I know this. It is so sad that it weeps with me and there is agony in the whirls. Its agony. It does not speak to me and I do not speak either. I am not sure that there was sound at all. But I do know that words were not necessary. I got to stay in this place for a long time and when I departed I knew I would not get to come back and It knew that I knew this. But when I left I had something that I did not have when I first went to that place...I knew. And I was never so terrified again and the pain was never so crippling again...all because I knew.

Good & Evil

Before we get all gung ho and full of courage let's visit once more and in greater detail about this concept of good and evil. This one concept dissuades more venturers than all others combined. Sounds silly on the surface but let us go further. As we begin to review our stories we stir our memories, awaken the spirits, rouse the ghosts. We lay open wounds that we thought had healed. We remember our most beautiful successes but also our most glaring failures. We face squarely the flaws and imperfections and idiosyncrasies that have, and continue to today, made our lives more difficult than necessary. We are taking a look at what isn't working and trying to repair it. The concept of good and evil repels many because of the morality that religion has linked with these ideas. We are not trying to figure out who is the biggest sinner. Remember, we are "both/and" creatures, not "either/or" creatures.

Over the centuries formalized religion has misinterpreted the meaning of the word sin. There is, in the natural world no place for the true meaning of the word sin. It belongs to the Spiritual world and is meant quite literally, "to fall short" or "to miss the mark". It amounts to the "creatureness" we all feel or would feel in the presence of that which is truly Holy. We all "miss the mark" of that which is truly Holy and this "falling short" of the Holy leaves us with a longing to transcend our unworthiness, to seek atonement, to be washed clean in the presence of Holy.

The most natural, earthly <u>analogy</u> is morality, hence the association of sin with good and bad, right and wrong. The fact that morality is an <u>analogy</u> was somewhere in history, forgotten, and as such, a literal doctrine erupted that has been disturbed and distorted by religious dogmatism to the point that "either a man run from religion or be urged on to inner collapse by virtue of his imperfectness and need for deliverance".

In the words of Theodore Parker,

> *"They (the heathen of classical antiquity) were conscious of wrath, of cruelty, avarice, drunkenness, lust, sloth, cowardice and other actual vices, and struggled and got rid of the deformities (defects, corruption); but they were not conscious of "enmity(hatred) against God" and didn't sit down and whine and groan against a non-existent evil. I have done wrong things enough in my life, and do them now: I miss the mark, draw the bow and try again. But...I know there is much "health in me"; and in my*

> *body, even now, there dwelleth many a good thing, spite of consumption and Saint Paul."[11]*

The "Wrath of God", the "Fear of God", "sin", "transgressions", the need for "deliverance", for "atonement", for "redemption" have, for those without formal Theological training, served to create a God that many have viewed as punitive and punishing, a God that they could never possibly please, that they would never be able to pacify, an angry God.

Paradoxically, it has been the *most honest* that have chosen to walk away from the church. It has been the *most honest* that have questioned Religion out loud. It has been the *most honest* that have admitted that they cannot be as "good" as the church asks them to be. Now, let's not take this too far, there is a place for morality and earthly sin or transgression and it is important but the point is that in the Spiritual world we stand before the Holy and in awe and trembling fall short and feel our unworthiness.

Hypothetically, I am standing before the Holy and I may say "Oh Lord I am a sinner, I am not worthy"—what I am saying is that I am but a creature and am not worthy to be in your presence—what I am NOT saying is "Oh shoot I did a bunch of bad stuff yesterday. Busted." In an earthy sense we all "fall short" daily, we all know, in the moral sense, right from wrong and good from bad. We are imperfect and God knows that. We are not God, we are human. We are not trying to be perfect; we are attempting to make progress. We are not in a race to get good; we are on a pilgrimage of becoming. We are not on a quest to cleanse our souls, atone for our sins or rid ourselves of that which is labeled sinful and bad. On the contrary, we are in the process of creating a piece of artwork called our stories, our lives. And as we re-collect, re-count and re-examined what has been thus far created we are learning to see the worth in the cracks, the value in the flaws and the pricelessness in the imperfection. We are learning to see the beautiful union of the paradoxes and in doing so are learning to embrace the "both/ands" of our beings and to own them all.

In psychology, they call these areas that need improvement an "illness" and the aim is "health". In Religion, they call the weak areas "sin" and the aim is "repentance". In Twelve step programs, they call these areas "character defects" and the aim is to "have them removed". We will call it owning our past, embracing our "both/ands" and choosing to become conscious authors of our future. This is not a search for the bad in ourselves. It is rather a search for ourselves. As gypsies we will explore our stories, ride the mighty dragon up and down, in and out of the moments of our lives and as troubadours we will return with a song to sing, a story to tell and with utter honesty, poetic grace and elegance of spirit we will share the memories of our past, the peace of our present and a new found meaning for our future.

In recounting our stories we are owning our history. We are stepping away from fear of self and from self-deception and choosing to face ourselves squarely. We are choosing to remember and recognize where we have fallen short and to see with open eyes the ways in which we have learned to adapt, through instincts, family and societal pressures and maps that we assumed we should follow. We are choosing to see the bad with the good and to identify what we choose to change and re-adjust from this day forward. We aim to pivot, to change our view. By telling our stories we are releasing pent up anger, resentment, fear, regrets and choosing to re-file and store these events as memories rather than allowing them to run rampant and govern our present. It takes courage to look, it takes courage to look with utter honesty, it takes courage to be thorough, it takes courage to own it all, it takes courage to share it with another. But look we must and tell it we must. Holding back nothing. Sartre called self deception the *mauvaise foi*, the bad faith. In his words it is, "the attempt to flee what one cannot flee—to flee what one is."[12] We are "both/and" beings. The good, the bad, the beautiful, the ugly, the wise, the stupid, the heartless, the compassionate, the mean, the caring, the hateful, the loving we are all of it and it all belongs in our stories.

We are historical creatures and we have pasts colored with events, people and behaviors. Today, this very moment, is the connector of my past and my future. We recall the past, in all its details, not because we can fix it. It is unchangeable. Nor do we recall the past because we think our lives have been just so darn interesting and that everyone would love to hear our story. We recall our past so that we may possess our present, so that we are not possessed. We own our history so that it does not own us. We lay claim to our stories for if we do not, they will lay claim to us—they will lay claim to our present and they will author our future, the story yet to be written. We can care and press onward into the mystery that is "self" or we can continue to hide behind all of the "pills" that we use to quench the longing. But if we do, we will be choosing to forever be, "tense before our own heart's curtain."

I disclose my story to you for if I do not dis-close my soul—it will surely close…

My days in the Sioux Falls hospital were tough ones but my pain improved little by little as with one surgery after another my bones were set and were finally allowed to start healing. What I remember the best is that physical therapy started. I was no longer just waiting for my injuries to be addressed but I was actually working on getting better.

A couple of weeks had past when I was taken down to physical therapy for the first time. I had spent so many weeks disconnected from my mangled body that I was truly unaware of the toll it had taken. I was taken to physical therapy flat on a gurney and transferred to a weird looking flat table to which I was strapped down. I felt the table move and little by little it began to tilt and raise my head and lower by legs. I had been flat in bed so long that the mere transfer to the vertical position was a trauma for my battered body. Slowly I reached the 45 degree angle position and the room began to spin around me. I felt the sweat bead up on my face and neck and I wanted them to put me back down and slowly the table returned to the horizontal position. Oh boy I thought, I suppose they are gonna lug me all the way down here tomorrow and do the same thing. And they did. Day after day I was taken via gurney down to physical therapy with my first rehab goal being to make it to the vertical position. No one even mentioned the idea of walking—they were just focused on getting me to vertical. The whole idea seemed crazy to me but I had long given up any attempt to control anything in my life. My entire world had been taken out of my hands and placed into the hands of others who were trying their best to get me healthy enough to take it back.

The day I made it to vertical was a monumental occasion—one of victory and one of horror. My mom and a family friend named, Wayne Eskew came with me to physical therapy to observe the tiny yet prodigious event. As the table whined vertical approached, the hugeness of the event lasted only seconds. Vertical was reached, the table came to a standstill, onlookers cheered and there before me was a ghostly image of a pale girl strapped to a table. I did not know her. Had she not blinked I might have thought her not alive. She was a tiny frame of bones that appeared almost without substance covered only in a white nightgown with royal blue hearts. The only evidence of substantial flesh was on the left lower leg where six pins protruded out of the skin and connected to a larger contraption that served to hold the bone together. I reasoned that there must be something solid beneath the gown or the chunk of metal would just tear apart the "paper-doll" girl that I did not know.

It was the first time that I had seen myself since I had been injured. I could not tell if my mind was actually connected to her body or if I was observing from somewhere separate. I remembered a young vibrant exquisitely conditioned 15 year old gymnast. Five foot five inches, 115 pounds of young healthy muscle and unperturbed skin. That girl was not here and I struggled to figure out how my mind could have gotten from her to the girl I was looking at now. This was the first time that I wondered if that other girl was ever coming back and in one of those silent divine moments I knew that she was not returning. What was left was a 75 pound broken body that looked as if it did not belong vertical.

After a little over 5 weeks in the hospital and numerous surgeries I was discharged to home. At that point I was able to sit upright and ride in a wheel chair and to take a few steps with crutches if someone strong had a hold of a large leather belt that was secured around my waist. At discharge I weighed 74 pounds. I did not return to school my sophomore year. My days after discharge consisted of physical therapy and people trying to get me to eat. I worked at physical therapy. Calorie consumption was more difficult. I continued to have attached to my left leg a large metal appliance called a Hoffman apparatus that was suppose to hold my badly broken left tibia in a position where it could heal. The apparatus made bathing difficult so each day after physical therapy was complete they would lift me in a hammock contraption and lower me in to a large metal hot tube where my long immobile joints and muscles could loosen up and where my mom could wash my hair and bath me.

Despite the physical therapy and the efforts of all I became weaker not stronger and within 6 weeks I was back in Sioux Falls in the hospital. Weak and frail with a broken spirit. There seemed to be no end in sight. My grandma would sit with me and peel oranges and force feed me whatever she could get her hands on. I went back to surgery twice to help break up contractures in that had formed in my left hip, knee and ankle that had developed from disuse. My spirit had plummeted into an abyss deeper than any I could ever have imagined. As my friends ran track and field and prepared for prom I worked on my ADLs (activities of daily living) like being able to bathe myself and brush my teeth while standing upright. Finally the doctors sent a psychiatrist up to visit with me. I would not speak with him. I already knew what was wrong with me and I knew, because of my visit in the blue and purple place with the navy blue surround that I would make it through. Physical therapy continued and progress was made by the time I was discharged a few weeks later I was stronger, I was walking with a cane but the leather belt was still required. I returned to Huron and my home for less than a week before I was to leave it forever when my family moved across the state to Rapid City. My friends through me a "going away" party but I knew that the girl they all knew had gone away on March 12, 1980. I have one picture of those days and it is from this party. I still can't look at myself without a visceral reaction and a sense that I do not know that girl. A move I had been so excited about just a few months earlier. I tried to be excited about healing and getting to train with the coaches in Rapid City, but again in the silent, dark moments I knew that I would never compete again.

5

The Voices

At this point we are thinking "Voices" indeed! A "not quite rightness", instincts gone awry, old maps, society, "good and evil", where are we going with all of this! Where we are going is that we are about to change the "voices". That is by telling our stories and leaving our personas, old reactions, old maps and old "connections" behind, and wandering, like bohemians, like artists, through our past we are discovering what is real in us, we are re-discovering *the self*.

The self is the only person capable of masterfully completing this piece of artistry that we call our stories. And when we emerge from this wandering through the vicissitudes that have thus far written our stories and we share our adventure with another human being, we are freeing ourselves from the strings, the chains, the walls, the fences and the voices that have held us captive, that have stolen our freedom. With our freedom freed, the voices become one voice. The voice that has been drowned out little by little from the moment our essences came into being. The voice that has manifested itself as a gnawing deep inside. The voice that has been smothered, stifled and squelched by the clamoring of the outside voices that have always been louder. The voice that, in spite of being astoundingly outnumbered, would not be silenced. The voice that continued to scrape and grind and claw and cause dis-comfort, dis-cord (from the Greek *chord* which literally means *gut*) and dis-stress until it was heeded. And, although this voice may have been, at times, snuffed out, ignored, discarded and disregarded, it remained bellowing in an echoing cavern and it will remain until we take our last gasp of air and our stories have concluded. For this voice resides in the very core of our beings, the spiritual core. It resides in the part of us that holds our moral conscience, our love and our creative center. And in this spiritual core is contained that which springs eternal…hope. The voice never quits because it has an abundance of one thing…hope. It is the same voice that has finally yelled loud enough for us to begin this journey and soon it will be able to speak to us in but a whisper as bit by bit the other voices fade away.

<u>Where am I?</u>

Philosophers, Theologians and Thinkers have, through the years recognized the value of detachment in the search for a deeper meaning in life, a life of value, a life fulfilled and a life that makes sense. Discovering ourselves, our identities, requires orientation. It requires a clearing of all that distorts and covers and confuses, and it requires an acclimation, of sorts, to where we have been and to *where we are* now. We get this acclimation in two main ways; it comes to us by way of a topographical depiction of the terrain that we are exploring. Okay fine, we need more maps. But these maps tell us only where we have been and where we are now. They are not maps telling us where we are supposed to go.

1. These maps help us see clearly where we have been. And you guessed it, the best way to explore thoroughly where we have been is to tell our stories. Not to think about our stories, to tell our stories to another living, breathing human being.
2. These maps give us a good idea of where we are now. We must know from whence we are to start tomorrow and we can only do this by figuring out where we are now and we can only answer that question by taking a good look at where we have been.

In other words, these maps have a "you are here" arrow. If maps don't have a "you are here" arrow then they are useless to us. We can read our maps all day long, even memorize them, but if we don't know where we are on our maps our mastery of them does us no good. It is our stories, the narratives of our lives up to this point that positions our "you are here" arrows. Without our history to connect us to the present our lives lose their unity.

As much as some of us would like to wipe the slate clean and start over, that does not work in the quest for self-hood. Ignoring the past implies that our lives up to now have been nothingness which leaves us frantically kicking in a sea of senselessness. Our pasts are more than one day after the other with no sense and purpose to them. Experiences and events in our past are what help us sort out what is constant, ingrained in our very essence and what have become our ways of acting and reacting to the world around us.

Our past is what tells us what we have come to value and believe. It tells us what we esteem, what we cherish, what we respect, what we regard, what we stand for. Our beforehand experience has been a series of lessons teaching us what these things are and how they fit in to our beings. They are a series of sifting, sorting, trying, failing, trying again, trading this for that. The significance of events and people and circumstances in our past cannot be viewed in the rearview mirror as isolated events. They must be examined via a bird's eye view to truly ascertain how they have fit into our lives and what part they have played in the chronicle we are reflecting on.

The self can only be known and understood through a narrative, an unfolding story. That narrative tells us *where we are* by telling us from whence we have come and the *where we are* enables the unfolding to continue. Our lives exist in time and space, and to orient ourselves to that time and space requires tracking the road we have traveled and putting our "you are here" arrow on the present. Who and what and *where we are* can only be understood by how we have become. As Soren Kierkegaard so eloquently put it, "Life can only be understood backwards, but it must be lived looking forward." We cannot point ourselves toward the future until we know *where we are*, what direction we are facing and which way we wish to go. Our stories tell us all of these. And we need these to complete the tapestry we are creating with our lives.

A brief tutorial on the "You Are Here" arrow...

It was an energetic task to begin with, we had loaded four children all under the age of nine into a forty foot RV in Tulsa, Oklahoma and had made our way to Michigan to visit relatives and show them the area where dad had grown up. The trip had been a blast and relatively uneventful until today. We had decided last minute to drive from Detroit to Lake Michigan, on the other side of the state to play on the sand dunes and the waves at the lake.

We made it to the lake okay. (It is big and kind of hard to miss!:)) Finding the sand dunes was another thing all together. A map would have helped but we decided that road signs would suffice. So, in our forty foot RV we weaved our way down road after road searching for the dunes. One road in particular was winding and narrow with low hanging trees. Bob Seger was interrupted half way through "Night Moves" by a screeching sound followed by a distant crash. We pulled off the road and wearily stepped from the metal beast that we had been calling home for the past 7 days and nights. Although it was difficult to view from our vantage point on the ground, it was quite apparent that the air conditioning unit on the top of our RV no longer had a cover. A short stroll down the road confirmed the like along with a large tree branch that had given its life in the abduction of our air conditioner cover. C'est la vie! Onward to the dunes!

We concluded (a stroke of genius) that we had taken a wrong turn and made the next, in a long series of brilliant decisions, to turn our beast around on the narrow road and head the other direction. Next came the crunching sound...we completed our turn and once again dismounted the beast. Can't image who put that boulder there! It was probably someone who never imagined that someday someone would get the bright idea to try to do a u-turn in a forty foot vehicle at this precise location. The gash in the rear of the RV was not life threatening but not subtle either. So much for that $2000 deposit at the RV rental store. C'est la vie! Onward to the dunes!

At this point we had completely thrown caution to the wind as the two girls and two boys in the back continued their "Night

Moves" dances from their respective seats. We made our way back to the sign we had missed, paid our park fee and pulled our beast into a spot marked "RVs only." We all six hopped from the RV grateful to be free at last and anxious to "arrive" at the beach. SO, with three kids in tow and one (a 1 ½ year old) on dads back we headed down the path that was marked with a sign that said "beach" with an arrow just in case someone got the crazy thought to cut through the thick forest I suppose. We walked and we skipped and we jogged and we walked and we walked and we walked and 40 minutes later (I would like full credit for having the thought, "Gosh maybe we should have checked to see how long the hike to the beach was or maybe we should have looked for a park right on the beach.") there it was the dunes, the beach, the waves. I have to say it was worth the trauma and worth the wait. The day was picture perfect and remains even today one of the most fun days that I can remember. We spent 6 hours jumping waves and building sand castles and sliding down the dunes. The kids (all 6 of us) were in heaven. Had it not been for the severe hunger pains we would have stayed longer but we decided that nutrition was becoming essential and we packed up and headed down our path back to the RV. To our good fortune there at the start of the path was a large wooden trail guide to steer us back. As our three older kids made their way down the path on which we had arrived several hours earlier we stood with the toddler on daddy's back and stared at our "guide". It was a bulky wooden sign with the parks 6 trails etched beautifully into the wood. It even gave the distances from point to point. What it did not have however, was, you guessed it, a "You Are Here" arrow. And we had no idea what trail we had taken. C'est la vie! How hard can it be, we will just backtrack. Rrrrright!

As we trudged our way down the trail that had so graciously led us to our spectacular day the toll of the day of play began to weigh heavy on us all. Little and big kids both. The back pack I lugged was making sure that I was aware of how insufficiently I had applied sunscreen to my shoulders and the toddler on dad's back was making it clear that skipping naptime was no longer working for him. We walked for about an hour and were amazed at how many "Ys" and "forks" there were on our path. Hmmmm?

And it had seemed so straight and direct on our trip in. Much to our relief we could see the trails end ahead and the opening into the clearing where we had parked in our "RVs only" spot. We all entered the clearing together ready to sigh that wonderful sigh of relief as we stepped off the wooded path and into the clearing there it was…a large beautiful field full of wild flowers blowing gently in the summer breeze. There was no parking lot, there were no spots marked "RVs only", there was only a very large field full of colorful flowers and 2 grown-ups and 4 children. No more C'est la vie.

Although it was light outside the woods were growing dark and the mosquitoes resembled small birds. We were all dead tired and dehydrated from hours in the sun and this was NOT funny. No more grown-up kids, we needed to find our way to something, anything that resembled civilization. The uni-bomber in a log cabin would have been acceptable. We made the decision that we needed to head back toward the beach and depart again, marking our trail as we went. Kids straggled behind pushing their little legs as much as they were able. We were no longer in a pack, now the trail was dotted with little bodies in age order. First mom blocks ahead looking for anything familiar to guide their turns, then the nine year old, fifty yards behind her was the 7 year old, a good one hundred yards behind him was the six year old followed by dad and the 1 ½ year old who now seemed to weigh a hundred pounds. Two hours past before mom's voice bellowed through the woods, "I found it! I see the RV!"And they all lived happily ever after.

Thank you for reading this brief tutorial. Take home message: Without the "You Are Here" arrow even the prettiest maps are useless.

But Who Am I?

What else? What else do we need to place the "you are here" arrows on our maps? We need a framework to build upon. You guessed it, it is in our stories. Our framework is this…a set of valuations.

1. What is it that matters most to us?

2. What do we value and hold above all else?
3. What do we see as trivial?
4. What do we see as worth doing?

Before we can decide where to place our "You Are Here" arrows, we need to determine who we are, who we are not, what we believe in and what we value. We need to know all of these if we are to weave a future that is fulfilling, that makes sense, that gives us meaning both individually and as part of the greater Whole.

Rabbi Zusya is quoted as saying, "In the coming world, they will not ask me why I was not Buddha, they will ask me why I was not Zusya."[13] The future will only be fulfilling, make sense and have meaning if we color it with that which matters the most to us, that is, if we color it with what and who we are and blend it with what we value. If we color it with what those around us value, surely the future will be nothing but shades of gray. In the coming world they will not ask us, why did you not weave your threads with someone else's needle, they will ask us why did you not weave your threads with your own needle.

Value is worth that only we can give to something. And we give value to those things that we hold in high esteem, those things that matter to us. A key feature of these appraisements is that they cannot be measured. That is, they cannot be measured in the traditional sense. The reason our personal valuations cannot be measured is because they are personal, hold value and are intimate to each of us uniquely. Someone else cannot decide how important or how valuable something is to us—only we, as individuals, can determine the power, the merit, the import or the stature. Remember, they will only ask, "Why were you not you?"

Charles Taylor describes an "identity crisis" as an acute form of disorientation and uncertainty of where one stands as a person. A plain and simple fact about human beings is that we have an Ego or a persona that, whether we like to admit it or not, matters to most of us. That is to say we, as human beings, have a self-image and we strive to look good in the eyes of others. We tend to cover our true character with social norms, family bias' and whatever it is that those closest to us think is "cool" at the moment. It is the bias of the social sciences that, "the ideally strong character would be maximally free of them, would not be deterred by the adverse opinions of others and would be able to face unflinchingly the truth about himself or herself."[14]

Yeah well, that is all good and fine and, indeed, this is in part what we have been trying to do by recounting our stories, but the point is, whether this is "ideal" or not, we as humans are not quite that simple.

1. We do care what others think and feel,
2. We cannot cease being human,
3. Others will always play a part in our lives, we cannot exist in a vacuum.

As Charles Taylor neatly lies out in "Sources of The Self", the "self" cannot be studied as an object. We cannot be described or "captured" outside of our surroundings. We cannot even describe ourselves without some relativity to the people and things that we value and disvalue. To know who we are, is to know, or least to have some concept, of what we stand for.

Our stories provide our most privileged access into our true identities, into our values, into those things that we give higher meaning, into what matters to us. What we are searching for here is the core, the spiritual core that makes sense of our lives. If we could refrain from being part of the "us/them", if we could stop being part of the corporate or cultural "we" and start being that first person singular 'I', what would we stand for, what would we be passionate about, what would add meaning to our lives, make our lives worth living? The greatest fear of most previous cultures was the fear of not being able to live up to impervious, rigid demands required to secure their place in the afterlife, in heaven or in a higher order of the next life. That fear has shifted for us moderns, for us the greatest fear is of emptiness, of meaninglessness.[15]

Hello!!! People, we have no idea what matters to us anymore! We do not know what we value. We find something that we think matters and then we realize that really it just matters to the gals down at the clubhouse but we are not sure that it really matters to us. We fear emptiness and purposelessness because we have lost touch with our cores, our spiritual cores. Our spiritual cores, that place that holds what we value. For many moderns the world has become spiritually senseless. It is not surprising to learn that psychoanalysts, who since

Freud have had the bulk of their patients suffering from phobias, fixations and hysteria, have recently reported a shift in pathology and report that the main complaints today deal with a sense of emptiness, flatness, futility, lack of purpose.[16]

What a paradox! In an era, known for its emphasis on individuality, for its "me first" mentality, for its supposed valuation of independence and uniqueness, we have an epidemic and it is called "identity crisis". Again, we have "an acute form of disorientation and uncertainty of where one stands as a person". In the midst of millions of autonomous individuals, identities are lacking. Taylor calls our modern independence a "very shallow affair." Stating that, "...masses of people each try to express their individuality in stereotyped fashion." Concluding, "...that the existence of a traditional culture of independence itself empties individuality of meaning." In other words, we are still traveling in herds. Like buffalos. It is just that now we like to pretend that we are very different from the buffalo traveling next to us. Few are the renegades truly prepared to dissect their stories, learn their lessons, slay their dragons, peel away their egos, pronounce with conviction, "This matters!" and grasp for themselves the meaning of it all, the reason for it all, or as Hegel sees it The Reason.

Along with our "identity crisis" and despite our technological "advances", we are also an era famous for its loss of community, for its loss of connectedness. In our communication Meccas and amidst the texts, the tweets and the IMs we have lost our connections. More accurately we have lost the art of connecting. We work and produce and consume and work and produce and consume at a frantic pace. The more lost we feel the harder we work, the more we produce, the more we consume. We consume more of anything, alcohol, drugs, money, stuff. And then we wake up tomorrow and do it all over again. Our sense of community stops at our usefulness to each other.

People did you hear what I just said? We are not individuals and we are not a community! No wonder we are floating out there wondering if there is meaning in it all, wondering just what the "experience of living" is all about. It is no wonder that we are at a loss for words no more profound than, "I just want to feel better"!!!

We like to pretend we are organized, driven and successful. We keep our lives in pocket sized communication devices that we used call telephones and use to stay connected to loved ones. We call it all progress. Like BBs in a box car we just keep pinging and ricocheting and buzzing from one meaningless point to another. Until one day we hit something soft, something that slows the pace, something that allows a pause, something that forces a halt and we realize that this isn't working. There is no meaning, no purpose, no rapture in being alive. We have striven to be unique in a herd of other uniques and it turns out we have all ended up being identically unique. Stampeding directionless and assuming that surely one of the buffalos up front knows where this is all going. We just expect that there is a purpose for this stampede. It is time, for a moment, to work our way to the edge of the herd, to slow to a gentle lope, then a trot, then a walk and finally to a pause. And in that pause we must reflect. What is the meaning in all of this?

Being part of the herd is not all bad...

It had been 5 months since I had been injured and though I had worked hard in physical therapy I was still left with an extraordinarily weak 80 pound body, electric pains down my leg, a brace on my foot and a cane to help me ambulate. We had moved to a new city and I had met a few new friends. They were mostly girls that I knew from gymnastics. My mom would take me to the gym once in a while and I would watch them train. Beyond this however I was fearful to go out or do anything with my new friends fearful that I would end up in a situation where I had to walk further than I was able to walk. Little by little my friend Kim convinced me to go places with her and she was always careful to make sure whatever we did was not too much for me. I clung to my cane as though it were a life preserver. My mom would encourage me to walk without it and on occasion I would limp around my house without it. But that is as far as it went. I was convinced that I needed that cane. It was my security blanket. It was also my excuse to stay home and to stay isolated. The isolation was not intentional but it was real. Somehow I had grown used to being the patient and being normal again was scary to me. I didn't want people to treat me as though I was a normal healthy teenager. I wasn't that and the cane made that evident to everyone. Without the cane people couldn't tell that I was weak and frail and injured. The cane made a statement so I didn't have to explain things.

I remember well, it was August of 1980 and friends of my parents invited my sisters and me to go to the big Harley Davidson motorcycle rally in Sturgis, SD. I wanted so badly to go along and I fussed for days worrying that I wouldn't be able to keep up. What if I got tired? What if I started to hurt? I'm not sure what I thought would happen if those things occurred I just know that those were the worries that went through my mind. Nevertheless, my desire to go won out and the day came and I had psyched myself into going along. We loaded up into the car and headed to Sturgis to see the 500,000 or so Harleys that once a year took over the little town of Sturgis, SD. It wasn't until we were about half way through the 40 minute ride when I made, what was to me, the most horrifying discovery. I had, in all of my haste and worry and fussing, forgotten my cane. I cried. What were they going to do with me? My sister tried to console me and by the time we arrived I was scared but calm. And so it went, I got out of the car and I walked. I walked without a cane. I walked slowly, but I walked all day. I saw the bikers, I smiled and I laughed and I ate ice cream and I walked. I walked and I never used that cane again.

The shield that told the world I wasn't normal was gone. The battle from here on out was to be a private one. The world would no longer see me as injured and struggling because for all appearances I was normal. The brace and the scars and the injured leg were all hidden. It was time to start being as normal as I could be, it was time to start being a teenager again. I was skinny, I was weak, I had pain, my foot didn't work but I walked and I knew that normal was coming soon.

The story goes that the great Hasidic Master the Baal Shem Tov was a normal man, Yisroel (Israel) ben Eliezer, searching for answers just like the rest of us until one day he turned around and walked out of the back side of his mind. Pretty cool huh? I can't do it. It is a task beyond the average person indeed. What we are trying to accomplish here is something "do-able." An earnest effort to have a life, that makes sense and allows us to experience the "rapture of being alive", has to be something we can do. It has to be something that will *just make us feel better.*

All of the esoteric albeit brilliant ideas and theories are good and fine but most of them do not help us to make our lives better right here, right now. Our search, our quest, our mission must be for a "way of life" not for an ideology beyond what we are capable of applying. So rather than delude ourselves into thinking that we are truly capable "walking out of the back side of our minds" let's proceed with the knowledge that we can never do this perfectly or even realistically come close. What we can do is free ourselves from the prison of self delusion. What we can do is recollect our stories, tell our stories out loud to another living being and try to view our narratives from a distance, to observe how our stories have played out thus far, to dis-cover how we have become, to distinguish between what is "self" and what is "Ego".

Change starts with objective observation. We cannot completely eliminate the persona, but we can, through our review of our histories as narratives, watch the persona, the ego in action. Self-consciousness is being aware that others are watching. We destroy the other "watchers" when we become our own true witnesses. For us "normals" (not Hasidic Masters) this is a very gradual process of becoming autonomous, of becoming first person singular beings. There is something rebellious, disobedient and courageous about stepping outside of the persona and into *the self.* There is something pure and fresh and clean about shedding our masks, both public and private.

Recollecting and telling our stories, while being as utterly honest, open and willing as we possibly can, allows us to make the modest but monumental leap from the ego, from the personality, to *the self.* When we are bold enough to face the instances where our instincts have lead us astray, when we are ready to wrap our arms around our family of origin and all that it has done to shape us, good, bad and ugly, when we are prepared to embrace the day and age in which we live and acknowledge how *every* culture before has brought us to this point in time, we are ready to step forward as first person singular beings. We are ready to eliminate what we have no use for and to weave ourselves into the beings we wish to become as we continue on the in this journey we call life.

What Have I Done?

There is one point that is critical here that we have yet to address, that point is dealing with the stuff in our past that we are less than proud of, the actions we wish we hadn't taken, words we wish we hadn't said, behaviors we wish we could take back. All of these need to be taken in and held and owned as part of the narrative that we have lived thus far. We must not dwell in the past. Just as we cannot become overly nostalgic and live in former glories, we also cannot and must not acquiesce to feelings of guilt or shame and remain stuck in a past that no one has the power to change. It is what it is. Telling our stories is what will teach us and what will allow us to "…not regret the past nor wish to shut the door on it".

Ok, ok, ok, I'm with you here. It sounds ridiculous to some of us. We are human and we have all done things we wish we hadn't. Some of us have REALLY done things that we cannot imagine not regretting. The courage to admit we are wrong, to make amends and to start again is indeed the most priceless, the most valuable courage of all, and we must *choose* it as one of those things that we value, as one of those things that we hold in great esteem. Put another way, the inability to admit we are fallible, that we are often incorrect and at times even wretched and profane, is one of the most grievous travesties of mankind. It is the travesty that costs us the only thing we truly have—ourselves. The travesty comes not in failing but in denying that failure, not in erring but in refusing to remedy the error, not in falling flat on our faces but in staying flat on our faces.

This is the deal—we cannot change the past, running from it isn't working, it is time to own it, make amends for it if they are indicated and learn from it. Step back as an objective observer and see where it fits in our narratives, see how it shaped us, changed us, twisted us, distorted us or made us better. What has it given us that we did not have before? Do we now possess a gift that we are intended to give away to other hurting beings?

I have had a lot of pain and suffering and bad things in my life. Some out of my control but many of them are direct results from decisions that I have made. However, I can stand before you today or before anyone and say with unqualified honesty that God has wasted no hurts on me. I may not fully understand them all but I am at peace with that. My story, my whole story, is what it has taken to get me where I am today. My history is rich and raucous and real, it is disturbing and harrowing, it is colorful, intense and enchanted, it is monotonous and ordinary. Above all it is oh so human. My files are full of memories that are far less than glamorous, memories that are humiliating, hurtful and hateful. I own them all, I clean up my side of the street by making amends that I owe whether others involved choose to do the same is not my business. I can only clean up my stuff, other beings will need to clean up their own stuff. No one can make my story 'right' for me. If there are issues left unfinished, amends that have been traded for silence then I need to address the unfinished business before I am free to file away the memory. I need to silence the sirens of disease before the events in my story will rest peacefully in the record of my past. Once my failings, flaws and faults have been addressed then I am free to file them away as memories and to draw on the endowment that the experience has left me with when I or another is in need of it. To ignore my failings is to stack one wrong on top of another.

There is no agent more infectious and more contagious than the agent of humility that approaches another human being with an outstretched hand. In holding out our hand to another in sincere apology we are opening the door of healing far beyond our own personal stories. We are starting a web of interconnected beings that in joining together as a whole and are infecting the world with the humility and healing that makes us all Whole. The discipline is a lonely one until the ever expanding web weaves its way back to us and one day someone comes up to us with an outstretched hand and says, "I am sorry. I was wrong." Then it is not lonely. It is love. It is the unconquerable love of humanity.

A "Love Story"...

    It was early 2003. I was living in Tulsa, Oklahoma with my husband and my 11 year daughter and our 3 year old son and 5 year old daughter. My 11 year old daughter Olivia decided that maybe she wanted to move back to Arizona to live with her dad in Phoenix. After much thought and deliberation we decided that we would give it a try for a semester and in early January we loaded her up and took her back to Phoenix. It took her about one month to decide that she wanted to be back in Tulsa with her mom. For the sake of continuity we decided to have her finish the school year in Phoenix and come back at summer time. For both mother and daughter May could not come fast enough.

    Like a bullet between the eyes May came along with papers from my attorney stating that Olivia's dad was filing for primary physical custody and that he was not planning on allowing Olivia to return. It made no sense, I felt like I was going crazy. This was not part of the deal. We had agreed on a trial to see how she would do. It had been the longest four months of my life and Olivia's too. Thus began a legal battle that I was destined to fight in the Arizona court system. I travelled back forth to Arizona all summer long. The summer came and went and the case dragged on. My heart would bleed at the sight of my 11 year baby that just wanted her Mama. Night after night I would talk to her on the phone and hear her little voice ask when she was going to be able to come home and night after night I would have to tell her, "Mama is working on it. Soon Baby soon."

    IT was mid-September and the school year had begun when our case finally came before a custody evaluator. After an exhaustive 3 day evaluation the conclusion was in, Olivia was coming home. My God the relief. What a nightmare we had been through but it was over and my daughter was soon to be under my roof again. One week later she was home. But the nightmare was only beginning. On the day that after I had welcomed my baby home and at long last held her in my arms the DEA showed up in my office.

For the past 2 years I had been being treated by a local pain doctor for chronic debilitating pain from the crushed pelvis injury that I obtained at the age of 15. Although I had always had some degree of pain from the injury it was during my last pregnancy that it became intractable. Since the birth of my son I had been on long acting narcotic pain medication prescribed to me by a pain specialist. After a year and a half on the medication I became addicted and began self medicating and self prescribing. A local pharmacist had turned me in to the State Medical Board for writing prescriptions to my nanny and picking up those prescriptions myself. And he was correct in his assumption, the medication was intended for my own use. I was in trouble, big trouble in more ways than one. Not only did I have the DEA and the Medical Board to answer to, I had a severe chronic pain problem and a career ending addiction to narcotics. The only thought that went through my mind on that horrible day was, "Oh my God, Olivia, they will try to take Olivia back to Phoenix."

Over the next two weeks I tried desperately to hold it all together aware that sooner or later I was going to hear from Olivia's dad, likely via his attorney, and that he would be trying to take Olivia back. I was truly powerless. There was nothing I could do but begin to clean up the mess that I had created and wait for the axe to drop. I travelled to Dallas, Texas to see a pain doctor who proceeded to implant and intra-thecal pain pump to control my pain and enable me to get off the oral narcotics and hopefully salvage my career. I made arrangements to check myself into a treatment center for addiction. I would be there for three months as that was the minimum requirement for the State Medical Board.

Despite the wreckage I had created in my life it did not compare to the pain that I had caused my little girl. She had finally made her way home to her mom and now I was leaving for three months. She cried daily. She was trying so hard to make the adjustment back into her Tulsa school and she needed so badly for her life to settle down. After many long conversations Olivia made the decision that she would rather go back to Phoenix with her dad than stay with her step-dad while I was gone. And I knew that this would be best for her. The subject was broached with her dad and again, a bullet between the eyes. His response was that she had told the custody evaluator that she wanted to go back to Tulsa and that she was going to have to live with her decision. "For God's sake she is eleven years old!" Olivia was devastated. I was numb with disbelief and crazy with desperation.

On my 38th birthday I left Olivia and my other two young children in the care of my husband and checked into a treatment center for narcotic addiction. I talked to my family nightly. Olivia would cry and ask me why her dad wouldn't let her come back. Her pain was acute and intense, and she could not be consoled. My husband would tell me that things were going smoothly at home and that Olivia was doing well in school but that he would hear her at night on the phone with her dad sobbing and saying, "Dad I'm sorry, I'm sorry. I want my mom or dad. Please dad." He felt as helpless as I did and a little eleven year old girl was paying the price. Two months into treatment Olivia's dad agreed to bring her out to participate in the children's program. Finally I got to see her and hold her and she looked good and was happy both to be with her dad and to see her mom. She spent her half a day in the three day program before her dad pulled her out and drove back to Phoenix and sent Olivia back to Tulsa. I did not get to say good bye. All I knew was that her happiness was fleeting and she was now back in Tulsa wanting either her mom or her dad and that neither one was there for her.

Her desperation continued the entire time I was in treatment. Shortly before I was discharged papers arrived from Olivia's dad again filing for primary physical custody. He now wanted the daughter that he had left alone and scared for the past three months. Two weeks before I returned to Tulsa Olivia was sent back to her dad in Phoenix. I was allowed to see her once a month in Phoenix. My legal council had very little hope that given my recent history and the fact that she had gone back and forth so many times already, I would ever be able to get physical custody of Olivia again. The feeling was that of despair and hopelessness and I focused on getting as much visitation with her as I could. The progress was slow and it took nearly 9 months for her to be able to return to Tulsa for a visit. I concentrated on caring for my two young children and I let their love heal me. I saw Olivia as much as I was allowed and I continued to clean up the wreckage of my past. Olivia continued to ask about returning to Tulsa to live but she knew, as I did, that there was very little hope of this happening. I wanted her in Tulsa with me, she wanted to be in Tulsa with me and there was nothing either of us could do about it. She was growing up 1500 miles away. Years past and Olivia's longing to come home only grew. She had been in Phoenix three years and she had friends and a life there, but she wanted her mom. Attorneys gave me very little hope of winning any legal battle for her return and recommended that we continued to focus on visitation. Olivia was almost 14 years old when I told her that I had been told that the legal doors were for all practically purposes closed and that we could not win a legal battle. I still remember her reply, "Mom, I am coming home. I will get myself back to Tulsa." And she did.

In the summer of 2007 Olivia did something that no one can do better than a teenage girl...she made herself intolerable. She challenged her dad at every possible opportunity. She wrote lists that were pages long of why she should be able to return to Tulsa. She ranted, she raved, she through teenage tantrums. She badgered, she begged, she hounded, she pestered, she tormented, she tortured. And by the end of July, 2007 she returned home. Home at last.

I can't give Olivia back those years and I cannot erase the pain that she suffered. What I can do is own it. I caused a lot of her pain. If I had not started abusing narcotics she would have been safe at home with me. My decisions left her flailing in a sea of uncertainty at the age of eleven. I can make amends to her, not just by saying that I am sorry, but rather by staying in recovery, by being a good mom, by making sure she feels safe and loved and that she knows that I would go to the ends of the earth for her...that there is no place too far. To be healthy and whole for her I have had to forgive her dad, it took years, but I have. To Olivia I have made a living amends. And I will continue to do so, for the rest of my life I will continue to show her my love by living the kind of life I want her to live.

Today Olivia is a beautiful, happy, healthy 16 year old high school student. If you asked someone to describe her in one word they would probably say "stunning" because she is...if I had to describe her in one word I would say "jovial" because she is. A mother and daughter could not be closer, our bond is sacrosanct and untouchable. Our tightness is hard to describe. And it does not need to be described because, like most things with Olivia and I, words fall short and they just are not needed. She will be a senior in high school this year and we are looking at colleges. Last week I received a text message from her out of the blue at about 10am (Uh hello? What is your phone doing out at school?)it read, "I want to just live at home with you forever. Can I?" Tears filled my eyes and I whispered, "You are home Baby, you are home."

To Olivia-

When darkness falls upon our heart and soul
I'll be the light that shines for you
When you forget how beautiful you are
I'll be there to remind you
When you can't find your way
I'll find my way to you
When trouble comes around
I will come to you
I'll be your shoulder
When you need someone to lean on
Be your shelter
When you need someone to see you through
I'll be there to carry you
I'll be there
I'll be the rock
That will be strong for you
The one that will hold on to you
When you feel the rain falling down
When there is nobody else around
I'll be
And when you're there with no one there to hold
I'll be the arms that reach for you
And when you feel your faith is running low
I'll be there to believe in you

When all you find are lies
I'll be the truth you need
When you need someone to run to
You can run to me
I'll be[17]

Now that is a true "Love Story"...

_____

Part III:
Hitting The Bottom

6

The Spirit

Our journey thus far has taken us through instincts gone awry, authoritative maps and societal norms. We have packed our bags said goodbye to our beloved personalities and prepared for the journey into the depths of our beings, to the very *bottom of our daemons*. The question that remains is what will we find in these depths when all that is familiar has been left behind? As Eckhart Tolle famously described, when Michelangelo was asked how he created the statue of David he answered, I took a large piece of marble and I chiseled away all that was not David. We have to take away all that is surface to find what lies beneath and what lies beneath is *the self*.

So here we are at the *bottom of our daemons*. We have whittled away the apparent and we are left with *the self*. Stripped of all that has, over our life time, gradually covered us, we are free to ask, "Who are you? What do you stand for? What do you value? What do you believe in?" The answers to these questions are in the very core of our beings. The answers to these questions are what build *the bridge* that connects our past with our future. The answers are what will enable us to journey on into a future that has meaning and value and peace. That journey into an unknowable future cannot take place until we build *the bridge*, right here, right now. We build this *bridge* by finding our truth, by finding and owning what makes sense for us. We build the *bridge* by answering for ourselves the question that mankind has been asking itself since the beginning of time. Is there something more? Is there meaning in all of this? People from every culture that has ever existed have felt the need to make sense of it all. They have felt the need to be connected with something more, something Bigger, something Ultimate.

Choosing The Spiritual

Although the questions are universal the answers are quite personal. The answers are spiritual. It is the spiritual, no matter what a person believes, that is the foundation of what each of us is all about. This chapter is difficult for me to write for two reasons. First, because I believe spirituality to be extraordinarily intimate, individual and private; explaining what and how I believe is like trying to tell you what a rose smells like. Second, because describing what I believe seems to break into pieces something that can only be understood whole. Breaking it into explainable parts somehow destroys the whole. I don't experience my spirituality in parts and I don't think of it in an "I believe this or I believe that" way. Rather, I simply experience it. It is experienced as an invisible flowing ribbon of air that weaves and wanders up, rises above, meanders down, writhes within and loops around me. It can float quietly near me and it can coil tightly around me. And in my most precious moments I believe that it is me. It cannot be possessed it possesses. It is the end and the means. It cannot be given it must be felt. It cannot be told to another, it must be heard. It cannot be owned only sought. The seeking in never done, it is part of the passing through.

Despite these difficulties I find it necessary to try to tell you about how I experience spirituality as I cannot tell my story and open myself to you without this for it is such a part of who I am. If I left this out you would know very little about me even if my narrative contained all of my innermost secrets. Writing my story without including my spirituality would be like reading the Mahabharata and skipping the Bhagavad Gita.

With about one hundred thousand verses, long prose passages, and about 1.8 million words in total, the Mahabharata is the perhaps the longest epic poem in the world. It is roughly ten times the length of the Iliad and Odyssey combined, roughly five times longer than Dante's Divine Comedy. It forms an important part of The Hindu Mythology. The Bhagavad Gita (Sanskrit भगवद्गीता, Bhagavad Gītā, "Song of God") is one of the most important Hindu scriptures. It is revered as a sacred scripture of Hinduism, and considered as one of the most important philosophical classics of the world. The Bhagavad Gita comprises 700 verses, and is a part of the Mahabharata[18]

Spirituality, or lack thereof, is an essential part of each person's story. Stripping away the beliefs we've been given and have tried to adopt, sometimes successfully and sometime not, is essential to the "being", to the true "self" in each of us. Again, what we believe and what we value is our spiritual core, our innermost essence and, until we are able to wrap our arms around this quintessence, the *bridge* to meaning cannot be built.

Our spirituality, no matter what its nature, shades how we view and interpret and interact with the world and its people. Spirituality deals with, not only what the Ultimate nature and meaning of our lives is meant to be, but also with, in a more earthy way, the inner life each of us experiences. Our spirituality tints how we receive all of the information that is out there. It sprinkles our inner beings and our personalities with colors. It pivots our perception to its own unique angle; it bends the light with which we see. Without it we wither away, it is like living without love, something shrivels and our very essence begins to vanish. We cannot *choose* to own it, to grab it and then check it off the list as something done. But we can *choose* to seek it, to reach for it, to open our beings to it, to heed it, to listen for it and to embrace it…or perhaps more accurately…let it embrace us, let it envelop us. We can *choose* to allow it.

Finding The Spiritual

First of all we need to figure out *where we are* starting from. For some of us it is the faith of our parents, for others that faith has long been discarded and replaced with something new or not replaced at all. Something uniquely modern is that we have become a reasonable and detached people. Due to many interacting variables, we have become a society that tends to step back, reason it out and then make a decision. This factor alone has impacted tremendously our willingness to accept faith based on our familial or societal authorities. We need, and indeed are conditioned to, decide for ourselves. For many of us, how we believe, our spirituality has been changed dramatically by our life experiences. Major events are pivoters of faith. Major events can give us faith, can change our faith or take our faith away. Hegel wrote that all of history has been directed by Reason, that it has all played out and continues to play out according to this Reason and therefore it is in history that we can see reason becoming Reason.

Whoa! Nevertheless, I find something valid in the idea of history and spirituality, especially as it applies to the individual. In our history, in our stories, lie the details of our beings becoming. In the dive to the *bottom of our daemons* we find out where we are and why we act and react the way we do. It is at the *bottom of our daemons* that we discover who and what we are. Our histories tell us how we have become, what we *choose* to do when we get to the *bottom of our daemons* will dictate what we will come to be. What we *choose* to seek does not matter. What matters is simply, that we *choose* to seek.

A ravaged faith...

She was 21. He was 22. Friends from high school re-united by fate and delighted to share some new common passions. They were both considering medical school and they had both gone away to college and found a renewed faith. Campus Crusade for Christ had lit a fire and the idea of missionary work around the world had been planted deep into both. They spent 6 months together. Growing, sharing, playing and falling, yes, falling in love. She had hung the moon and stars in his eyes since the first day she arrived at his high school. Could this really be happening 5 years later? She had never been all that interested in anything other than friendship but now there were common bonds and love was growing, pure, simple and real. Faith in God was growing.

They talked of faith, they talked of God, they talked of a future together, they prayed and praised and studied and taught. Both volunteered at the local Job Corp a state run live in training facility for troubled teens. Once a week she would head to the girl's dorm and he would head to the guys and they would lead Bible studies and spend time with the teens that needed an ear. Together they worked well and a future together seemed obvious if not predestined.

She awoke one day to a box on her doorstep, in it something she never could have imagined, something that would change her forever. It was a hat, a Russian Ushanka, and a note. The note read, because of your past I cannot spend my life with you. You are better off in God's hands than in my arms. She never saw him again. The past that he was referring to was that of a marriage that lasted less than a year. In the eyes of the law she was divorced, in the eyes of the Catholic Church the event had been annulled, in the eyes of her love she was tainted and not free to marry again.

Broken hearts heal, shattered faith has to start over. What he had taken when he left was her faith. How could she worship a God that saw her as somehow less than, where do you start when all that you have believed in views you as the unforgivable, the flawed beyond repair? You start Godless and Faithless.

It changed her. It changed her forever. It changed her faith that at one time had shown so bright, so pure and so utter. She would talk to God and tell Him how big her faith problem was until one day when she decided to turn around in her mind and tell her faith just how big her God was. Her God was in the blue and purple space with the navy blue surround. Her faith would return broader, bigger, deeper, stronger, all inclusive. For her, people would not be judged. They were and would always be equal no matter their past, their present, their religion, their status, their ethnicity, their nationality, their beliefs, their education, their successes, their failures, their strengths or weaknesses...she gave up the claim to have some sort of privileged access to the one true

God...she learned to love another's truth as much as she love her own.

He became a missionary. She became a doctor.

We experience spirituality in moments, in events, in words, in people, in nature, in objects...in being part of a greater Being, a larger Whole. Life is a spiritual journey regardless of exactly what we each personally believe. We all find it in our own way. For me, organized Religion quit working, authority confined me. I am wary of the "rightness" that every Religion claims. For some it may be perfect. Still others believe in something Bigger quite undefined, a Higher Power.

Just as we are the only ones that can tell our own stories, we are the only ones who can decide what and why we believe.

> *Albert Einstein:* "I have found no better expression than "religious" for confidence in the rational nature of reality..."

> *Blaise Pascal:* "The eternal silence of those infinite spaces strikes me with terror...When I consider the short extent of my life swallowed up in the eternity before and after, the small space that I fill or even see, engulfed in the infinite immensity of spaces unknown to me and which know me not, I am terrified and astounded to find myself here and not there."

They both speak of an Awe at the "sense" of our world. What they each personally believed or why they believed matters not, just that they believed.

My most intimate experience in this world is the chronicle of my life. It is the time and space that I have been given. If there is sense in it all, if there is meaning in it all, if it is sacred, as I believe it to be, then I will find it in the story that is my life. My life is a paean to the Holy, it is the salutation that I dance as I navigate the twists and turns and convolutions and peculiarities that I have been given. Life is daily. The meaning that I put into those days is what makes it sacred. Ordinary is ordinary…until it is not. As I learn to embrace and marvel in the ambiguities and the questions, as I become patient enough to allow the mysterious and the mystical, as I come to appreciate the fleshy, scarred, gnarled and flawed humanness of myself and those around me, I find God. God is in the ordinary and when I behold that, it becomes extra-, supra-, beyond- ordinary.

What I can discuss on this topic can only be penetratingly personal, it can only be my experience and will therefore be presented as I experience it, in the first person.

For me, that which is much Bigger than us all is best addressed as spirituality. The term seems to better allow for the differences in what all of mankind can relate. I allude above to the rational that is so characteristic of our modern times and since my space and time on this planet is in modern times it is what I can best relate to. We are a people that have been trained to be rational, to think it through, to reason it out. The difficulty arises when we are dealing with something like spirituality as, I believe, it cannot be fully understood, that is it is beyond our capacity to figure it all out. That is why it is called faith. Faith is not understanding, not seeing, but believing anyway. And in some ways, faith is intuition going mach 5 with its hair on fire. Still throughout the existence of mankind the questions of, "Who am I?", "What is the meaning of all of this?" have abounded. How do I reason out the unreasonable, how do I define the indefinable, how do I comprehend the incomprehensible? I don't know. But I can tell how and why I believe and experience something Bigger and in doing so I must add that I have been influenced immensely from the depths of history and the thinkers with minds deeper and more imaginative than mine to find a faith that, like my story, is uniquely mine.

The Rational

I see, *the rational,* as that coming from our capacity to reason, from that which just makes sense. From this comes the part of my spirituality that feels like a gentle amazement at the rationality and reasonableness in nature, in the cosmos. It is that subtle inkling that this cannot possibly be all "chance" without any intentional design. At a young age I read something that I have never forgotten, I do not know where

I read it or who wrote it and for this I am sorry as I would like give credit where credit is due. It goes something like this, "Common sense antagonistic to faith is rationalism; faith antagonistic to common sense is fanaticism." Herein is how faith works for me, my God is big enough to be indefinable and smart enough to be sensible.

I think that few capture the essence of rational faith better than Albert Einstein. Obviously a mind trained to think reasonably and rationally, but also a mind so brilliant that the more it uncovered of the laws of nature the more it realized that there was reason in it all, that there indeed must be a plan. In his book, *The World As I See It* he wrote, "A knowledge of the existence of something we cannot penetrate, of the manifestations of the profoundest reason and the most radiant beauty, which are only accessible to our reason in their most elementary forms, it is this knowledge and this emotion that constitute the truly religious attitude; in this sense, and in this alone, I am a deeply religious man." Albert Einstein found his rational faith in science and the reasonableness of it all, but describes an amazement in the emotion generated by the sheer prodigious complexity of it all. Others find their faith from *the rational*, not necessarily from some keen understanding of physics, but rather by simple wonder at the predictable cycles of nature or the like.

This *reasonable faith* is what helps me to not look upon those with a claim of "rightness" and say, "You are a freak, get away from me!" It helps me to not "throw the baby out with the bath water" so to speak. It is the, "I believe this because something or someone told me it was true, I can't it explain any of it but it is the ONLY right way to believe and if you don't believe this way you will be condemned to eternal damnation," that has tempted me and many others to throw up my hands and say, "You are a bunch of nuts, this faith thing is not for me!" When the truth of the matter is in my most simple moments my sincerest thoughts are, "Wow, how could I not believe?" I think belief is person penetrating, it is profound, privy and can only be felt by the individual doing the feeling...or the reasoning.

Another way that *rational faith* works for me is in how, Socrates, Plato, Aristotle and hoards of others to follow, saw "the good" in reason. Their *rational faith* had to do with what they saw as mankind's innate, "built-in" ability to know good from evil. Although they each called it something different, such as, virtue, Idea, good, truth, God, to what they were referring was the capacity of human beings to know what is good and right. They all argue the point, in one way or another, that, as reasonable beings, we are capable of discerning what is good. Although my over simplification is extreme, I do think that this is another way that spirituality grows and takes hold. Everyone is different and we would each choose our own words but the bottom line is that we do know good from bad, right from wrong. If we were asked to say in a word what the Ultimate Good is most of us would come up with compassion, love, dignity, brotherhood or the like. And the fact that our sense of good or right leads us all to a similar Ultimate puts *rationality* into how we are made as human beings. We are made with an ability to reason it all out. I am an idealist and a romantic but I think true, honest, untarnished love is in each and every one of us and that we need and want and crave it and that perhaps love and spirituality are the same thing. Regardless, we were born rational and able to tell good from bad, to tell love from hate.

...Hmmm? What is love? Well, I know for sure that it is NOT a second hand emotion. I may not be able to define it but I can describe it...it is wrenching, excruciating, blissful and divine all at once. It is costly, yes; it is definitely not free at least not to the "feeler". It is, however, free to the "feelee" with the subtle paradox that no one can be a "feelee" without also being a "feeler". For when it is not reciprocated love becomes infatuation or obsession or lust or something else lacking in divinity. I think love is a need much like food or water or air. Without food we can live for three weeks, without water we have three days, without air just three minutes. The cruel reality however is that without love we die slowly...little by little. Love is that "thing" we all seek intuitively. It is sort of like God, we don't know what it is but we know we want and need it and we know when we've been touched by it. And maybe God is love and therefore love is God but I think only in its purest most unadulterated form that to be true. Regardless of what it is I know I believe in it. I believe that it makes everything better... everything. I believe that love is the mystical healer. I believe that

with love all things are possible, with love life is more precious, with love peace and serenity are reachable and reasonable, with love laughter is more special and blessings more cherished. Or more simply put…love is Grand.

The Non-Rational

Enough of this reasonable stuff, no matter how good it sounds to my intellectual side I must admit that there is a huge part of my faith that is what Rudolph Otto would call *non-rational*. The *non-rational* is about the *mysterium, tremendens et facinans*[19] of my spirituality. It has to do with that intuitive sense that, even if I had no reason whatsoever, I would feel my God. I would know that there is something Bigger than me. The *non-rational* is all that is Mighty, all that is Mystical, all that is Mysterious. It is what makes my God infinitesimal and ineffable. I need to point out that, when I say it is *non-rational*, it is completely different from saying that it is irrational. What I mean by *non-rational* is that it is beyond my reason, not that it is non-sensible just that it is beyond the ability of my senses. It is a feeling. For me this is the feeling of absolute Reverence of God. It is the awe that goes beyond itself to become Awe, mystical Awe full of mystery, something beyond my comprehension and apprehension. An Awe so full of mysterium, so daunting that it produces shuddering and trembling. It is what is meant in the Old Testament by the "Wrath of God". It is not the wrath that we use in everyday language that gives the feeling of anger but rather an element of Holiness that has no parallel. It is an energy completely foreign, overpowering, incomprehensible and yet blissful and wholly and completely positive.

The *non-rational* exists for me in subtle, quiet ways. I find it in masterful musical composition, in the art work of the masters, in quiet meditation and in oracular utterances of worship that in the everyday world make no sense like the 'om' of Eastern meditation or other more common words familiar to me but only heard in masses of ancient tradition such as Kyrie Eleison or El Shaddai. The *non-rational* is experienced for me in the darkness of temples and catacombs. It is that sacred, spiritual feeling that looms in the air in the silence of monasteries and temples or in the silence between the notes in a musical

126

composition. It is in the ritual of incense, in symbolic breaking of the bread and in the sprinkling of Holy water. It is experienced by native tribes around the world as they adorn their traditional garb, chant and raise their hands and dance around the fire in fits of ecstasy not seen in everyday life. The *non-rational* for me is what reminds me that my God is vast and measureless, over, above and beyond the bounds of what I could ever imagine Him to be.

I think there is every day *non-rational* as well. We see it in miracle, coincidence, intuition and serendipity. Those things that happen that really have no plausible explanation; those things that have a billion to one odds of happening but happen anyway or the happy little fortuitous surprises that stop us in our tracks, deter us from one thing and lead us to another. Like I said, I am an idealist and a romantic and to me these things are not happenstance or good luck...I tend to just smile and say to myself, "God is directing traffic." I realize that there is such thing as good luck and coincidence and I am not a fatalist but, come on, you have to admit that some things are more. I don't think it was a coincidence that there was a surgery resident in the emergency room the night I got hurt. My injuries were far beyond the skill of a family practice doctor who, in all but the rarest of occasions, are the only physicians in Huron, South Dakota. When, with our current state-of-the-art trauma centers and doctors specializing in trauma medicine, the mortality rate for my injuries right now, almost 30 years later, is 97%, how was a tiny rural hospital in a small town in South Dakota able to find 23 units of B-positive blood and save my life? "God was directing traffic!"

Magic or Miracle

It is important here to distinguish the difference between magic and miracle. *Magic* is a slight of hand, a trick. *Miracle* is an interruption in the laws of nature. There is a big difference and it is more than semantics. At the risk of what Keen calls "ghettoizing" the argument, we are going to talk about addiction. For the addict or the alcoholic, the drug or the drink become the *"magical"* cure for an "angst" that they cannot explain. The drug or the drink makes everything better, at least for a period of time. By the time the chemical stops working these unfortunate individuals have turned on a switch, so to speak, in the brain that makes them unable to stop despite the most horrendous of consequences. It is a disease that Carl Jung called hopeless and deemed that, "...a spiritual or religious experience—in short, a genuine conversion, that while such experiences had sometimes brought recovery to alcoholics, they were...comparatively rare." The *magic* of the drink or drug is the addict's effort to control, to fix how they feel. The *miracle* of spirituality is God's remedy. Modern medicine classified addiction as a disease in 1955. The only known treatment for this disease, in a medical climate where heart transplants have become routine and daily, is spiritual. It is no coincidence that the Latin term for liquor is *spiritus*. For the addict, the drug is the *magic*, spirituality is the *miracle*. The analogy of addiction is a deliberate one, for this reason, it is characteristically modern to find something to fill the void, to fix the incompleteness, to remedy the angst. We are a quick fix society. There is no shortcut to spirituality. It is a *way of life* and it is a continual process. Anything short of spirituality, be it sex, status, shopping, being the best..., saving, power, winning, money, beauty, control, fame..., is sleight of hand, is toying with magic. Like the drink for the alcoholic, it will eventually fall short, will ultimately fail. It will leave us scrambling, reaching, clawing, thirsting, empty. The alcoholic or the addict learns that he must find a spiritual basis for living else he dies. Quite literally. This ultimatum facing the addict makes the choice of spirituality an easy one. Those not afflicted with a life threatening addiction have to make the spiritual choice based solely on faith that life can be meaningful, faith that there is a more fulfilling way to live, faith that Faith will fulfill. Not infrequently you will hear an alcoholic say that he or she is a grateful to be an alcoholic. The first time I heard it I thought, "Yeah rrrrright! Blah, blah, blah!" Now I know that what they are speaking of is this, they would rather be an alcoholic and be required to have a spiritual basis for living than to be a non-alcoholic and risk making the decision to try to live without it. For those who are not addicted to drugs or alcohol spirituality is a *choice*. God either is or He isn't. What is it going to be?

Choices...

It had been six months since I had been injured and the number of surgeries was well into the double digits. Wheelchairs, walkers and crutches had released me from the prison of the hospital bed and I was finally able to walk with just a brace and a cane by the time I started my junior year at my new high school in Rapid City. I had spent the summer in and out of the hospital and in and out of physical therapy. My daily routine included an electrical stimulation machine that was applied to my partially paralyzed left foot in efforts to help the damaged nerves to regenerate. I held on to hope against hope that somehow, someway my left foot would start to move again. I would sit and stare at my toes and try with all of my might to will my toes to move. Sometimes I would think I saw them move and I would holler at someone to come watch, desperate for my delusion to be reinforced. They did not move and eventually I came to accept the fact my foot was never going to move again. I had retained some nervous system function in the calf muscles of my left lower leg but that was it. I could not walk without a brace to hold my foot in position so I wouldn't trip over it. I couldn't walk without tripping over my own foot. It was maddening. Unfortunately I could still feel it and electric like pains would shoot into my foot unpredictably. It felt like a cruelest of all worlds. I couldn't move it but the shocks came intermittently to remind me it was still attached. I was able to walk with a cane, a brace, special shoes.

I went to the gym every day and would try to do what I could with the gymnastics team, mostly I just watched and made suggestions and tried to help the girls that were competing in any way I could. They were kind to me and liked having me around. The coach let me travel with the team and although it was obvious to all that I would not compete again they made me feel like I was one of them. I had started to put some weight back on but was still not even strong enough to hold myself up on the uneven parallel bars. My body was done with the gymnastics but it would take another two years for my heart to let go.

In the fall of 1981, a full year and one half after I had been *hurt, my mother and I travelled to Denver Children's Hospital to an Orthopedic surgeon who specialized in pediatrics to see if there was anything else that could be done with my permanently damaged left leg. I had adjusted to walking with the brace and the cane and sometimes I would even hobble without the brace. I don't know what I was expecting. I had gone through so many operations that I had become numb to it. This was our third opinion and all I could think about was that they were going to stick needles in my foot and leg again and do all of the painful tests again—for the third time. Dr. Eilert was a great big man with a muscular build, blondish hair and kind blue eyes. My mom and I listened carefully as he explained that he thought that he might be able to make it so I could walk without the brace, but our hearts dropped and the numbness returned as he described the series of major orthopedic operations that would be necessary. He rambled on about fusing bones and transferring tendons and putting some sort of a button on the bottom of my foot for a period of time. Many surgeries over many years and many recoveries with many months on crutches and MAYBE I would one day walk without a brace. It was something but somehow the news didn't feel like good news. I remember standing in an old fashioned red telephone booth at Tamarac Square shopping Center and telling my dad that Dr. Eilert thought there was something he could do. His reaction was subdued and he said, "Well we'll have to talk about it." I knew that he thought Dr. Eilert's plan was more than my little body could handle. I knew both of my parents thought that enough was enough. I knew that they were so grateful to have me alive, able to get around and back in school. I knew they didn't want their baby girl to hurt any more, to struggle any more. I knew they thought we should accept my injuries, move on and be thankful for how well I was doing. But I also I knew…that they knew…that I knew…that I was going to walk without a brace. I knew…that they knew…that I was never going to quit trying to be normal. I knew…that they knew…that I was planning a trip back to Denver.*

One of the best gifts that my parents ever gave me was freedom… the freedom to make this choice

Freedom and *choice*, these are at the root of our beings. These are what remain when we have wandered through our stories and addressed instincts gone awry, life experiences, familial influences, societal norms and the pressures to conform from government, religions and institutions. Stripped of all that has shaped us we are left with nothing but our very souls and the freedom to *choose*. Deep down at the very *bottom of our daemons* we find *the self*. And so I ask you,

1. What do you find at the very *bottom of your daemons*?
2. When there is nothing left but you, what do you believe?
3. If it is just you, and no one or nothing else is there, what would you say? Is there something or is there nothing?
4. Can you find a God of your understanding?
5. Is there a personal, intimate ineffable God there with you?
6. When at the very bedrock of your daemons, when in the deepest darkest crevice of your being, with all that you have known absent, do you feel something Bigger?
7. With absolute freedom from all that has shaped you what do you *choose*?

It is here, at the *bottom of our daemons*, that we find our faith, our own personal, private, individual faith. In darkness, in silence, in utter aloneness we find a freedom to believe and a foundation of faith. We find that which we can move forward with and build upon. We find a meaning and a purpose and a good that is ours and that, if allowed to, will frame our narratives as we venture back up and out of our past, onto the *bridge of the now* and onward into the course of time as our beings continue to become. All we need to journey onward is faith in something Bigger, not in religion, not in the faith of our fathers, not in anyone else's God, not in anything in particular, just in something Bigger than us. From here we will build, shape, mold, construct, chisel and weave a tomorrow with value, worth and sense. Not a tomorrow that can be planned and laid out in front of us but a tomorrow that we will experience differently, an adventure unlike any before...one that we will feel, see, touch, taste, smell, undergo, meet and go through one day at a time, one moment at a time. A tomorrow that will enable us to experience the "...rapture of being alive."

Discovering our foundation of faith gives us a starting point, a spiritual core to enlarge upon. What I believe is what makes my story a myth…not because it is "make believe" but because it is "what I believe". My faith is how I view the world. It is what brings the characters in my story to life. It is what animates them and it is what makes them into vital, living, dynamic, spirited mentors and allies and villains and guardians and shapeshifters and tricksters. Faith makes my story more than a tale. Faith makes my story bigger and brings it to life. Faith gives me the thread to weave my part in the Greater Tapestry. Faith brings my beautiful story from the past into this very moment. Faith is the *bridge* in my story that connects my past to the present. And it is what enables me to battle the mighty dragons that will, if left untamed, tether me to a past that I cannot escape. Faith lets me go backward and make sense of my story and it is what shows me how to step into tomorrow and experience the "…rapture of being alive."

Now we are not talking about going forward on some spiritual plain that is hypothetical and sounds peaceful and ideal for someone who doesn't have to live in the real world. We are talking about real life…real daily life "the experience of living". We are talking about a nidus composed of the secular *and* the sacred to build upon as we "go about living". We are talking about letting go of the plan "to arrive" and embracing the process of becoming. We are talking about releasing the delusion that we can "fix it" or "get it right" and, beginning to, with our own, personal, intimate beliefs, set forth on an unfolding, an evolution. We are talking about, admitting that we do not and cannot know, and becoming comfortable with the fact that we do not need to know. We are talking about a twisting, turning, delicate harmonizing of where we are, what we are, why we are and who we will become. We are talking about choosing faith over no faith, choosing completeness over incompleteness, choosing fullness over emptiness, choosing the Whole instead of the hole. We must ask ourselves, "Do I want my life to be larger than me? Do I want it bad enough to make the leap to an unknown God? Do I have the courage to just jump?

I wanted my life to be better. I was unwilling to accept what I had been given and I chose to take that leap of faith into the arms of an unknown God and entrust Him with an uncertain future.

So to back to Denver we went and went and went. I remember my first surgery in Denver well for what now seems like a silly reason. My first operation was the one where they fused the bones in my ankle and they put a button on the bottom of my foot. My foot was still so painful and I didn't want a button on the bottom of it. The button didn't particularly hurt but I knew it was there and I wanted it off. I'm not even sure what the button looked like because I couldn't see it but they called it a button and I wanted it off. The button stayed with me for four long months while the fused bones healed. The day I finally went back to Denver to have the cast and button removed was mental torture. I didn't care that they were going to remove a cast and move my leg that had been immobilized for four months or that they were going to stick needles in my foot again or that they were going to make me try to step on my leg, I just cared that they were going to touch that damn button and I didn't want them to mess with it. They cast and the dressings came off and the slightest movement of my leg was excruciating. Muscles and tendons and joints that haven't moved in four months are not very fond of being moved. I sobbed and screamed as I stared at my left lower extremity that no longer looked like a leg. It was withered and white and shriveled and it looked like it must be attached to a corpse. The pulsitile paroxysms that shot up and down my leg reminded me that it was attached to my leg. I couldn't catch my breath and my mental control that had served me well in the past was gone. Tears and sweat dripped down my face and pleading words for them to stop kept coming out of my mouth but they continued to mess with my leg as though they didn't realize that it was connected to a person. And then they started talking about the button, "Oh my God they are going to take the button off!" I just knew that this was going to send me over the edge from where I would never return. Dr. Eilert held my toes while the room full of muscular orthopedic residents watched with curiosity at the results of the first of several ground breaking surgeries. Although my protests continued and were loud they didn't need to hold me down. Any movement on my part hurt too badly and so I laid there on the table frozen like a statue screaming. I heard Dr. Eilert say, "That's it" and he and his procession of residents filed out of the room. The nurse put a cold rag on my forehead and whispered in my ear, "The button is off"and she followed them out of the room. I laid there wet and shaking and alone, but somehow the fact that the button was gone comforted me. I didn't feel him take it off and the button had never been painful but I didn't like it. This was just the first of several surgeries that Dr. Eilert had planned for me but the surgery with the button was over and I clung to that as if it had some sort of significance.

Over the next year my mom and I would load up the car and make the eight hour drive to Denver almost monthly. I remember every one of them and little details about every hospital stay. I remember my roommates ages 2 to 16 and nurses and Dr. Eilert coming in and deliberately bumping my bed to determine my pain level. He didn't know that I was on to his "technique" until one day as he walked into my room at 5 am I said, "If you bump my bed today I am going to put you in time-out for the entire week." He and his flock of residents laughed and Dr. Eilert never bumped my bed again. One of my roommates was named Crystal and she was 3 and had to have surgery on her stomach. I remember her after her surgery watching TV with me and every time a Coke commercial came on she would say, "Cokey mommy. I want Cokey." To this day, "Cokey mommy" is code in my family for, "I'm thirsty."

The part of Denver I remember most was my last visit. We were sent over to a shoe store to be fitted for a new brace and shoes. It was called 'Jerry's Stylo-pedics." Major league red flags! Panic set in immediately. My mother, my friend Kim and I stepped slowly into the shoe store with the frightening name. My hesitancy turned to absolute horror in a heartbeat. This tiny little store with dirty carpet and a funny smell had the walls lined with rows and rows of the ugliest shoes you have ever seen. They were hard soled, tar black or poop brown leather shoes. They all looked the same to me although the gentleman that was trying to help me kept inviting me to look at all of the different styles. My mind kept yelling, "No, there is no way I am going to where these to school much less all summer." My best friend Kim held her composure for about ten minutes before succumbing to out loud laughter at my reaction.

Kim was the gymnast that I never got to be and from my first day in Rapid City had become my best friend. She somehow always managed to get me through the toughest of times. I had been dealt this hand of crutches and wheel chairs and braces and being a normal teenager was not an option for me. Kim could have been normal but she hung with me instead and never failed to find some way to keep me going forward. I remember having to go to school in a wheelchair and Kim shrieking with glee when she realized that I was going to be given a key to the elevator at our high school. She didn't seem to even notice the hassle of lugging the wheelchair in and out of the car or pushing me around, she was just ecstatic about having a key to the elevator. For most of my junior and senior years in high school I was the injured girl and for the most part the regular rules didn't apply to me. Tardy bells, hall passes, do not enter signs…they didn't apply to me and Kim quickly discovered that as long as she was known as the hurt girls buddy they didn't apply to her either. She drove a little yellow Mustang and were it not for Kim I would have spent most of my high school weekends with my mom and dad.

Anyway, it was clear that Kim was going to get me through this shoe nightmare with humor. She tried hard to hold back her amusement with Jerry's Stylo-pedics, the ugly shoes and my utter dismay at my shoe choices. When the sales clerk casually mentioned that I would need to get my shoes two sizes bigger than my actual size I thought I would die. The tears came. Kim turned her back toward me in her efforts to hold it all together but I could see her shoulders shaking as she laughed uncontrollably. "This is horrible. I can't believe you would laugh!" I shrieked. I will always remember her answer, "I just kept picturing you jogging down the beach like Bo Derek in your stylo-pedics this summer. I bet you'll be able to jog this summer." As usual, she made my tears turn to laughter. She was right. This was the end of this part of my journey. I was just months away from seeing if I would be able to walk without a brace. The journey was long, painful and treacherous but it was one that I had chosen and one that, despite lots of love and support, I had to take alone. Late nights in the hospital always reminded me that I was on a solo trip. I chose this trip because it was going to make my life better, I knew it would work and I knew I would walk without a brace one day. It was a scary choice...a step into the unknown...but a step closer to what mattered the most to me...a normal life.

Part IV:
Facing the Facts

Okay let's re-orient for a moment….what we are working on is telling our stories. Our stories are much more than a series of events in our lives. Our stories are full of thoughts and feelings as well and that is what we are going to talk about in the next three chapters. We are going to talk about our thoughts and our feelings because without them our stories will be nothing but a recanting of a series of empty events. Our stories become epics and gifts when we include our deepest thoughts and our most sincere feelings. And when we share our deepest thoughts and our most sincere feelings that means we are going to share our secrets. Our deepest darkest secrets. Our secrets consist of three main things: resentments, fears and sex. Whether we care to admit it or not, these are the three things that take up the most space in our heads. So if we really plan to recollect and tell our stories we better plan on addressing them all. If we are to really tell our stories we must include these. Just go with me here. I don't want to know what you've done, I want to know what you thought and how you felt.

We've covered instincts and maps and finally spirituality in the last chapters, because these are things that we need to get a handle on as we prepare to tell our stories. What we are going to cover now are things that lie a little deeper. Things that are not resting on the top but are rather buried a little deeper and do not come quite so easily. These things are, however, central to how we see and interpret the world and they are central to how we think and feel about everything. To tackle these one thing is essential, there is one thing we cannot do without and that one thing is faith. Believing in something Bigger than ourselves is necessary if we are to REALLY tell our stories, reconcile our pasts and proceed to a future that we are free to author. Again, just go with me here.

So blah, blah, blah, blah………………What is key here people is that we cannot tell our stories and teach with them and learn from them unless we have a few skills. And a faith in something, in anything, is necessary to develop and practice these skills. I don't care if the door knob is the Power you believe in. What is essential; however is that you believe in something Larger than yourself. We must concede that we are not God.

7

Resentment and Fear

At the *bottom of our daemons* is where we find our spirituality. Stripped of our instincts gone awry, of our familial conditioning and maps, of the events that shaped us, of societal norms, we find ourselves free. Free to *choose* what to believe. We have made our way down through all that has shaped us and in sifting through our pasts, have established a foundation of conviction, a foundation to believe in and a foundation to build our futures on. It is time to wander back up from our depths and to step on to the *bridge of now* which is where we begin to tell our stories. By reaching down to the very *bottom of our daemons* we found faith. We found a God or a spirituality of our understanding that "works" for us as unique individuals. We have *come to believe.* Our next step is to *become willing.* That is, *become willing* to use that faith to embrace our past and to capture our freedom of *choice* as we go on to write our stories in the future.

As we climb back up from the recesses of the *bottom of our daemons*, all that we have shed to find a spirituality of our own comes back upon us. We are human and our instincts, personalities, family influences and social conditioning are real and are the reality that we live. Einstein said, "Reality is merely an illusion...", and after reaching down into our *bottom of our daemons* and discovering that which is authentic in ourselves, it is easy to see what he meant. Albert was no dummy, however, and he did feel the need to complete that quote by adding,

"…albeit a very persistent one." The authentic self deep inside may be what is real and pure and true, but the world is where we live, and if it is indeed an illusion, it is an inarguably persistent one. The key here is that what we have now *come to believe* is real. What we have *come to believe* is what, if we allow it to, will change the way we see this illusory reality. Knowing what we believe in is what enables us to go back into the past and make some sense of it all. What we have *come to believe* is what will enable us to reconcile the events of the past and step forward on the *bridge of now* into to the future.

But more than change the way we see reality, it will change the way we experience reality. You see, our faith is about to alter our illusion. The world as we know it will not change, nor do any of us have the power to change it. We do, however, have the power to change how we see and experience it. To change how we see and experience reality, we must *becoming willing* to apply what it is we have *come to believe*. And we must *become willing* to apply it as we tell our stories. Our stories are full of not just things we have done but they are also full of how we think and how we feel and what we believe…so let's go…

Before we move on I want to address specifically those that are still stuck on the came to believe part. For me, faith has come quite naturally and I think this is because of experiences I had when I was a teenager. I recognize that for some faith does not come easily. For some, God is still that man with a long white beard that throws lightning bolts when we do something wrong and that image of God can be difficult to shake. If believing is beyond where you are right now I am going to ask you to do one thing…I want you to believe that I believe. Nothing more, just believe that I believe and walk on with me. My hope is that perhaps journeying on will tickle out something that you can believe in. Your spirituality is your own, no one can give it to you. Sometimes we need to become willing first.

There is a big difference between wanting and becoming willing…

I make my living today as a cosmetic surgeon. Every day I see patients who want liposuction and are presently involved in that age old battle of the bulge. Usually what I do is shape up an area that isn't responding to diet or exercise or we proceed with liposuction as a "jumpstart" to an attempt at losing some weight and adopting some new lifestyle habits. Needless to say a frequently asked question is, "Dr. Masters what is the best diet? What diets work and what diets don't?" There are a million diets out there, Atkins, South beach, Mediterranean, low-fat, Slim fast etc. etc. Dieting has become an American past-time which is good in that we know there are health risks to being overweight. There are even television shows on prime time, The Biggest Loser and now Dance Your Ass Off. But for the purposes of this discussion I am using dieting as a metaphor for life. It is truly baffling. You see, every diet works. But I think it is part of our humanness to want to "fix" everything now and to look without rather than within. A diet working or not working is not the question. Knowing what to do to lose weight is not the question. The key here is you can't wish it or simply want it. You have to become willing to actually do the deal.

Easier said than done, I know, I know. But the analogy holds. Just as we can't just want a diet to work, we cannot simply want spirituality to make everything better. We have to become willing to see and experience things differently. We cannot control the world and the people in it, we have to become willing to experience the uncontrollable differently.

Freedom

Where do we start? It is a mind game. Yep, in the mind. By telling our stories we start to see how our minds, our 'way of thinking' has led us into actions and reactions that did not always serve us well. In telling our stories we are forced to look at events of the past that were often painful and disturbing. These events can stick with us and haunt us and make us unable to move onward out of the depths of our story into the present. They hold us tethered to the past. Our stories also bring up reminders of people we have hurt or wronged and people who have hurt or wronged us. Again, these things get us stuck; they keep us from moving on. Bottom line: our stories are full of people, places, things, events, behaviors and habits that hold us hostage to a past that is the history of our becoming up to this point.

But now, at this moment, we are about to make the past into a wonderfully organized epic of all the memories that have shaped us and taught us and that we can draw upon as we navigate our lives from this day forward. Our pasts need to be embraced and treasured but left where they belong—in the learned file of our memories. To free ourselves from the parts of our stories that cling to us and hold us prisoners we must take a look at our 'thinkers', our minds and re-train, if you will, how we think, see and experience the now and beyond. The words hostage and prisoner are chosen deliberately as the first step into a more meaningful now and a purposeful future is the step into freedom, we must *become willing* to *become free* of all that binds us.

Freedom comes from *becoming willing* to reconcile the past and then leave it. Like we have talked about before, spirituality cannot be gotten, it must be experienced. So it is with freedom. We cannot grasp it or claim it we must receive it and experience it for what it is …a gift. What we have *come to believe*, our spirituality, is the giver. It is our spirituality that will *gift* us the essential tools we need to build a now and a future with meaning and joy.

The first of these gifts is freedom, without freedom we cannot open ourselves to the gifts that follow. We must cut the chains that bind and file the past in a file that we are free to use as a resource. We must put the past in its proper place which is in a memory file that is useful to us. We must learn to use the past as something that we are able to draw up and draw upon. If we fail at this lesson it will surely draw us down and continue to draw upon us.

Freedom is first and foremost. Freedom from all that we have tried to control and all that we have clung to, for by holding tight to these things they have come to rule us, to control us. Only by letting loose of them will we be free to experience the *gift* of *freedom*. Our efforts to control and cling have made us prisoners. Prisoners are not free, they are under control. Freedom is experienced when we cease fighting anything and anyone, when we surrender. Whoa! Wait a minute, surrender sounds like something a prisoner does!

Such is the first great paradox of spirituality. We must surrender before we can be free. Surrender traces back to the Latin root *reddere*, which means to *give back or return*. Surrender is the ultimate spiritual paradox, only when we surrender, *give back* control to our God can we experience the gift of *freedom*. By claiming control we are controlled, by letting go we are let go. Only by surrendering to the fact that we are not in control of people, places, institutions, events or life, by *giving these things back* are we in a position to experience freedom.

Freedom is not earned or attained, for both of these imply that we have some degree of control. No, *freedom* is *gifted* and then experienced. We start by letting loose of it all. We start by realizing that what we have *come to believe*, that the God of our understanding, has got it and He doesn't need our help. We have *come to believe* that we can, "drop the rocks". We start by seeing that we all have one thing in common. Every last one of us has something in common. We are not God and we do not get to be in control. "There is a God, I'm not It."

Our stories are not to be forgotten they are what our God has given us. They must be told for they are what we have to give the rest of humanity. They are also full of examples of us struggling with our own humanity and trying to hold on to, manipulate and change what only God can control. The absurdity is this, as we hold tight to everything we think we need and want we lose what is most valuable—our *freedom*. We become prisoners to the things we are trying to control. We must learn to, "drop the rocks".

Forgiveness

Enough of the fluff, let's get real shall we? If we are going to live in the here and now and build upon it and truly experience the "rapture of being alive" there are a few things we need to get filed appropriately. Let us start with resentment. We've talk about this briefly before when we talked about *fighters*, but everyone does battle with resentments. Each and every one of us! The word itself literally means "feeling again". Which is appropriate since that is what it does, it makes us feel a pain over and over and over. Resentment has been called, "The number one offender." The number one offender of what? Of freedom. There is nothing that cuffs us to the past quite like resentment. It is anger, attached at the hip. It is anger that cements us to the past and makes us feel it again and again and again and in doing so it controls our now and our future. Simple anger is healthy and normal. It is when we lose control of it that it controls us. Anger out of control is rage, anger that we cannot let go of is resentment. J. Geils called it "Rage in the Cage" and what an appropriate metaphor as it indeed imprisons us. Resentment takes a hold of our 'thinkers' and distorts and taints and mangles and perverts and warps and garbles how we see and experience reality. It is cunning, baffling and powerful. And it is a forceful and merciless abductor of our freedom.

We are all victims at one time or another. When we harbor resentments we volunteer to remain victims. How do we rid ourselves of this anger that won't go away? Two musts: number one, we need to accept what we actually do and don't have control of and number two, we need to own our part. What we have control over is our own actions and reactions. Likewise, what we need to own is our own actions and reactions. So when something has been done against us and we cannot let go of our anger and sense of betrayal what can we do? We can *choose* to not remain eternal victims and this involves another *gift*.

The *gift* of *forgiveness*. Like *freedom*, *forgiveness* cannot be grabbed or owned or willed. It can only be experienced. *Forgiveness* is one hundred and eighty degrees from resentment. Its opposite. Why is *forgiveness* necessary, because we cannot change the past and we cannot change another person. We cannot rewind history and make things turn out differently. Try as we may to "re-boot", wish as we will to "un-do", search as we might for the "control-alt-delete" escape, in life these do not exist. We cannot cancel the pain or the hurt or the anger or the betrayal. All we can do is not allow whatever it was to continue to tether us to the past. In the here and now we can choose to let it go and forgive or to hang on and live in it and with it forever. Without *forgiveness* we cannot fully receive the gift of *freedom*.

When we do not have *forgiveness* we do not have it for one of two reasons:

1. *We cannot forgive.*

We know we should, we know we need to close a chapter, we know we need to allow healing but try as we may we cannot. We say, "I have tried. I have really tried but it keeps coming back. Everything that reminds me of that person brings back the resentment."

2. *We refuse to forgive.*

We refuse to even consider it saying, "I will never, as long as I live, forgive that person."

So how do we experience this thing called *forgiveness*? In 1989 a study was published by researchers that looked at just this phenomena.[20] What the study showed was that *forgiveness* is something that happens to us and it happens quite spontaneously. No matter which of the two groups above we fall into *forgiveness* can and does happen. The researchers go on to uncover a truth long known in religious and philosophical thought, we experience *forgiveness* by feeling, by realizing that we are forgiven. Not by a conscious, "Well, he forgave me so I guess I should forgive too," but rather in a subliminal, unconscious way. The researchers were able to connect, via every six month interviews, the experience of being forgiven with the experience of *forgiveness*. Interviewees were prone to saying something like, "Wow, I guess I have forgiveness now but I don't really know when or how it happened." By documenting significant events in the lives of the participants the researchers found that an astounding number of the participants spontaneously forgave not long after an incident, trivial or not, when they themselves were forgiven. *Forgiveness* is an experience that lands upon us gently, quietly and unexpectedly...when we *become willing* to live according to what we have *come to believe*.

Those of us that are not even near the willing to forgive have a little bigger mountain to climb. Which is why this section is titled, *become willing*. We must at the very least be able to squeak out the words, "Maybe I will try. I really dislike or maybe even hate this person but I will entertain the idea that for myself to heal I need to let go of this and quit letting it control me." Whew! There is a start. It is not easy and there are things that seem beyond *forgiveness*. We must remember this, we are trying to forgive to help ourselves not to help the other person. The forgiving is to free ourselves and it is not to hold the other faultless. If they were faultless then they would not need forgiving. That is what forgiving is, the word literally means "to give up". In other words, we are "giving this up" to something Bigger than ourselves.

(hence the need for the *coming to believe* part!) We are forgiving and that is entirely different than trying to forget. We are forgiving to file this as a memory, as something we remember. Not as something we forget.

I am not sure who came up with the saying, "Forgive and forget" but I think it is a really dumb idea. Really dumb. For two reasons,

1. *By forgetting we devalue the very experience of forgiveness.*

Why forgive if we are going to forget about it anyway? God may be able to forgive unconditionally but we are human and cannot and should not forget. Remember, "There is a God and I'm not It". Forgetting depreciates the entire experience. Good, bad or ugly, the experience mattered in our lives and if it was important enough to harbor a resentment over then it is important enough to remember. We are all responsible for our own actions and behaviors, and consequences come with bad actions and behaviors. Now that is not to suggest that any of us have the right to assume the position of judge, jury and punisher. But it is to suggest that forgetting implies the erasure of consequence. When we erase all consequence the message sent is covert and threefold:

   a. I don't value you enough to hold you responsible for your actions;
   b. I don't value me enough to hold you responsible for your actions and;
   c. There are no consequences for hurting me, so step back, re-load and let me have it again. Forgetting says that the experience did not matter.

2. *By forgetting we do not learn the lessons we are meant to learn and sometimes these lessons serve to protect us.*

Perhaps a cheating spouse can be forgiven once, but when he cheats a second time it is no longer a moment of weakness…it is a pattern. A pattern that we hopefully someday we will forgive but, in the name of self-protection and self-preservation, never forget.

As for forgiveness when every bone in our bodies screams, "No way. Never!"

I can only tell you what worked for me. It has to do with when my daughter's father left her hurting and scared with a step-father that cared for her but could not console her. First I said, "No way. Never!", then I talked to people and they told me what they did, what worked for them. (You see the value in stories!!) Finally, I chose to take the advice I was given and "try". My heart was not in it. My mind knew it would not work but I did agree to try. The advice that I was given was to pray for him. "Yeah right. Screw that." Was my first, second and third reaction. Prayer, for me, has always been something that I have done but wondered a lot why I did it. It usually came spontaneously and just felt like the thing to do although I doubted that God was up there saying, "Well Leslie really seems to need this so I'm going to just go ahead and give her this one." Early on in my life I decided that prayer was for "thank you" and "give me Your strength" but for me it couldn't be about asking for anything beyond this. For some reason I have never believed that my prayer was going to change what God decided to do next. Blah, blah, blah. Anyway, one evening I sat outside, lit up a cigarette and though I wanted to say, "God give him everything he deserves." I managed to say, "God please give him everything that I would want for myself." And that was it. I said that same prayer night after night sometimes even rolling my eyes in a look of skepticism as I did so. I do not know if prayer changes things. And I do not know if praying helped me to experience forgiveness but I do know that forgiveness came and rested itself on my heart. I have always said that I could forgive almost anything you do to me but hurt one of my children and there is not a chance. I was wrong.

Sometimes the only thing we can do with a lingering resentment is *become willing* to experience *forgiveness*. Other times there is more that we can do and this is own our part in the situation. In almost every situation there are two parts played, ours and the others. For the most part, we always have a role in the resentment. And ridding ourselves of the chains that lock us in the past and hold us away from freedom involves owning our part in the problem. Yes this means making amends, saying, "I'm sorry" and yes, saying, "I was wrong to…" We have no control over what another person says or does but we are responsible for our own side of the street so to speak. In making amends we are keeping our side of the street clean. The other person may decide to clean their side of the street too…or they may choose to leave it cluttered, dirty and chaotic. That is not within our control. We are making amends not to be forgiven but to experience *forgiveness*. We are making amends not to "fix" some situation, but to clean up our side of the street, to take care of our own unfinished business. We are making amends to lose the resentment, to open ourselves up to the gifts of *forgiveness* and *freedom*.

What happens during the amends making is not one of those things we get to control. The amend does, however need to be sincere and real, it needs to be a complete owning of our part in the problem. What it cannot be is an excuse or an explanation or a re-stating of why we did what we did. It is simple. It is just a stating of where we were wrong. Whether the other person 'had it coming' or not is not the point. The point is we want our side of the street to be clean and we want to live in the now and to be excited about the future not hobbled by the past. To continue with our previous example of the unfaithful spouse, if I am the victim of a cheating spouse my amends may sound something like this, "I am sorry that I lit all of your clothes on fire and slashed your tires. It was wrong for me to do those things. I am not proud of my behavior." And leave it at that! I have owned my stuff, made amends, cleaned up my part and chosen to open myself to *freedom* and *forgiveness*. Obviously forgiveness will need to come into play sooner or later (and often much later) but owning our part is an essential part of the healing of the resentment.

Before we move on from "the number one offender", resentments, I want to mention two other kinds of resentments that we often don't think of, resentments toward God and resentments toward ourselves. These resentments are just as real as those that we harbor for another person and the remedy remains the same. We must acknowledge that we are not God and that we cannot and will not understand everything that happens in this world. We must accept the fact that we are human and that we will fail, we will do bad things, we will hurt people and that we, like everyone else, need *forgiveness*. We must realize that what has happened is in the past, we cannot change it. Children get sick, people die, car accidents happen. When I was injured any resentment toward God was quashed quickly and I am not sure how or why, just that I remember my Grandmother saying, "Oh my God, oh my God why did this happen? Why you?" And I answered, "Grandma why not me? If we understood it all we wouldn't need God." My experience in the blue and purple place with navy blue surround had left me with a peaceful accepting feeling that told me that I didn't need to know and I didn't need to understand. I just needed to take what I had and move on and never forget.

Forgiveness of ourselves requires us not just to accept our part but to accept ourselves for what we are—human, not God. *Forgiveness* of others starts with the awareness and acceptance of a shared weakness, being human. *Forgiveness* of ourselves starts with the same steps that we talked about earlier but demands that we look further. Once again, our thinkers are deceiving us. Self-condemning for wrongs done is reasonable and honorable. Self-condemning does however need to come to an end. Once we have owned our part and made amends or are working on amends (since living right can often be the only amends we can make) we need to drop the self blaming attitude. When we don't drop the blaming we are choosing to remain in the chains even though they have been unlocked and we are free to walk away from the bondage. If we are free to walk away and we choose to stay there must be something in it for us. There must be something that we are getting out of the damnation we are dealing ourselves.

Believe it or not, self deprecation is pride in cognito and our need becomes *humility*. *Humility* comes from the Latin term humus, which means earthy, grounded. In modern terms it means being right sized. Not more than and not less than. And it is another one of those gifts. *Humility* is a gift that comes when we forgive ourselves and accept that we are not gods and we are not beasts. We are just humans, all of us imperfect. Self-condemnation is a form of narcissism. Just as Narcissicis fell in love with his own reflection, in self deprecation we fall in love with ourselves as martyrs. We fall in love with the specialness of ourselves as the only human being that is unforgivable. We are saying to ourselves, "I may be really bad but I'm a very special really bad." When we cannot forgive ourselves we need to look at what it is about being the martyr, the eternally damned, that is working for us. We are saying that every other human deserves forgiveness but we are somehow 'special'. It is that very specialness that puts us above or below others. The very act of non-forgiveness of the self says we think we are somehow 'more' or 'less' than the rest, different, unique, not as human as the rest of the folk. Forgiving ourselves is therefore a matter of getting right sized, accepting our place in humanity, admitting that we are 'just another bozo on the bus'. We are not more than and we are not less than. We are the same as every other human being, imperfect, faulty and limited. Human and *humility* come from the same root, humus-earthy, grounded. To get grounded we have to come back to reality, and guess what pal, that means that just as we don't get to be perfectly good, we don't get to be perfectly bad.

Reality check...

She was on her hands and knees weeding the garden when the phone call came in. "Hello my name is Officer Joe Goe(yes, that was really the name) with the Tulsa Police Department I need speak with Leslie Sibley." "This is she, "she replied slowly. Her pulse had jumped to 150bpm in an instant. "Dr. Sibley I need to set up a time to visit with you regarding the diversion of narcotics for your own use in the summer of 2003." Oh my God! It was the Fall of 2004 surely they are not going to file charges against her now! The two years that had passed since she had been to treatment for an addiction to narcotics that resulted from chronic narcotic use due to pain from a crushed pelvis injury when she was a teenager. Although she had only been on narcotics for two short years it had been long enough to become addicted to the medication and toward the end of that two year period she had started writing her own prescriptions and self-medicating, above and beyond what the pain doctor was prescribing. Big no-no!!!
But why was this happening now! She had done everything

she was supposed to do. She was better now. She had gone to extremes to get off narcotics. The permanent pump that bulged out of abdomen proved it. She had travelled to another state and had the pump placed so her pain could be controlled without needing oral narcotics. She had dealt with the medical board and was doing everything they had asked of her. She spent three months away from her family to go to treatment. This was not fair. She had jumped and was still jumping through every hoop they asked her to jump through. The consequences had been tremendous. They had sold their home and exhausted their savings, she had lost custody of her 11 year old daughter, she was on 5 years probation with the medical board and still trying to figure out what to do with her career. She did random drug screens every week, went to AA meetings daily and dealt with the anguish of having a pump protrude out her once flat abdomen. What else did they want from her? Enough already.

It just didn't make sense that two years later they wanted more from her. She was behaving and doing what she was told. She had never been in trouble before. She was not an under the bridge addict. It is not like she was producing Meth or selling drugs. She just made some bad decisions while in the midst of an addiction. She was sick but she was better now. Right?

Wrong! Reality check! Forgive and forget doesn't work with resentments and it doesn't work when you break the law. There are and there should be consequences for our behaviors. Forgetting says that the behavior didn't matter. It also says that the person doesn't matter. By forgetting the offense the person is either devalued to someone not responsible for their actions or the person is treated as though they are extra-special and the rules don't apply to them. Forgetting says the experience was not important, let's just disregard it. Forgiving says it was important and let's file it in the memory bank and grow from it. I matters…it all matters!

Serenity

Resentment traps us in the past, fear suspends us in time. And like resentment, it takes away our freedom. Fear possesses us and controls us. We have become unknowing captives of fear. Fear of failure, fear of economic insecurity, fear of loneliness, fear of looking like the fool, fear of abandonment, or how about these, fear of not being respected, fear of not being liked, fear of not looking good, fear of not being good, fear of not being good enough, fear of not being in control, fear of appearing weak, fear of being found out, fear of not winning, fear of being hurt, fear of losing face...

To abate these fears we cling, we mold, we morph, we manipulate. As long as we are consumed with these fears we are not free. Spirituality cannot *gift* us *freedom*, it cannot lift the weight off our shoulders, cut the chains that bind or trigger the relief valve until we *become willing* to let go of fear. And we can only let go of fear by believing, by trusting utterly in what it is we have *come to believe*. The silly thing is, that we have very little control over any of these things that we fear, but to silence the fear that engulfs us we fool ourselves into thinking we do.

Again, our thinkers need fixing. What we are doing is pretending, living in the illusion, subsisting in a fantasy, deceiving ourselves into believing that if I do this or if I do that it will all be okay. We become obsessed with the illusion that we can make the future behave. We convince ourselves that if we do everything just so, then all that we fear will not happen. Wake up call pal!!! The future is going to happen. We don't get to dictate how it happens. Remember, we only have control over our actions and reactions. We don't get to direct the whole show.

Until we can accept and embrace this fact, fear will control us and rob us of the next gift of *becoming willing—serenity.* Our refusal to let go, to let loose, holds us captive in a cruel fantasy land. By letting loose of all that we cling to we find *serenity.* Releasing brings us out of the illusion and into a place of peace. By demanding security, certainty and perfection from everything and everyone we are fooling ourselves. Our thinkers are tricking us into believing that we are the gods that get to control it all and by controlling it all we can cast away our fears. We stay locked in the frantic task of trying to keep all of the balls in the air at once. Fear has then consumed us, except we call it life, we call it normal and we accept the pace believing that we can make it all okay.

In truth, fear has led us away from what is real. What is real is what we have *come to believe* and what gives peace and *serenity* is *becoming willing* to simply be human and let God be God. By demanding control over the future, our 'thinkers', our own minds, deceive us. If resentment is the freedom killer from our past then fear would have to be the freedom killer from the future.

Why? I ask you, why do we do it? Is it that we just got caught up in something and don't know how to slow down? It is like the entire world is one huge high speed train and we don't dare slow down or the cars behind us will plow us over. My hypothesis is that it is a combination of two things and they are both fear. Fear that we won't get something we think we need and fear that we will lose something we have. These fears, which encompass pretty much everything, cause us to attach to people, places and things. And attachments hold us hostage. We cannot attach and let go simultaneously. Fear is one hundred and eighty degrees from faith. Its opposite. God either is or He isn't. We can *choose* to detach and let go of it all ("drop the rocks!!!") or hold tight and live in fear and angst forever.

Blaise Pascal called our attachments, "enslavements to the ego" and named them, libido dominandi, libido sentiendi and libido sciendi; the lust for power, the lust for intense sensation and the lust for knowledge.[21] Hmmm? Power, pleasure and knowledge, sounds good to me. And no one is saying that these are bad in and of themselves. It is when we become obsessed or consumed by any of these that they undermine our freedom and fuel our fears. They begin to control us and drive us. When we attach to the "lusts" of everyday life we ignore what we have *come to believe* and we become anything but willing to let go. They key is being rightly centered with regard to all of these, to participate in them, but not attach to them and allow them to drive us. Lust simply means a general want or longing. These are good things until we become attached. When we become attached our fears kick in. Then they begin to control us, our thoughts and actions begin to center around them, our demand for them increases, our *wants* suddenly become *needs*. We need air and we need water, the sense that we are being deprived of either sets us into a panic. So it is with our attachments, when they flip from being a *want* to being a *need* our panic or our fear that we may not get what we "*need*" sets in and we grasp and cling and attach as if our very existence depends upon it. A story from The Spirituality of Imperfection further clarifies.

Ibrahim Adham, a great spiritual leader of the Sufis, was wont to live in much pomp and splendor, surrounded by a large number of servants. Even his tents were pitched with golden pegs.

A wandering dervish once happened to pass by his tents, and was enormously surprised at this display of wealth by a Sufi. So he went, begging-cup in hand, to Ibrahim and questioned him thus: "It is strange that you call yourself a Sufi, and yet you are surrounded by luxury and material wealth of a kind, that even your tents are fixed with golden pegs."

Ibrahim welcomed him, and bade him to rest awhile and asked his servants to feed him well. After some time he asked the dervish if he would like to go along with him to Mecca, and the dervish readily agreed. They both set out on their pilgrimage, the princely Sufi leaving all his wealth and luxury behind him without a thought. They had not walked far, when the dervish suddenly remembered that he had left his wooden cup in Ibrahim's tent and wanted to go back to fetch it. Ibrahim smiled and said, "My friend, I left all my wealth behind without the least worry. Yet you are so much attached to a cup of practically no value that you cannot proceed to Mecca without it. The golden pegs which so much surprised you were driven into the earth, not into my heart."[22]

Gratitude

When the future becomes something we are to conquer, attain, win, get or own, then our thinkers are messing with us again. When we attach, our *wants* trick us into thinking that they are *needs* and fear is sure to follow. Detaching, letting go and trusting in a Power that is greater than us allows us to live in *serenity* and peace, in a place of faith and utter trust. Letting go allows us to stand up from the director's chair and adopt a new posture on life. A posture of *gratitude*. It is a posture that links our thinking with thanking. And you guessed it, it is another one of those gifts. It quietly reminds us to appreciate.

Gratitude is more than thankfulness; it is a demeanor, a way of being. Grateful comes from the Latin root *gratus*, meaning pleasing or full of pleasure. *Gratitude* is a posture that graciously accepts gifts it does not win goods. *Gratitude* rests in the pleasure of what one has. One scale recently developed to measure *gratitude* in people is called the GRAT. The GRAT assesses gratitude towards other people, gratitude towards the world in general, and (big surprise!) a lack of resentment for what you do not have. A recent study showed that this scale, like others, is simply measuring *a way of approaching life*. Two other recent studies have suggested that *gratitude* may have a unique relationship with well-being, and can explain aspects of well-being that other personality traits cannot. Both studies showed that *gratitude* was able to explain more well-being than 30 of the most commonly studied personality traits.[23] *Gratitude* lands on us like an unanticipated gift when we "let go" of the control illusion, surrender (give back) the fear and live by what we have *come to believe.*

Fear never says, "thank you", it says, "take more". Fear is a cunning foe, a stealer of freedom and a saboteur of faith. It slithers into our psyche when everything is just fine and says, "Worry." It says, worry, you may lose something you think you own or not get something you think you need. The reality is that we do not *own* and we do not *need.*

If resentments are the wreckage of our past, then fear is the wreckage of our future. Sounds nuts doesn't it. Fear is like "pre-worrying". Instead of being grateful for this day, this moment, the now, we say, "No thank you, I think I will trade this beautiful day for a bucket of worry about stuff that hasn't even happened. You know I hate to get behind on my worrying so I thought I would start early." It is one thing to have concern or worry over a here and now crisis, that is called being an adult and dealing with life. It is entirely another thing to fear wreckage that is not even here. Fear of the future is called the absence of faith.

Change happens. And change is always associated with a bit of discomfort because there is an innate fear of the unknown. The future is an unknown. But it is an unknown that will always be there. The future is not a single event or a single change that we can just "get through" by swallowing a bit of fear and discomfort. The future will always be there and, lest we become eternal victims of the fear of "what might be", we need to find a new way to adapt, to embrace the unknown and to trust. And this is why telling our stories and *coming to believe* is so crucial. Once we *come to believe* we have access to a new way of *seeing* the future and the unknown. Once we have something to *believe* in we can take that modest leap into an unknown future with faith rather than fear. We can *become willing.* Faith is believing you can close your eyes.

Resentments from the past and fears of the future rob us of the freedom of the now.. They steal the "rapture of being alive." They distort our thinking and play with our minds. Resentments tie us up and hold us as eternal captives of the yesterdays that we cannot change. Fears suspend us in time and, like Botox, paralyzes us, rendering us unable to move into a future of possibility. Resentment and fear are what make us restless, irritable and discontented in the now.

We *came to believe* in something Bigger than us, now it is time to *become willing* to live as if that something Bigger is actually real. It is time to surrender, to *"give back"* the illusion that if we stay angry we are somehow in control, to *"give back"* the will that tells us we can make it all happen according to our own plan. You see, our stories will forever remain jumbled as nothing more than ruminations if we are unable to reconcile our resentments and allay our fears. The beautiful, exquisite stories that we have lived and have to tell will forever remain a snarled, ball of useless string until we make peace with the dragons that hold us to the past and threaten our future. We will be unable to sew the tapestry that is our life thus far unless we have become willing to address our resentments and our fears as we tell our stories. ___**Our fears and our resentments need to be in our stories!!!**___ And then they need to be filed away. And we step into tomorrow naked and bare with wreckage addressed. And when we create more wreckage, (and we all will!!!) we clean it up promptly; and each and every day we teach our selves to "drop the rocks" ....again and again and again.

Freedom, forgiveness, humility, serenity and gratitude are gifts that are ours when we *become willing* to live according to what we have *come to believe.* They come and rest upon us when we *become willing* to clean up the wreckage of the past and when we *become willing* to trust God with the unknown future. They envelope us when we start living what we have *come to believe* and *become willing* to walk even when we cannot see the path. We do not have to walk perfectly but by *becoming willing* we are allowing hope to sneak in and tell us that perhaps, just perhaps, we can.

Two and a half years had passed since I had been injured and I had spent those precious teenage years in the hospital and learning to walk again. I had done everything that I could possibly do to get back to normal and now I was on my way to college at Arizona State University. No one knows me here I thought. They don't know my past and I can be normal. I can be just like everyone else.

But I was not like everyone else. I was two weeks out of the brace that had been my unwelcome companion for the past two years. My leg was weak and shriveled and though I could walk I walked slowly and with a bit of a limp. My leg was not the only thing that was behind. Here I was at Arizona State University with young girls from all over the country and I was quick to realize that what they had done in high school was very different than what I had done. They were worldly and wise and daring and bold. The experience steamrolled me back into my reality instantly. For the first time in my life I felt quiet and shy and conservative.

Overwhelmed by the social experience of a Pac Ten University, I chose to focus on the books. Classes were academically easy but physically difficult. It took all I had each day to make my way in the bustle of thousands of students to each class. The campus was huge and the trek between classes was taxing on my leg. It was here that I came to terms with the cold hard fact that my leg was as good as it was going to get and that try as I may, I was never going to be physically normal. I was never going to have a normal leg again. It was an excruciating realization but mercifully it came slowly, little by little, in doses my heart could handle. I had undergone over thirty operations and hours of physical therapy to become normal again. Now I needed to face the truth that I was now as normal as I was ever going to get. I needed to pull myself out of the world of hospitals and doctors and unrealistic hope and into the world of the here and now. I needed to find that oh so elusive acceptance. And I did. It was a painful time for me emotionally. Sort of like a yearlong slap in the face. I left Arizona State after one year. It was a bitter sweet departure but the experience had given me a gift that would serve me well. The experience had forced me off of the merry-go-round of, "I'm going to get better, I'm going to get better" and helped me onto the swing of freedom. I was finally free to say, "Look mom, no hands."

8

Sexuality

Oh come on, just go ahead and say the word…SEX. See that wasn't that hard (no pun intended)! Yes we are going to talk about sex. We are going to talk about sex because it is a huge part of who we are as human beings. My goodness, we are sexual beings and for some reason we just keep stuffing that part of ourselves into the proverbial closet. It is as though we think that if we don't talk about it the person next to us won't know that we think about it and yes, oh my god, we actually do it! How, I ask you, can we tell our stories and ignore this part of who we are? We can't. So we are going to talk about sex. BOOM. Over and done. Decision made. We are going to talk about our hang ups, our fears, our insecurities, our escapades, our fantasies and the even darker side of sex, the bad things that have happened (and they have happened, to one degree or another, to almost all of us). But first…

We have worked our way through our givens, addressed our instincts, familial influences and societal stereotypes. We have also, at the very *bottom of our daemons* found faith, we have *come to believe*. We stood proudly on the bridge of now and faced squarely our resentments and our fears. Now we are asked to stand on this bridge and *become willing* yet again to face a mighty dragon that locks us into the past… sexuality. We have *become willing* to use our faith to work our way through our stories and this indeed is the Minotaur that will not be ignored. Our stories are incomplete and our freedom is fleeting if we leave out our sexuality.

We have "Felt The Need", "Gathered The Info" and now we are "Facing The Facts". And let's face the facts people...so much is written about how to forge *The Road Less Traveled* or how to have *A Purpose Driven Life* and it all works great until we get into intimate situations and then it all goes to hell in a handbag. Our *spirituality* leaves immediately because it is sure there is something "sinful" and wrong going on. Our *minds* twist themselves into some impossible yoga position and can no longer think straight. Attempts to express intelligent thoughts are hijacked by the stupid gods. You know that, "I cannot believe I just said that!" feeling. Whoa! And then there are the *feelings*, it is like someone dips them in LSD before they get expressed. Yikes! And it seemed like such a beautiful heartfelt emotion before we expressed it. Now the *body* on the other hand, this fella is more than willing to jump right in and participate. Problem is this...the body can be a cunning, baffling and powerful convincer. The body has immediately left the realm of reasonable and he is all about convincing us that to see, to touch, to hear, to taste and to smell are all that is needed so let's get to it. You see, today's body was raised in post modern times where sensuality means you kiss first and sex means the genitals get to play and intimacy....well heck if the genitals played you were obviously intimate right?

Ha! Ha! My point here is this, the average American person gets up Sunday morning and goes to church (or doesn't) and then spends the afternoon with the family in one way or another, watching football, doing yard work, whatever. Traditionally speaking we, as a society, have set Sunday aside. Something handed down to us from hundreds and hundreds and hundreds of years of religious tradition. And, obviously, sex is not a topic generally discussed in church, but then comes the next six days and the flood gates open and we talk and joke and jest and take free license to act and think any way we desire. But how about this idea, how about allowing *sexuality, sensuality* and *spirituality* to be kin, how about taking the dirty out of *sexuality*, taking the suggestiveness out of *sensuality* and taking the "Thou Shalt Not" out of *spirituality* and allow the experience of the carnal be sacred. There is no human experience so enveloped in divine promise and so engulfed clandestine sacrilege, so exalted and yet so defiled as sexual intercourse.

Sex is an instinct just like fight, flight or freeze. The sexual instinct, like the others is present in all the species. That is how we and they procreate and propagate our respective species. The difference is that this particular instinct has been humanized. It matures. It matures in three stages.[24]

1. In the first stage there is the "goal", tension reduction. Obviously masturbation can serve this immature stage.
2. In the second stage there is an "object", another person. However, just because the "tension reduction" has developed into sexual intercourse does not mean that the instinct has matured. This is seen clearly in the fact that at this stage of sexual maturation the partners are interchangeable. The intercourse may be with another human but this other human is yet to be humanized.
3. In the third stage of maturation of the sexual instinct, the humanness of the partner is fully realized, internalized and embraced. This is when the uniqueness of the partner is actually comprehended. This is when the partners, who are two separate "I's" become "thou's" to each other and the result is monogamy and, yes, love.

Let's stick to this subject of sexual maturation for a moment...
Stage one is the "goal". If this is the stage one is arrested in then the instinct may be addressed by simple pornography.
Stage two is the "object". If one is stuck in this stage then prostitutes will suffice. Hey, let's call it what it is. When partners are interchangeable the result is promiscuity.
I think the brain fuck (no pun intended) comes when we step back and look at our society and realize that we acquiesce to the open expression of these immature stages of the sexual instinct and that we call that acquiescence being progressive or enlightened. No judgment here, just and observation.
Think about it...

So here is our sexually schizophrenic society…we vacillate between books explaining every sexual position possible with vivid technicolor pictures next to the explanations (just in case we don't understand the text), to books that neatly lay out the anatomy and label each part with a little arrow pointing to the appropriate anatomic site as though there is going to be a test afterward before actual exploring with a real live human body is going to be permitted, to books that teach us that even the thought of sex prior to marriage is itself a sin and after marriage it is permitted in the dark, after showering and only in the missionary position and oh yeah, never on Sundays. Volumes have been written on celibacy as the only pure decision and the only way to achieve true enlightenment. Women's magazines vary on what men prefer most, demure, inexperienced little ladies that always allow him to make the first move or sensuous women who have tried it all and are going to take charge and show him how it is done.

Yikes! It is as though we are supposed to pick one of the above. News flash…we aren't. Remember, we are free human beings and it is in the telling of our stories that we grasp the freedom to address how we really feel about sexuality. It is in the telling of our stories that we get to address the sexual dragons and then *choose* for ourselves how sexuality is going to be for us. In other words, by sharing our sexual thoughts and feelings in our stories we are liberating ourselves to *choose* how we will experience our sexuality as we go on to experience "the rapture of being alive" in all of our tomorrows.

The Body

We were given bodies to be *participators*. Our bodies are what take us beyond marvel and wonder from afar and place us into the exquisite tapestry of which we are part. Our bodies are what engage reality and bring to life that which is touchable. When children do it we call it play. The infant and the child experience their environments completely. Every sight, sound, smell and touch captures their attention and prompts their innocent fascination. They experience their senses wholly and spontaneously. The body was made to interact. Our bodies were meant to sense and make sense of the environment that surrounds us. Our bodies were meant to be an active part of the life we were brought into.

Chaos, intensity, speed and stress create uptight bodies incapable of being moved by inspiration and fascination. Artists and poets will confirm, bodies tense with anxiety cannot create because they cannot feel. Bodies focused on defense mechanisms and regimented demands cannot simultaneously engage with and participate in the erotic and exotic mystery that surrounds and envelopes us daily. Erotic, like sensual, has been sexualized but originally is from the Greek term *erotikos* meaning, *of love, caused by love, given to love*. The body was designed in love and caused by love and is meant to be given to love. The love of the world we live in is meant to be brought to life by the body. Love is a verb. It is an action word. The world was meant to be experienced, interacted with; not merely observed. Observers are data processors that take in and record information. If we were intended to be mere observers then we would need brains and eyes and a score sheet. Sadly, that is how many of us live. According to Thoreau, "We need pray for no higher heaven than the pure senses can furnish, a purely sensuous life. Our present senses are but rudiments of what they are destined to become."

Thus goes the "split-minded" mental illness of body image...

To add fuel to the roaring fire and only to propagate the tragedy that has besieged the erotic body comes the books telling us what the splendid body is supposed to "look" like. These books focus on diet, exercise and fitness, stress the "ideal". And for god's sake, for some reason we all bite on this "ideal". So we work and grind and then when we are all svelte, trim, hard and fit, we become obsessed with not missing our next work out. We are tense with the compulsion to maintain. That or we've given up all together and gone in the direction of sloth and gluttony.

Media bombards us with ways to take control, whip that body into shape with body balls, thigh masters, rubber bands, more weight fewer reps...no wait, I changed the channel...less weight more reps body...new channel...whoa! The Beach Body in just six weeks. That sounds cool. I think they are telling me I have to strap my body to the ball like contraption and roll around...no thanks think I will check the next channel. Oh swell, now there is some chick throwing a football to some antique former NHL players and they are all just so happy that they have lost weight that they want to play catch on TV. Paaaleeez! Oh boy here is one for you, "Turbulence Training Time Efficient Research-Proven Workouts That Boost Muscle Growth And Blow Torch Body Fat." I'm just going to say, "Ouch!" and leave that one alone. Eureka! Here is the answer at long last...Exercise Pill designed to enhance body functions during exercise. Hooray a workout pill!

Did you know that when I Googled "get in shape" I got 34,200,000 hits, when I Googled "lose weight" I got 36,700,000 hits and when I Googled "sensual body" I got a measly 433,000 hits. We are obsessed with how we look people! We care more about how others think we look than how we actually feel! I mean come on gals be honest, would you really wear those three inch heels if there was no one around to notice how sexy they made your calves look?

Society and the media are consumed with telling us how to lose weight, get in shape and they all promise the quickest and fastest remedies. God knows we would want the quickest ways. We are challenged to assume crazy yoga positions and say, "Om" and to practice ancient relaxation techniques that we incompletely understand because someone else tells it would be good for us. Look, there is nothing wrong with taking care of our nutritional and fitness needs, my beef is with the reasons we do it. It needs to be for ourselves and our health not to chase the proverbial Barbie and Ken ideals.

Perhaps it is time to move away from what "they" say is sexy, allow sensuality, sexuality and spirituality to intertwine and to immerse ourselves with proud humility in the earthiness of the stunningly unique bodies that were given to each of us individually to have as our own.

Cult and Commerce

<u>Religious condemnation</u> and <u>over stimulation</u> have diverted our senses and robbed us of our sensuality. The bodily senses have been paltered in the biggest rip off known to mankind. We have traded the vessels that we were gifted to navigate and experience the world in over to fanaticism and frantic 'progress'. We are now creatures that live by "Thou Shalt Nots..." or by pings, dings, rings, bleeps, beeps and rhythmic tones of technology. The trade has left us deaf to the joyful melodies of daily life, frigid to the touch that heals and oblivious to the natural world that does "everything to git attention". Nothing has done more to shut down our senses than <u>cult</u> and <u>commerce</u>. Together religion and economics have conspired to de-sensualize and de-sensitize contemporary culture. We have sacrificed the body, our sacred feeler, for the sake of religious phobia and the "more, more, more" mentality. Who, I ask you, decided that the body was so bad, decided that it was so defiled, filthy and bedraggled that it should be looked upon as something banal and lowly and nothing more than a necessary evil? When was it decided that it was okay to shut off all of the pleasure centers in the body because working and getting and spending were just so damn important? How did these sentiments get so seared into the human mentality that we became willing to forfeit the gifts of the body as if it were one of Gods accidents? Who decided that sexuality, sensuality and spirituality were unrelated? For crying out loud the body is what God gave us as a means of taking it all in!!

Cult

Historically, the Christian church stood firmly against Gnosticism and Manachianism, the two main streams of religious practice that viewed the body and the earth as dirty and vile, nevertheless, it remained ambivalent with regard to exactly what was okay about the body. It was as if from the beginnings it found itself unable to separate promiscuous sexuality from wholesome sensuality and therefore decided we best steer clear of both. Genesis and paradise lost were entirely too confusing. Sensuality was therefore labeled as one of those proverbial 'forbidden fruits' with the resultant and predictable consequence of only making it more mysterious and more taboo and more titillating. "What is allowed, we scorn; what's not allowed, we burn for."(Ovid) When the church chose to remain quiet or to dub sensuality as bad, secularism was all too willing to pick up this hot potato, shout loud and steer society into the very thing the church feared the most...a sexualization of sensuality.

The sexual revolution started in Europe and spread to America and suddenly sensuality <u>was</u> sexuality, all touch contained sexual undertones and sensuality, like sex, suddenly became a genital phenomena. The wondrous 'exploring with the senses' that defined childhood and the divine use of the body as a beloved interactor had been perverted and pillaged. Aaaaahhhh!!! Sensuality was lost and sexuality ran rampant through society. Eye contact during a conversation or a gentle touch that says, "I am listening and I am sorry that you are hurting" is immediately misconstrued as sexual interest. "Free love" and "sport fucking" became the name of the game and everyone from scientists to self-help writers jumped on the band wagon. Erogenous zones were diagramed in detail for the individual wishing to maximize the experience that now involved two relative strangers combining genitals as means to a pre-determined end—the orgasmic climax. The mighty orgasm that was to make up for the all of the self-imposed sensate deprivation we so bravely endured. The responsibility for all of the sensate needs of the human body now rested on a single organ, the genitals. Not only was the wholeness of the human body shattered but a sacred act full of divine promise had been dissected studied and destroyed in the process. The sanctity of appreciating with the senses had been abandoned and eventually all but forgotten. Sensuality had been demoted to fornication.

Commerce

We have talked about the fast paced intensity of the world that we live in today, where the ability to multi-task is a marketable job skill. We are bombarded 24/7 with constant stimuli. Phones, pages, post-its, memos, texts, instant messages, email, twittrs, flickers and more. Advertising has broadened its horizons and now covers busses, park benches and even the clothing of the rich and famous. In this sensory overload we have lost an appreciation for the earthy, vibrant, steamy, crude, lush, lavish, precious, miraculous world that we live in. Prisoners kept in dark cells and meditators who isolate themselves and employ sensory deprivation begin to hallucinate. How often do we finish a day feeling as though we are in a different world, feeling "locked-in" to our own beings? We are sensually deprived in a world that that throws stimuli at us at every turn. Ours has been called the age of alienation. What the term actually means is coolness, disaffection, estrangement. In other words, we are connected up the wazoo but never actually get to face or touch another human being. We are constantly bombarded with communication from other people via every gadget imaginable. At no other time in history have people been so accessible. Modem hook-ups, cell phones, apps for every occasion, have us hooked up and, according to the *New York Times*, "terminally in touch"[25]. We live in a society that worships independence, but ask someone to turn off their cell phone, to disconnect and the sky starts to rumble. Our era travels and communicates at breakneck speed. We are over-the-top, out-of-this-world over connected. Not only do these conveniences deprive us of solitude, they engage us in working, producing, planning all of the time. In a culture that no longer recognizes the value of sensuality, computers, and heaven have mercy, even our cell phones seemingly offer it all: stimulation, knowledge, news, alonetime, relationships and of course, sex.

More information please...

Our current society has a tension level off the scales. We live in a world that has most of its members wound up so tight that they are suffocating. We operate at lightning speed and if you can't multi-task in the double digits you just aren't competitive. We have even complicated a task as simple as kicking back to watch the evening news. There is no such thing as simply watching the news. There is a ticker tape running across the bottom so we can read and listen at the same time and while the sophisticated anchor person reports on Capitol Hill the right upper corner flashes international new headlines, the right low corner tells us what the markets are doing and the left lower quadrant keeps us appraised of the weather and time. (I think the clock is to see how long it takes us to absorb all the info simultaneously.) And they wonder why the ratings for the evening news have dropped—duh—it's because they give it to us all at once!! Why sit through the whole broadcast when you can get all the information with a single glance. Scary thing is our brains are now conditioned to operate in this fashion. I am a firsthand witness to the fact that teenagers can study efficiently, while having 3 separate text conversations, 4 facebook conversations, downloading iTunes, burning CDs, eating dinner and catching up on One Tree Hill. Sure it is bad study habits—HELLO—that is not the point. The point is that they can literally do it and do it well. We consume ourselves with worry that teens are maturing so rapidly, that they shouldn't have phones in school, that the city wide curfew should be better enforced, that they may be having SEX, that they may be experimenting with drugs or alcohol, that there are dangers on facebook and the web and by focusing on each separate issue we are missing the big picture. We are producing children equipped to handle a sensation overload and a stress overload like never seen before in the history of the world. Aaaaahhhhh!!! There are days that I go to work and function just fine until some critical mass of stimulation over load is reached and I can't tell you what it looks like but I clearly have an "I have had enough, my plate is full, my brain is going to explode" look. My office manager can spot it from 100 yards away. It is called body language.

Attempts at revival of pure sensuality have been viewed with suspicion and with few exceptions have been deficient. Satisfactory language and experiential wisdom have been insufficient in re-kindling sensuous embers. The contemporary *sense* of sensuality has become stuck in a murky bog and with wheels spinning is spitting mud onto those attempting to free it from the trap "free-sex" it was pre-warned of. Brown artfully emphasizes that, "The resurrection of the body has been placed on the agenda not only by psychoanalysis, mysticism and poetry but also by philosophy and its criticism of science." Our society is in dire condition with regard to our need for sensual revival and a redefining of sexuality. We are dying of sensory deprivation in a world of over stimulation.

We have completely lost the art of interacting with sensual glee, loving compassion and mysterious intimacy. The body no matter what it 'looks' like is ours and it is what we sense and make sense of the world with—stretch marks, scars, bulges, droops and imperfections are real, fleshy, and perfectly imperfect, perfectly human. Our own unique, flawed bodies are able to feel, touch, inhale, detect, savor and relish the magical creation we live in with skillful precision, gentle fascination and breathless awe.

Intimacy

For the most part the sexual revolution has played itself out partly due to the fact that participators in the frolic in the proverbial Garden of Eden came to their own realization that the fulfillment that they were seeking was not to be found in fun and games and multiple partners. Fears of the new more frightening sexually transmitted diseases put a final cap on it all. So here we are today facing the unquestionable, factual truism that obsession with sex worked no better than repression of sex.[26]

The word intimate literally means *to make known*. Intimate refers generally to the innermost nature or fundamental character of something. Intimacy refers to a familiar and very close connection with another as a result of entering deeply or closely into relationship through knowledge and experience of the other. Genuine intimacy with another human being requires communication, openness, vulnerability and reciprocity. We waited to discuss this subject until this point in the book because if one fact holds true it is this, we have to know our *own self*, our inner *self*, in order to make our *own self* known to another. And up to this point, that is what we have been working on, we have been learning to learn, specifically about our *own self*. We get into trouble in intimate relationships very quickly if we do not know our *self* well. To sustain intimacy for any length of time requires full engagement of the spirit, the mind, the heart and the body. Like a pendulum that swings, we must be able to come together and go apart comfortably.

Psychologists call this ability to come together and go apart comfortably self-differentiation. We are going to call it owning our centers. Knowing who we are, what we are, where we are and what we stand for is essential for true intimacy. I cannot give myself to another if I have no idea who I am. When we cannot go apart comfortably from another that we have become intimate with we have given away our centers, we have given away our *self.* Or at least we have tried to. Scientists call this symbiosis which means quite crudely when one organism lives off another. Not exactly a picture of health! We attach our self to another self. Instead of being two I's who are Thous to each other we become one I who wishes that the Thou would get off his back. It is our right, our duty, our responsibility and our privilege to be a *self,* an individual. God challenges us to get to know our *own self* and then share the beautiful *self* He created with the world. When the Bible tells us to give ourselves away, symbiosis is not what He had in mind! We must know our *own selfs* and then let our *own selfs* be known.

Why, I ask, when relationships are so hard, do we all want to be in one? Is it that we all want someone "special"? Or (more likely) is it that we all want to be "special" to someone else? Probably the latter. No matter how healthy we get it remains "all about me". And besides, we have friends and families don't they make us feel "special" enough? And if not, then maybe it is all about sex and that limbic drive to procreate, but that is out there, sex can be found without the entanglements and heartache and work of an intimate relationship.

We are getting closer—it is ontological (rooted in our nature of being). It is a drive so deep that for many of us it feels like a need and not just a want. It is love, plain and simple it is love. It is our God given desire to love and be loved, and intimately speaking, to know and be known. We need to go back to the original definition of erotic, of love, caused by love, given to love or as Plato used the term Eros to mean to love or desire ardently. The love is just love, the desire just desire, neither have anything to do with sexuality.

How about a little myth to clear things up...

Plato's Eros came from his myth of the androgyne, the three types of human beings; man-man-, woman- woman and man-woman.

These human beings were attached at the back, had four arms, four legs and one head with a face on each side. They, therefore could never face one another and they ambulated by cart wheeling end over end. Eventually Zeus took pity on these magnificent creatures and split them down the middle so they could face each other. However, in splitting these creatures each half, though free to ambulate normally and to face the others, they would always be incomplete and each would forever feel compelled to search for its other half. Therein lays the explanation of why we as humans are driven by Eros to search endlessly for our other half, our missing complement.

Greek philosophers in general considered Eros or love to be the principle motivator of all things human and non-human. Love was the inspiration that made all things seek fulfillment. Therefore, erotic potency does not mean sexual puissance...it means the power of love. It sort of turned into that game you play in grade school where you all sit in a circle and one person whispers something in the ear of the next person and so on until the last person says what they were told and it never resembles what it started out as. Somehow we messed up the meanings of the words, but kept the idea that love and that missing half were the answer to fulfillment. We just need to go back to the 3rd century B.C. to understand where we made the fatal mistake.

Sacramental Sexuality

Plato aside, historians would probably lay it out something like this. We westerners have romanticized and democratized love. We invest all of our time and energy and passion into work, into the accumulation of money, stuff and power. Love and romance are private and we expect them as the reward for it all. We grow up expecting that the "happily ever after" will happen and that marriage will be that sanctified just bounty of love, romance and sex that will make it all worthwhile. Our partner will be all things to us, companion, lover, friend, assistant and protector....we will build a home, have children and grow old together, through thick and thin, until death do us part. Ah but the bitter truth hits us square in the face, romance dies away, the burden of sex alone to shoulder the task of holding together a marriage where romance has fled is too much, reality and divorce statistics attest that our fairy tale ideas of romance, sex and marriage do not sustain. Let's face it folks, we Americans are disillusioned by marriage and intimate relationships. We expect them to fulfill all of our needs while we focus most of our energies working, producing, consuming and spending.

Perhaps it is time to rediscover sexuality at its sacramental depth.[27] The ancient definition of sacrament is this, "An outward and visible sign of an inward and invisible grace." What is sacramental about sexuality is this, it is our chance to fulfill our deepest, darkest longing; a moment in time where we can wash ourselves clean of that which has itched and burned and burdened us from a very early age; it is our opportunity to strip away the dysfunctional instincts that continue to taunt us, to peel off the layers of familial influence and demolish the levees that culture has built around us. It is our moment to give up being somebody that time has created and morphed and molded and to simply be the *being* beneath it all. It is in this sacramental sexuality that we are at long last freed to purge the mind of all regard, to unlock the soul, raise the curtain and allow our beings to stand naked in all their wondrous glory and to give up the charge of being a solo individual and in another's arms let two solos become a solitary duet. The burdens of the personality are laid aside and then in a mysterious, enchanting and spellbinding experience "…when two I's who are Thous to each other become We…"[28] the boundaries of the self are swept away. And the pendulum swings.

So how do we define sacramental sexuality? I think it is best defined by what it is not. It is most certainly not any kind of sexual union that objectifies another, it is not a mutual satisfaction of genital desires, it is not a piece of ass, a conquest or a reward. It is not sexual intercourse with a replaceable person. It does not pull or push on one person or the other past the bounds of their individual comfort. It does not desecrate or violate. It is not sex, it is sacred. Remember, "an outward visible sign of and an inner, invisible grace". Sex, like Eros, will answer its promise when it is united with something enduring, utter and blessed. Nietzsche said, "The degree and kind of a man's sexuality reaches up into the topmost summit of his spirit." Without the spirit, love we will remain in an erotic crisis. There can be no performance, there can be no audience. True sexuality and true spirituality do not permit it.

In sacramental sexuality, as in spirituality, the same ontological longing exists, that is, a longing to relieve ourselves from the burden on our aloneness while simultaneously retaining the individual *self.* We both desire and resist the loss of *self* whether it be in the arms of a lover or in the arms of God. It is as though we are asking "How can we be alone together?" And so it is in spirituality, as it is in sexuality, the pendulum must swing. There must be a coming together and a going apart. We commune with our God and then we must move out into this secular world that we live in and be what He made us… human. We unite with our lover, we surrender our individual *selfs* to one another and we must for the sake of self preservation let the cadence of the chroniker separate us as individuals, solos. If the swing ceases is the game is over. The *self* cannot survive alone <u>or</u> in an infinite connection to another. When the *self* is sacrificed it will most surely be destroyed. And so the pendulum <u>must</u> swing.

Two Thous separated…

It was February of 2000 and we had all survived the turn of the century without cataclysm. I was completing my final year of fellowship training in Medical Oncology and had re-married and given birth to another daughter. My children were 8 and 2 and life was busy, but my body was strong and that made all of the difference in the world.

One morning I received a phone call from my parents who were escaping the South Dakota winter by spending a couple of months in Puerto Vallarta, Mexico this winter. My dad had awoken one morning to chest pain and shortness of breath and they were rightfully concerned. The decision was made and my dad arrived in Tucson later that day. He was to be seen by cardiac experts at my hospital, The University of Arizona Hospital, the next day.

He arrived in Tucson tan from the Mexican sun looking happy and healthy and much younger than his 60 years. My dad had always been healthy, a track star in college and an avid runner most of his life. He loved sports and outdoor activities. Hiking in the breath taking trails of the Black Hills of South Dakota was his favorite. As we prepared to leave for the hospital, I found my dad outside in my backyard. I asked him how he was feeling and he answered, "Happy, joyous and free, I feel happy, joyous and free." My dad went for a cardiac catheterization that day to evaluate his coronary arteries. Blockages were revealed, recommendations were made and my Dad was planned for elective bypass surgery. He was to spend the night in the hospital and go for surgery on the following day. My mother arrived that evening as did my sister from Dallas. My Mom, my sister, my two daughters and I all sat in his hospital room that evening light-hearted and laughing and relieved that we had caught this in time and that he was in good hands.

Surgery was later in the day and the waiting was the hardest part. By 7 pm the doctor called us in the surgery waiting room and told us that everything had gone well and that he would be moved to the CCU shortly. Although we had not been overly concerned about this serious but elective surgery a big sigh of relief was felt by all of us to know it was over. My Mom stayed at the hospital and my sister and I headed back to my house.

I was awakened the next morning to my mother's voice. She just said, come back to the hospital and her voice was worried. I flew out of bed and hollered down the hall for my sister to do the same. My husband had left for work so I ran across the street to wake up my neighbor's daughter to watch my girls. Funny what one remembers but I remember my sister trying to get her belt on and watching it go flying freely into the street as we loaded into the car. I remember thinking "Why in the hell do you need your belt?"We drove done Sabino Canyon road toward the University hospital. We were calm and feeling mostly like my mother got worried about something and just wanted us there. We moved swiftly but were not racing.

As we made our way into the CCU my heart stopped. The nurses, all of whom I knew well, were signaling for us to go into a front private waiting room. My sister was oblivious and followed their directions, but I knew. Oh my God, I knew, I knew what those rooms were used for. I had directed families of my patients into those rooms too many times. He was dead. I knew he was dead. We walked into the room where my mother sat with a nurse. She just looked up at us and said, "Dad coded. He is gone." My sister shrieked and sobbed. My emotions went flat. I felt nothing but the need to take care of my mother and sister. I couldn't cry. I couldn't fall apart. I just remember making phone calls to notify my sister and my parent's closest friends. A nurse came in and told us that it was okay to go into his room if we wanted and I did. My mom and my sister were not sure if they could do it but I lead the way. I am not sure if they followed. I walked into the pale tan room that I had seen dozens of patients pass through. At this moment, however, it was my Dad's room and he lay there motionless, appearing so strong and solid and healthy. I reached for him and touched his muscular, tan leg. He had a runner's legs. My chest tightened and my eyes darted around the room that had been cleared of any evidence of the chaos of an actual code. I suddenly had the uncomfortable and foreign feeling of being a doctor and a daughter all at the same time. I knew what had just gone on in this room and though it tied my heart in knots I needed to know more. I knew the residents that had coded my Dad were residents that I had trained. My friends coded my Dad. I couldn't get the thought to register in my brain. As I exited his room my eyes met those of the senior resident and as though the look on my face had already asked the question he said, "It was a clean code Leslie, it was a good code. I'm sorry."Codes can get crazy and sometimes they run smoothly and sometimes they do not. For some reason I needed to know that everything that could possibly have been done had been and those words were what I needed to hear.

I turned to go back to the private waiting room and saw a face I knew all too well coming down the hall. It was Wayne, from the morgue. I had spent an entire year doing autopsies and had always admired his warm manner with families as he talked to them about corneal and skin harvesting for transplants to other patients. I saw him reach for the waiting room door and I just screamed, "No Wayne, no!" I could not stand the idea even coming into my head. They were not going to take his beautiful tan skin or *his soft blue eyes. "No Wayne, no!" was all I could say. I did not even want him to speak the words. Not to me and for sure not to my mother or sister. "I know what you are going to say Wayne. Please don't even say it. The answer is no. Just no." I know my mother wondered why I wouldn't let the man speak but she just went with what I said.*

My dad was gone. My rock. The only person that had ever made me feel brave and not alone.

I looked at my mother and for the first time my eyes welled up. For her I could cry. She had just lost her other half, the person who had been by her side since she was a sophomore in high school. How do you marry your high school sweetheart, give birth to his children, set up a home and raise kids and endure the tough times together and reach retirement and prepare to at long last enjoy just each other and then lose him...how do you go on, what do you do next?

My Dad, my protector, my guardian angel, the first person to call me doctor, was gone at the age of 60. He died happy, joyous and free.

Any marriage or long term relationship needs to be a spiritual journey that two separate individuals, who will always remain a mystery to each other, set out together as two I's who see the other as a thou and who in occasions of mystery, ecstasy, passion and ardent Eros become a We. And then they once again come apart into two I's. They set down the fairy tale illusion, become worldly-wise and reality-ready and grow together into soul-friends and spirit-lovers. And with *a trust that is indistinguishable from faith* they choose to proceed on a solitary journey, called life, together.

A trust indistinguishable from faith is a lofty goal. It was Soren Kierkegaard who coined the term *leap of faith* and it was his conception that this is the only way a man could "believe in God" or "fall in love". According to Kierkegaard, faith is a decision. Just a decision, as there could never be enough *evidence* to justify the kind of *total commitment* involved in religious faith or romantic love. The decision of faith means we make the commitment anyway. We take a *leap of faith.*

Somewhere in my heart I want to leave this chapter on this flowery, beautiful note....to let the reader just go off humming into the next chapter, but I know we are not finished. If I were to stop here then once again sex would be pushed into the proverbial closet. We have danced around it, made it sound lovely and surreal and ideal, but we haven't really talked about actual, real-life sex and that is what needs to be in our stories. In real life, sex is bare and naked and carnal and fleshy. It is secret and sultry and wet and wild. It can be scary and dark, vile and dirty or light and lovely, erotic and ethereal. No matter what it is naked bodies touching, flesh on flesh, and more often than not, it is two people each placing their own meaning on the encounter.

What is essential to remember here is that even when a person has evolved into the higher stages of the sexual instinct the more immature stages remain in each and every one of us. Happily married, completely fulfilled men (and women) still masturbate and they are still lured by the intrigue of porn and yes, by the idea of raw, raucous sex with other women. Seventy percent of men have extra-marital affairs and 30% of women do. Most don't ever get caught. Most will go to the grave with these encounters.

Although our sexual pasts do need to be in our stories, it becomes more than evident that we need to use caution when we decide who we are going to tell our stories to. I beg you now, however, to at least one time tell your entire story, including your sexual encounters and experiences to another trusted or anonymous human being. Full freedom comes with utter honesty. We can and should tell our stories over and over to hosts of others and in those stories our sexual histories can be left unspoken, but once, at least once we must expose these dragons and shake the hold they have on us so we can walk forward on the *bridge of now* as free beings.

She was single, he was single. They had both been through marriages, they both had children and between them a spark was ignited. A relationship ensued and the couple grew close and intimate. They shared with each other their most penetrating moments. Sex was exotic and erotic. They relished in the flesh of one another and explored every inch of each other's skin. Fantasies came alive and they danced, skin on skin in the reverie of the other. They reached for one another over and over and the sensual dance they shared continued for almost one year. They were clearly two "I's" that were "Thou's" to each other and in moments of blessed abandonment came together and became a "We".

The relationship grew and evolved and despite the events of everyday life they held tight and endured. They spoke of marriage and a life together. Although the vicissitudes of the journey were difficult they continued on. And the time to make a commitment before God came and they hovered on the finality of the decision.

And then a day, like any other day, came when in a casual conversation with friends a brutal truth was laid on the table for examination. The name of a particular woman came up and he casually stated to other men in the group of friends that he had "nailed her".

"What? Are you serious?" she said. "She is half your age." Her insides twisted and churned and felt as though they were going to erupt.

"It was 9 months ago, when we were having a hard time." He responded casually as if it were completely justified and no big deal.

"Aaaaaahhhh!" her mind erupted into frantic and heinous and hideous and gruesome thoughts. A filth came over her. A yuck like she had never felt before. There was no sense of betrayal feeling, just a yucky, dirty, execrable, revolting feeling. And then the merciless truth landed at the very bottom of her soul. It would never be the same. A one-night, nothing experience to him had just severed the communion they had enjoyed and reveled in.

No anger, no bitterness, no sense of betrayal. She just had a yuck, I cannot reconcile the image of them together feeling.

And she turned and walked away from the man that for so long had been her beloved "Thou."

They sat in a small group of women, each going through one of the most trying times in their lives, trying to heal. They were there to support and love and nourish and guide one another.

Heather spoke first. She was a professional at a very prominent Corporation and had recently been transferred to Washinton D.C.

She had finished work late on a Friday evening and had decide to stop for a glass of wine on her way home. All she could remember was that she had several glasses of wine and now she was somewhere with a man.

"I cannot get the image out of my head." She sobbed "I just remember looking up and I was laying there and he was on top of me. This old, ugly, dirty man and he was doing things to me and I couldn't move. And then he was inside me. This grimy man that I didn't know was making love to my body. He kept asking what I liked and if I was enjoying it. And he had my body naked and wide open. I wasn't being raped, I was being made loved to and I was being enjoyed and I couldn't move. All I could do was watch him test and taste every part of me."

She sat perched in front of the computer. A beautiful Ukaranian girl. 30 years old with deep green eyes and a heavy Eastern block accent.

"What is a cunt?" she asked innocently. "I am on MySpace and he sent me a message calling me a cunt."

"Well," I hesitated and grinned, "Literally it means vagina."

"Why would he call me a vagina?" she asked.

I could see the language translation in her brain churning. She had been dating a man her same age that had recently graduated from college where he had been a football star. His transition into the "real world" had been a difficult a one. He was used to women swooning over the college stud. Those days were long gone. He had found a stunning Ukranian woman and tried to settle down. Recently however the idealized settling down had exploded. She was left searching. He was left angry and hurt and had regressed to his college days. Her MySpace page was covered with obscenities and vile language that she didn't understand and could not translate from her native tongue.

"Cunt is a bad word. You never, ever say that word. It is one

of those swear words that you just don't ever say. It is probably the worst thing that he could call you." I tried to explain.

She proceeded to show me text messages and MySpace messages that in the most horrendous language detailed all of the sexual encounters he was having with other women. She then had me listen to a voicemail from a woman describing what she was doing with my friends now ex-husband. The voice also described her follies with my friend's ex before he was an ex. It was disgusting and foul.

"Okay, I won't say cunt. But I just don't understand why he called me a vagina. I just want him to leave me alone. How do I make him leave me alone?"

"I don't know. Just ignore him until he goes away I guess." And that was the extent of my feeble advice.

Really telling our stories means that we have to set our egos and our fears aside and become rigorously honest. Sexuality is a sticky subject and it is one that many people have a difficult time talking about. Regardless it is a huge part of who we are and including our sexual history in our stories is so, so, so important. At least once to another living, breathing human being. Sexuality is wrapped, for many of us in fears, insecurities, guilt and shame. And this is exactly why it needs to be included in the stories we tell. Secrets hold us prisoner. Again, what comfort we would bring to others if we were to tell them our secrets. Why? Because their secrets are very similar. We keep secrets because we think we are so damn unique when the truth of the matter is that we are unbelievably similar.

Forty five to seventy percent of women masturbate. One hundred percent of men do. I told these statistics to a girl friend stating that if you do not masturbate you are in the minority. Her response was, " Then I'm in the minority. I wonder if they have scholarships for that?" Ha, ha! My first thought was this...I wonder if she is telling the truth or if she is just reluctant to disclose her truth. And that is fine. I don't expect anyone to disclose their secrets to the general public. I am simply saying chose a person and include your sexuality in your story at least one time.

As my conversation with my girl friend continued I made the comment that if I really start thinking about sex with a man that I care deeply for I can actually go to that erotic place and climax just by thinking about it. Her response was, "Remind me to never ask what you are thinking!" Aha! Again with the jokes that shuffle around and keep us from actually having a conversation about sex.

So often our conversations about sex shift us back into the earlier stages of the sexual instinct. Many of our actions have occurred in these earlier stages of sexuality and these are okay. They need to be in our stories. We are not trying to tell our stories and prove to someone else that we are sexually mature. We are telling our honest and open stories that include our sexuality to bring all of our "stuff" to the forefront where we can own it and then file it away as part of private, personal histories. A story without sexuality is incomplete.

With all due respect to the Baptists, it is all about evolution. We are including all of our sexual "stuff" because without disclosing it we are not free to evolve into healthy, carnal, fleshy sexual beings. Tell it, file it and evolve.

9

Feelings

We have talked about *coming to believe*, our *spirituality* and about *becoming willing* to share our resentments, our fears and our sexuality. It is now time to move on to the disinherited prodigal son, the *feeler* or what I'm going to refer to as the heart. How we experience our feelings is essential to the stories that we tell and they are worthy of deeper dissection as we traverse the *bridge of now*. We cannot reach into our depth and truly tell our stories until we have a good handle on how we experience our feelings. All that we have covered up to this point affects the way we encounter, endure and test our feelings. Our instincts, our families, our churches, our society have all shaped how we understand our feelings and how we express our feelings. Now no one is quite sure where feelings come from but they are real just the same. It is essential as we delve into our stories and as we step out into the *experience of living* in the future that we understand how, we each as unique beings, handles feelings. This understanding will help us make sense of the past and, just perhaps, aid us as we step into tomorrow.

Now I am going to say that feelings come from the heart, however, other people may say they come from "the gut" or "the little voice in my ear". Funny thing is, we all know what we are talking about, we are just not sure where these feelings actually reside. And perhaps this lends itself handily to the fact that all too often we are not sure what to do with them.

The mind processes feelings and the body is moved by them so they must be real.   We become heavy with grief, tense or rigid with anger. We run from fear and dance with joy. We experience our feelings both mentally and physically, but we feel them somewhere else. They don't follow the reason of our minds and they don't follow the circadian rhythms of the body. They seem to have a life all their own. Ah the ability of the being to delight in the full life that it currently fears. Laughter is a good example of something we experience with our entire being. The being also weeps in sorrow, trembles in awe, smiles in delight and writhes in pain. Our beings are moved by emotion and feelings. And the full life of these emotions includes the bad with the good, the happy with the sad and everything in between. The whole range of emotions and our ability to feel and experience them is critical to wholeness and to being part of the Ultimate Wholeness that we all share in.

The tragedy of modern society is that we have all become so consumed with being spectacularly happy that we miss the bliss of contentment. We demand and act as if we are entitled to only the good side of the feelings spectrum. If it feels good do it. The true, soulful feeler knows that a full life of feeling comes only when the pendulum is allowed to swing from side to side, to encompass the whole range of emotions in all of their glory. And when the pendulum is allowed to swing freely, we will always spend twice as much time in the emotions that are 'middle of the road' than we will at the extremes of intensely good or intensely bad. Just as our spirits seek for something to *believe in,* our hearts scream to *be allowed* to feel.

There is sacred in all that surrounds the beings that we've been gifted just so long as we *allow* these beings to feel. In the child it comes naturally, they do not need to give themselves permission to feel and show emotion. As we approached adulthood, however, we learned to hold them in check, to experience and express them differently. What many of us learned was to control them, to deny them or to manipulate them. So often we were told how we should feel and how we actually felt was quashed and buried. In adulthood digging those feelings out is not always easy, as our ways of dealing with them have come to feel safe and secure. Uncovering them seems risky and changing the way we experience or don't experience them seems, well unnecessary. Why sign up for extra grief right? Wrong, our stories are full of feelings. To really tell and interpret our stories we need a handle on the ways these crazy little things called feelings have affected our stories. Not only this but as we go forward to author our stories in the future we must be prepared to successfully deal with feelings if we are to maintain our freedom to choose for ourselves. We made it this far...we can *become willing* for just one more thing...to allow feelings.

Too many of us have forgotten the art of feeling. Somehow we no longer know how to *allow* what is natural to come through. We have become masters at repression for a multitude of reasons. And those reasons matter less than the fact that the victims of this repression have been our entire beings (and more often than not, those we care about the most). We can have a mind and a body and a spirit but without the heart the entire creature withers. Feelings denied or repressed manifest themselves as tension headaches, clenched jaws, stress, anxiety, body aches, hysteria, stomach ulcers, nervous breakdowns and many other physical and mental symptoms that run rampant in our age. The symptoms are the cries of our hearts asking to *be allowed* to feel. When *allowed to* feel the dispirited body comes alive with energy, energy that Blake calls, "...Eternal Delight."[29] So just how do we go about *being allowed* to experience the earth and all of its creations in a subjective, real, personal way? How do we re-train ourselves to *allow* feelings?

Our feelers (our hearts, our souls or whatever does the feeling.) feel in three main ways.

1. They allow feelings in.
2. They experience them.
3. They allow feelings out.

Some of us do well letting feelings in and others are good at letting feelings out. Some of us are bad at both and some of us are *too* good at both. Key point here: unless we become good at letting them in and letting them out we will never be good at experiencing them. So how do we *allow* feelings? How do we adopt a posture of welcoming them, entertaining them and then letting them go?

Before we break this down further there is one thing that is key to know about feelings and that is that they can only be experienced in the moment, in the now. We can plan experiences that involve the emotions and we can anticipate how something may make us feel but we cannot plan the feeling. When we are present, in the here and now, and are not dwelling on the past or planning the future, then we are available to feel. Feelings only display themselves in the moment. Feelings from the past are nostalgia and feelings from the future are fantasy. Feelings put the realness in the now. Feelings put the humanness into our experiences moment by present moment.

Like the demure lover, genuine feeling dances quietly around us, asking shyly for permission to be noticed, whispering modestly, *"Allow me in."* This lover may be demure but she will not be ignored.

Detachers

When we are talking about the issue of *allowing feelings in* we are once again dealing with issues of control. So many of us have adapted to the demands of family or society and have taught ourselves to stay rational, reasonable, to hold it all together. Think it through, detach and reason it out. We have been taught to value the "level head." Feelings made us feel soft, vulnerable and out of control—somehow weak.

There are many reasons that we do not *allow feelings in* but they all narrow down to two basics types:

1. We get *positive feedback* for not feeling, as in the modern work place, or
2. We have, in the past or currently, received *negative feedback* for feeling and have learned that it is less painful to simply not allow the feelings in.

The most common type of *not allowing feelings in* is born of and nurtured in our society. Our commerce driven culture gives rewards for the rational, the reasonable, the emotionally detached. In the past these accolades for behavior void of emotion were seen primarily in men, however, the feminist movement with its efforts to level the playing field has rewarded this same behavior in women. When we receive positive feedback for not feeling we typically relish in that positive and that works for a period of time. Detachment and reason have been so valued and stroked in the work-a-day world that at some point we adopt the style in all areas of our lives expecting the same reward. What we are left with is hollow relationships and temporary fixes.

The negative feedback loop is when the feedback from the outside world causes more pain than the feelings themselves so we disallow the feelings access to our beings. We shut down. We adopt the, "If I don't feel, you can't hurt me" posture. In both cases, the positive feedback and the negative feedback, the adapting behavior is CONTROL and the pathology is DENIAL. We deny the feelings permission to come in. We disallow them.

Once again we are back at attempts to control. We are back to willing what cannot be willed and controlling what cannot be controlled and we are back to putting on the mask of what we are 'supposed' to be in efforts to cover and control what is real. Refusing to *allow feelings in* leaves many of us walking around numb, flat and unable to engage, for when we disallow feelings of one kind we typically disallow <u>all</u> authentic feelings and are left wearing the mask of make believe. Our interactions and expressed emotions are generally whatever it is we think they should be at a given moment. We live in a perpetual 'oughtness'. We act out how we *think* we 'ought' to be feeling, we express emotions that we *think* we 'should' be experiencing. We simply act the part, we act happy or sad or angry because that is what we *think* is appropriate. We *think* instead of feel. This is far from genuine emotion and is a recipe for emptiness, for soul-sickness. We perform, we don't feel. We feel empty because we are empty—we have refused to *allow* what is real to fill us. We have refused to allow feelings in.

Those of us that are operating under the "don't feel" rule tend to look for something to put in the spot where the feelings are supposed to go. That or we reach for a way to numb the discomfort of having our 'feeling space' remain empty. When feelings are not allowed in we are left with an empty area within our beings, the space that was reserved for feelings way back at the time of our creation. Leaving this space vacant causes pain so we try to fill it with anything that will lessen the pain. The space aches to be filled. So we reach for those ever familiar "feeling fixes". And they can be anything that we turn to instead of experiencing true feelings, the feelings that our bodies need (and want) to feel.

Although there are some "feelings fixes" that are more common than others we humans can latch on to just about anything and use it as a "feelings fix". I suppose the most common "feelings fix" is food and when used to the extreme this "fix" can be lethal. Obesity on the one end and anorexia nervosa on the other end are case and point. Let's see what else? We've talked about them before…shopping, spending, working, cleaning…hmmm? To what else do we turn to fix the feelings we are shutting out? Sex, love/relationships, 'conspicuous consumption', exercise or if you are a positive feedback non-feeler—power, prestige, status, ego, wealth.   And then there are always the 'numbers', alcohol and drugs.   "Feelings fixes" work because we just need something, anything to put into the spot that God or The Power of The Universe reserved for our own, unique authentic feelings.

When genuine feelings knock at the front door of our feelers we panic. Feelings make us uncomfortable, vulnerable, out of control. To fight this "out of control" experience that manifests as the emotions keep knocking and begin to riot demanding to be let in, we reach out for something we can control or something to consume us so we cannot hear the riot.…you guessed it, the "feelings fixes". Anorexics quit eating because it is something they can control. Shoppers feel a rush from buying. Relationship junkies get taken away in the excitement and vigor of a new romance and they bounce from relationship to relationship just to experience the "new relationship" high. We do anything to avoid the authentic feelings begging to get inside, in doing so we divide the heart from the mind from the spirit from the body and are left with inner angst. We are left with a longing for wholeness, a not quite rightness, a torn-to-pieces-hood…A fisher king wound.

Feelings are only experienced in the here and now and unless we learn to feel them, to experience them our navigation across the *bridge of now* into the *rapture of being alive* will be fraught with hazard and peril. Not *allowing feelings in* suspends us in a perpetual now. A perpetual now so artfully brought to life in the movie "Groundhogs Day". Do you know what the definition of insanity is? It is doing the same thing over and over expecting a different result. Like the proverbial "dog chasing its tail" we become suspended in the never ending drama of the fool attempting to fill a leaking bucket, trying in vain to fill ourselves with "feelings fixes". Problem is, the need to feel is permanent and lest our aim is to be gerbils on a spinning wheel going nowhere we must learn to *allow feelings in.*

Our goal is to allow the feelings to come in, to feel them and to allow them to float back out. So, let's go on and take a closer look at those of us that have managed to *allow feelings in* but are stuck, rather, on the act of *allowing them back out.* We are the ones that have the "jammed up out box".

Stuffers

The second way of not *allowing* feelings is when we allow them in but then we refuse to let them out. Unlike the non-feelers who won't allow feelings in we *stuffers* allow feelings in and we even feel them but then we stuff them somewhere and ignore that they exist and refuse to *allow them out.* Where the *detachers* deny to themselves that their feelings even exist, the *stuffers* deny to others that their feelings exist. *Stuffers* usually know how they feel they just refuse to let anyone else know.

We stuff feelings for all sorts of reasons but regardless of the reason, it doesn't work. Like *detachers* we put on masks and play the part and act like we feel the way we *think* we are supposed to feel. Remember the *hider* character? The difference between the *hider* instinct and the feelings *stuffer* is this; hiding comes from an instinct. This innate instinct tells us to hide or we are going to get eaten by the saber tooth tiger. This, God given instinct would never dream of telling us not to feel afraid. You see, instincts are built in survival mechanisms (that we sometimes take too far) but the feelings faux pas' are learned. There is no survival advantage to telling ourselves or teaching ourselves to not feel scared. Make sense?

The real danger for the *stuffer* is that the feelings are already on the inside and on the inside they will stay and fester and rot and ferment until, one way or another, they come out. Typically, when the feelings do come out, they come out sideways and in a flurry. Our efforts to control our feelings backfire ("Fire" being the key part of that last word). We store the feelings that we have allowed in under pressure until they blow and when they blow there is no control what so ever. If we are especially good *stuffers* and the pressure to blow is contained, our feelings come out as physical or mental pathologies. We grind our teeth, clench our jaws, experience headaches, stomach ulcers or we become obsessive or compulsive or we become control freaks or worry warts. One way or another, those feelings are coming out.

Big dreams, high hopes....

College was a series of moves from Arizona State to the University of Iowa, back to Arizona then home to the South Dakota School of Mines and Technology and finally, after 5 years of transfers and surgeries and recoveries and transfers and surgeries and recoveries I was on my way back to the University of Iowa to complete my senior year of college. It was May and the school year had just ended. I hadn't had surgery for quite some time and for the most part was a normal college student with one exception. I was a loner. With all of my transfers and moves I hadn't established many connections with other college students. It is easy to see this in retrospect, however, at the time I don't think I really noticed. I was just so happy to be close to finishing my Bachelors degree and to be a normal, non-patient person. I had no big plans for the summer, no job and had an itch to do something fun.

I remember sitting at the dinner table one evening with my mom and dad and my younger sister Laura. My dad had this thing about giving everyone nicknames. Mine was Turd and my sister's was Fred. Turd came from my dad's first reaction my dying our little white Bichon named Poppy pink for Easter one year. I thought it was cute and clever. Cars would stop out in front of our house to stare at the little pink Easter dog. My Dad was livid. You could see the fury in his face and the words that came out of his mouth were, "Leslie you Turd." It stuck. From then on he lovingly referred to me as Turd. It didn't matter who was around or where we were, he referred to me as Turd. My sister's nickname came from her tendency to lose her cool. My dad played softball with a guy named Fred who was always a hot head so he started calling my sister Fred. She was Fred ever since she was about 6 years old and even other people had started calling her Fred.

Anyway, here we sat at dinner Mom, Dad, Turd and Fred, and

I decided this was a good time to announce my plans. "I am going to go to Europe this summer and hike around and see the sights. " I said matter of factly. My Dad just said, "No you are not." I replied, "Yeah I am. I have friends that have done it and I think I'm going to try it." "Who are you going to take this trip with?" he said. "By myself" I replied. "No you are not." He said and that was the end of the dinner conversation. The dialogue continued over the next week. It went something like, "No you are not." "Yes I am" "No you are not" "Yes I am""No you are not" "Yes I am"… But I went ahead making plans and buying myself a backpack and a tent and printing out maps and buying books. It was a week later when once again it was Mom and Dad and Turd and Fred at the dinner table and this time my Dad said he had an announcement. He said, "Well if you are really taking this trip to Europe, which I am against, then I have decided that Fred is going with you. I bought her a ticket." My sister's mouth dropped. And so it went, Turd and Fred were headed to Europe for six weeks. Fred got a backpack and gear that matched Turds and we were off on a European adventure that Fred hadn't actually even volunteered for.

We arrived in England, made our way to London and then Dover and then onto a Hoover craft which took us across the English Channel to Belgium. For some reason we decided the ride across the channel would be more fun and less crowed if we hopped on the 4am Hoover craft instead of doing what normal people do which would be to sleep at night and get on the 9 am ride. Boy were we surprised! Our ride across the English Channel was a memorable one. It was Turd, Fred and 400 British GIs. Ha what a sight! The guy in charge put us in a little corner and assigned other GIs to guard by us. They escorted us when we needed to use the rest room and they went and got our breakfast for us. They didn't want us unescorted on the craft.

We arrived in Belgium and proceeded to spend the next six weeks trekking and riding our way through much of Europe. It rained a lot of the time and we spent many a mornings with our tent in the dryer at some little laundry mat. The trip is more fun to remember than it actually was to live through. But the memories are priceless. Now I was normal. I was doing normal things and crazy things and I felt free.

It was about two weeks after our return when my Dad and I loaded up my Blazer and his Wagoneer and headed for Iowa City, Iowa to move me into the apartment where I would live for my last year of college. My Dad never asked what I was going to do with a Biochemistry degree, but I know he wondered. I think he was just glad that I was finally finishing my degree after six years of traipsing around the country and struggling to be a normal college kid.

I started school and returned to Rapid City to see my folks over Labor Day weekend. It was a Sunday. My Dad and I had gone for a long hike in the Black Hills. My Dad was the best hiker. He always knew trails that no one else knew and he was careful to pick trials that I could walk with him, although he never announced that he had picked a certain trail because it was easier than others. He always acted like it was the trail that he wanted to hike that day. But I knew.

I knew he picked the trail that I would be able to conquer. We returned home late afternoon and sat together in the hot tub on my parents back porch. Our house in Rapid City was out of a fairy tale. It was a great big yellow farm house with a white porch that went all the way around it and a huge windmill (yes, a real windmill) in the front yard which was enclosed by a white picket fence. Norman Rockwell indeed! Anyway, we sat in the hot tub and just visited. Once again I decided it was time for an announcement. Why I had this tendency to keep everything inside until it was decision time I don't know, but I do know that I took my Dad off guard when I announced that I had taken my MCAT last spring and that I had decided to go ahead and apply to medical school. I guess I thought his reaction would be one of excitement. I thought he'd be so proud and full of enthusiasm. His reaction was silence. Silence for a long time. And then I saw tears in his eyes and I will never forget his words. I hear those words in my head almost every day still. He said, "Turd, your life has been so hard, so hard. I can't stand for it to get any harder and I'm afraid this will make it even harder. But I can tell you this," and a tear ran down his cheek. "If this is what you decide to do, I am behind you all the way and I promise you one thing. I will be the very first one to call you Dr. Masters."

And five years later my Dad was standing at the door as the University of Minnesota Medical School class of 1994 exited their graduation ceremony. He put out his hand and said, "I'm proud of you Dr. Masters. I am so proud."

But what if we don't fit in either of these groups? Then we usually fit into one of the other two groups the *charmers* and the *forcers*. These guys let feelings in and they let feelings out but they refuse to take ownership of them. These fellas are feelings givers because they give their feelings away. More accurately, they insist that others take them.

Again, the pathology is in the *allowing*. The problem happens on the inside where the actual feeling is done. We allow feelings in but rather than experiencing them we push them back out and onto someone else. As if to say, "Here, you feel them." We force our feelings onto others and by doing so we give them away. We don't own them, We don't allow them to be unique, personal, intimate or authentic. We don't participate in the feeling because we are fixated on getting the feeling out. Now!!! We insist that they be felt and experienced by those around us instead.

Charmers

If we are *charmers* then we take feelings in and we let them out. However, instead of owning and experiencing them, and allowing them to float back out peacefully; we immediately shove them out and on to whomever is unfortunate enough to be near us. In our desperation to not have to experience and authenticate the feelings, and let them set for a spell within us, we rush them out as quickly as they came in and search for somewhere else to put them. We want those feelings anywhere but inside us so we scream in silence, "Just get them out of me!" Then the scramble to put them on to others begins.

The feelings are pushed out so quickly that they take on a life of their own. They come out in a blast, extreme and insistent that those around us realize how very important they are. The classic example of the *charmer* is "the drama queen." The *charmer* insists that the people around them feel and experience their feelings for them and when the others don't feel the feelings as vividly as the charmer thinks is appropriate, when others don't join in the drama, frustration builds. As this frustration crescendos efforts are made (conscious or unconscious), to ramp them up the effort. We embellish, become more theatrical, add details (some true, some half true), add other characters to thicken the plot...anything to impress upon those around us how important our production is and how critical it is that they share the same dis-ease that we have. Our biggest fear is not of the feelings that we are insisting those around us adopt; it is in having to experience those feelings for ourselves. We don't force by might, however, we force by giving a grand performance. We force with charm and drama. "Charming people, like paranoids, are thinking ahead all of the time."[30]

Forcers

Very similar to the *charmers* are the *forcers*. The *forcers* are the people that insist others take their feelings, not with drama and charm, but with force. For them feelings are facts. Just as two plus two equals four for everyone in the whole wide world, how they feel is how they believe the rest of the world should feel. When we "feel" in this way we state our feelings as facts. Have you ever heard it asked, "Would you rather be right or would you rather be happy?" Well for this type of feeler the answer is easy, they we want to be right. They want how they feel to hold true for everyone around them and they push, force their feelings on to others. Forcers don't tend to charm, they just tend to "run the show". Actually, they feel as if they have no choice because, like the *charmers*, being left alone to feel and own and authenticate their own personal feelings without the rest of the herd to follow along and reinforce them causes a great deal of dis-ease.

Charmers and *forcers* have another characteristic in common. Calm is the enemy. They blow through life like a tornado, zigging and zagging, unpredictable, desperate and determined. As long as there is chaos and disorder they do not have to stop, be still and feel and own and authenticate their feelings. Bob and weave, hit 'em and move, perpetual motion is the name of the game. My best advice for when you are confronted with a *charmer* or a *forcer*? Well, what do you do with a whirling dervish? Get out of the way and let 'em whirl.

I have a friend that is fond of the quote, "Feelings are not facts" Hmmmm? Let's see...

<u>*Facts:*</u> *tangible, provable, concrete realities that hold true for all who observe them.*
<u>*Feelings:*</u> *intangible, non-provable, subjective realities experienced only by the feeler.*
<u>*Facts:*</u> *can be replicated and reproduced by all.*
<u>*Feelings:*</u> *cannot be duplicated or experienced exactly the same way by another person.*
<u>*Facts:*</u> *discerned in the mind.*
<u>*Feelings:*</u> *experienced by the entire being.*
<u>*Facts:*</u> *black and white.*
<u>*Feelings:*</u> *rainbows of every color the mind could ever imagine.*
<u>*Facts:*</u> *reduce them in to elemental components and the mind says go ahead.*
<u>*Feelings:*</u> *try to break them into pieces and the being rebels.*

Yep, my friend is correct. Feelings are not facts!
But they are real! ☺
For the self to be real, the feeler, the being must be allowed to feel. For the alternative is that we are all mind, all thinking, all facts, all the same. What need would we have for procreation when cloning would do? Facts are constant, determinable and universal. Feelings are fluid, immeasurable and intimate. Feelings make us each unique. Feelings and emotions, when allowed, make us soft, vulnerable and carnal. They also make us touchable, lovable and real.

By allowing feelings and emotions, and practicing the art of "feelings-in--feelings-owned--feelings-out", we are exercising the gift of freedom and we are becoming more real, more honest and (hooray!) more connected! Feelings want to be shared. The biggest pathology that comes from not allowing feelings is isolation. True that feelings are our own and we, the feelers, are the only ones that can feel our own feelings, however, feelings want company. They want to be shared. And they are critical in any kind of relationship we could ever hope to have with another human being. By not *allowing* feelings we place ourselves in a box. Either we refuse to let anyone else in or we are incapable of coming out. We are alone in a crowd, solo at the dance, lonely amongst friends.

The peace that comes from feeling our own feelings is not foreign but to many of us it has become a remote peace. For just a minute, let's look at just a few examples:

1. The catharsis of true laughter is an example that most of us can relate to and an example that most of us can pull from past experience.

The reason we can pull it from past experience is because it felt so good. The experience stays with us because it was real and raw and genuine. No one can fake a good belly laugh.

2. The purging felt when genuine tears are shed. Sometimes we just need to cry.

How many of us have walked around trying to hold back the tears all the while knowing that their release is really what we needed most. Grown men don't cry ha! Honest grown men do cry, little boys afraid of what people might think don't cry. I am as guilty as any of these men who walk around holding it all in. That is how I deal with things as well. And the conditioning of holding it all in can be so complete that when we finally give ourselves permission to let go we are unable to do so. "I feel like I just need to cry but I can't," is a strange statement but one that is not foreign at all to those of us conditioned to stay in control of our emotions.

3. The simple empowerment that comes from speaking our part

in an argument, the elementary act of getting angry, owning that anger and expressing in a mature controlled fashion.

To some this may seem strange but to many of us just a simple speaking of our most basic feelings is a challenge. For the person who has traditionally submitted to a stronger partner this simple act can be the most empowering feeling that they can remember. How wonderful it would be to have these isolated acts of owning our feelings be the norm rather than just memorable incidents of temporary breakthrough.

Feeling Tools

To learn to *allow* we are going to ask for help. We are going to ask our reasonable, deductive minds to help us learn to feel and to feel appropriately. After all, the mind and all that is us, stand to benefit from this rightness of feeling. Equipped with a few handy tools we are on our way. What are our tools? Learning to feel authentically requires that we feel safe and not threatened. Allowing feelings, correctly or incorrectly, makes us feel vulnerable. Feeling opens us up and removes the proverbial armor that we have all suited ourselves in, often times, since we were children. For many of us this feelings world is a strange new world, a strange new world that we enter into with fear and trepidation. The tools we take with us are these: a people picker, a worry wand, a remote control and a bullshit meter. With these we will be equipped to forge both backward and forward on the *bridge of now*, we will be equipped to begin to learn *to allow*.

People Pickers

Let's start with the *people picker*. There are people out there that are just not safe when it comes to the expression of feelings. Just because we are trying to set down the need to control everything doesn't mean that others are. Knowledge of this and the use of good judgment are critical here.

Some of us just have broken *pickers*. We repeatedly pick the wrong people with whom to surround ourselves and with whom to share our feelings. This is the cool part...we are not like the tin man in "The

Wizard of Oz"! We were born with brains! We simply need to be re-trained to lead with the brain and not with the heart. We need to be prepared with the fact that some people will take our feelings and twist them or pervert them or manipulate them or attempt to use them against us or attempt to convince us that they are not legitimate. No go! We will not be manipulated and we will not be convinced that our feelings are not real or not important. They just are. Period. Sometimes the brain needs to protect the heart.

Just as the heart must be taught that not all people are trust worthy, it must also be taught that not all people are "not trustworthy". Just because we are trying to be smart and healthy with regard to our feelings doesn't mean that we need to let our *people pickers* run amuck eliminating everyone in sight. Wisdom lies in the strangest of places and can come from the people we least expect. Reflection is good. Hyper-reflection lands us in a whole new pathology. Along this same line, it is important to remember that we are using our *people pickers* to decide whom we should and shouldn't share our feeling with openly. It doesn't mean that we are trying to eliminate from our inner-circles those unworthy, just that we are electing *choose* whom we open up to more carefully.

Although there are those fortunate ones that are surrounded by safe people, most of us are surrounded by a mixture of people. What is key here is recognizing that really good people who genuinely care about us are still just people and they too are fallible. When they are family or very close to us they have a personal interest in us and in our feelings, actions and decisions. Even the purest of hearts have trouble taking themselves and their interests out of the equations. The bottom line, sometimes feelings need to be shared with people around us and close to us and sometimes it is best to share certain things with those not invested in the situation or even with people that we do not know at all.

How do we learn to pick better? Pause, put your hands in your pockets, take three steps back and, as my dad would say, 'think, think, think'. Think it through. We need to listen with our hearts but pick with our brains.

Worry Wands

Onward! Besides proceeding on the bridge of now with our new and improved *people pickers* we will also be traveling with our *worry wands*. Our *worry wands* do not cause worry, nor do they make it vanish. Our *worry wands* make the worry "right-sized".

We have become a country full of worriers, "Did the kids eat a balanced breakfast?""Will the stain come out of the rug?" "Did my boss really like that presentation?" "My God have you seen the price of Cheerios?""Do I look fat in this dress?" "Why is my wife working out so much? Is there someone else?" "Is my teenager responsible enough to go away to college?" We worry and if that isn't enough we even pre-worry that we are not worrying enough. And herein lies the art of "letting go". Simple but not always easy. The good news is that it just takes practice.

This is what I do, I say...

> **"God grant me the serenity to accept the things I cannot change, the courage to change the things I can and the wisdom to know the difference."**

And sometimes I have to say, "People, events and institutions" instead of "things". Then I take whatever it is I am worried about and I put it into this little prayer. The prayer is my worry wand. If there is nothing I can do about it I need to let it go and trust the Power that is greater than me, if there is action that I need to take I set forth to do so, if I am confused as to whether or not there is change that I should participate in then I sleep on it and say the prayer again the next day and try again to find clarity. Sometimes when I am particularly troubled I have to say that little prayer 50 times a day.

> **Why? Because I am human and even when I try hard to let worries go I tend to take them back and I need to let them go again and again and again...**

It is like trying to swim with a large rock in my hands. I start to drown in worry and then I hear a voice holler, "Drop the rock!" And I do and I am no longer drowning but swimming along with ease and then I get this swell idea and I dive down and pick up the damn rock again. Now I am gasping for air and just as I am about to go under for good I hear the voice again and I drop the rock again.

It is exhausting but practice does help and I am better at only having to drop the rock once or twice than I used to be.

The answer to, "Is worrying going to help or change the situation?" is always no. However, there are real worries in this world and lest we err on the side of complete denial (remember the *runner* character?) we need to wave our *worry wands* over all worries just to make sure they are being given the "right-amount" of brain space. Sometimes the worrying is just our feeler telling us to listen to that little voice inside and take action. Worrying doesn't change things, but it is something that we need to address with our brains just to be sure that we haven't missed the wisdom.

Remote Control

Next tool! The good old *remote control*. Now the little prayer above works for this too in that I need to frequently ask myself whether I can control or change something. But just because I am trying to control stuff doesn't always mean that I am worrying about it. I tend to try to control stuff more than I worry about. And usually I am trying to control shit because I am frustrated and my feelings have begun to bypass my brain. This is when I need my *remote control*. You see, my remote control puts my mouth on mute long enough for my brain to catch up.

Part of getting right with feelings is giving others the freedom to feel the way they feel. That is after all what I am seeking for myself, freedom to feel the way I feel. When frustration starts to set in it is typically because the rest of the world is not going along with my plan and so I manipulate myself into being okay with my feelings by trying to manipulate others.

Oh wouldn't life be jolly if everyone would just be the way I think they should be! So…with my mouth on mute my brain has the chance to ask my being the following questions:

1. *Are you angry?*
2. *Are you hungry?*
3. *Are you sick?*
4. *Are you horny? (We are all different but I think more often than not the more appropriate question for women is, do you need to be held?)*
5. *Are you tired?*
6. *Are you lonely?*

If the answer to any of these questions was yes then my feelings cannot be trusted and I need to continue on "mute" and get myself right before proceeding with life. The remote control acts primarily in the department of damage control when I am not operating at full capacity.

I wish there was such a thing as a remote control that would shift automatically to "stun mode" for when I try to take the "mute" off too soon!!! But alas…I fear that no such device has yet been invented. : (

The *remote control* mutes my mouth while I take a minute to be sure that I am fully charged and acting rightly. The *remote control* puts me on "mute" when I am angry, hungry, sick, horny, tired or lonely which is when I am likely to act like a two year old on acid and demand that the world behave according to the laws of Leslie.

The danger, when I am not right, is not only in my making a fool of my temperamental self but also of creating a negative feedback loop where feelings are concerned. The more I "act out" when I am not right the more likely I am to generate negative reactions to the expression of my feelings and the less apt I will be to share them again. Of course this negative reaction would be all of my own making but real and painful just the same. The *remote control* gives me just enough time to tell if I am okay to proceed openly with my feelings or if I am in danger of "trying to direct the show" because I haven't checked myself lately.

Bullshit Meter

And finally there is the good old fashioned *bullshit meter*. My bullshit meter not only calls me on my own emotional bullshit but it also goes off when someone else is about to fling a load of the same in my direction.

The *bullshit meter* acts as an alarm of sorts. My bullshit meter goes off and alerts and protects me from having my brain shut off in the middle of an emotional crisis and then predictably turn back on during a moment of silence and say, "Hey wait a minute, that doesn't make sense." Or "You should've said this…"

When I head out into this world with my brain in the off position my feelings are left to fend for themselves. Left alone, feelings are apt to get scrambled and confused and leave me with the all too familiar, "Yeah but…" and "Uuuhhh okay…"responses. These responses are a sure clue that somewhere, somehow my feeler and my thinker got disconnected and my feeler was out there on its own trying to fend off the bullshit with pure feeling, a definite recipe for trouble.

My brain and my *bullshit meter* must come along for any venture I take into the dangerous world of feelings. Feelings make us feel vulnerable and weak because when they are all that we are relying on we are vulnerable and weak. Our minds were meant to think even while we are feeling. Our thinkers think, our feelers feel and they do it simultaneously. When we are all thinking or are all feeling we get into trouble. The *bullshit meter* is the minds way of protecting us when we are brave enough to feel our feelings.

So what is the best way to learn about our feelings? We tell stories. We learn about our feelings by sharing our stories and we learn about our stories by sharing our feelings. We tell our story and we listen to the story of another. We give ourselves to one another with love, compassion and tolerance, joined by a common weakness…humanity. "My self is given to me through your gift of your self to me and my gift of my self to you."[31] And when we do this we find that we are all on solitary journeys together.

Part V:
Practicing The Art

10

The Self

We have come to the *bridge of now* and looked back into the myth we have lived up to this point. We have looked into the past and gathered all that we needed to tell our stories. What we are going to do now is pause and recognize the bridge we have been on our entire lives for the first time. The now, this very bridge is where we have lived our every moment of our lives and it is where we must live all of our tomorrows. You see, we do not get to continue on this bridge into tomorrow. Tomorrow comes to us on the *bridge of now* and becomes today. We can turn and gaze off into the future but we cannot go there. We must wait for it to come to us...one day at a time.

If we are to co-author our future we must grasp this concept that we can only author our stories in the here and now. Right here on this *bridge of now* is where we will write the remainder of our stories. This bridge will remain the same old bridge until we reach into the past and begin to tell our stories. It is in the telling of our stories (yes, out loud to another living, breathing human being) that we begin to see this bridge for the first time in all of its exquisiteness. Our stories are what tell us how we came to be in the now that we live in. Our stories are what orient us and allow us to appreciate all that is superb and all that is subtle in the now that we live in.

With the drawing of this Love and the voice of this Calling

We shall not cease from exploration
And the end of all our exploring
Will be to arrive where we started
And know the place for the first time.

T. S. Eliot

Our *choices* are all that we have to author our future. And it is in the here and now that we will make these choices. It sounds so nice to say, "I will make different choices in the future." But the truth of the matter is that we do not get to make *choices* in the future. We only get to make *choices* in the now. This is why it is so essential for us to tell our stories and come to grips with how we got to where we are right now. How we deal with the present moment becomes part of the story we will tell tomorrow. If we do what we've always done we will get what we've always got. Telling our stories reorganizes our now and changes how we experience this thing called life.

Our bodies are our sensers and, yup you guessed it, we are not whole without including the *body* with the *spirit, mind* and *heart.* Our bodies are what make us sensual beings. It is hard to look back in our stories and say, "Here, here is an occasion when I was sensual." And that is not the reason for this chapter. At this point we are going to focus on how to see the now that we live in (and will always live in) differently. Our bodies are how we take in the world. Our senses are what allow us to interact with and experience all that is tangible. We see, feel, touch, smell, taste, hear through our bodies. Our modern culture has grabbed a hold of our bodies by one means or another and squeezed our senses to death. We have labeled sensuality as something bad or dirty and close the door on the most natural, innate way we have of interacting with our environment and experiencing our world.

Our bodies are what *bring it all to life.* As infants our senses, our sensuality, introduced us to this world. Polymorphous peversity. We reached out and touched everything placed in front of us, we were comforted by human touch and consoled with our mother's milk. A quest to become and to become whole and to become part of the

Whole would be incomplete if we were to not address the travesty that has been done to our sensuality and begin the process of re-claiming. Just as our spirits seek for something to *believe in* and our minds ache to *become willing* and our hearts scream to *be allowed* to feel freely, our bodies beg to *participate*.

The fantastical body…

It was 1991 and I was just completing my second year of medical school. I was focused on two things, boards part I and my upcoming surgery to be performed by the chief of orthopedics at the University of Minnesota Medical School. His plan was to re-break and re-set my badly crushed pelvis. He had never performed this operation before but thought he could do it and he had called in the orthopedic trauma surgeon from across town to assist. My plan was to take the boards and one week later go in for surgery. For two months I had been giving blood for them to store in case I would need a transfusion during surgery and by the time boards came I was feeling weak and tired a lot, but I managed to take and pass boards.

The surgery was a big one. Extremely painful, one of the worst, but it seemed at first to help the chronic pain in my pelvis and I was back on my feet in a matter of weeks. Two months later I got married to a man I had known since high school. Three months later I sat in my surgeon's office and stared at the most recent x-rays of my pelvis. It had moved back to its former position. I knew it before I saw the x-rays as the pain had returned as well. After several long discussions with my surgeon and the orthopedic trauma surgeon, the decision was made. The trauma surgeon would travel with me to Los Angeles to have my pelvis reconstructed by a surgeon that did this and only this, pelvic trauma reconstruction. It was a big deal, but they got me in.

Shortly before my consult across the country however, I found out I was pregnant. To me and my family this was nothing short of a miracle as I had been told that it was unlikely that I would ever be able to have children. The pregnancy was easy until I hit

28 weeks when I went into pre-term labor and was hospitalized on strict bed rest. Ever try strict bed rest? Bed pan, no showers, no sitting...torture I tell you, torture!! My miracle baby was born 10 days later. Two and a half months early, weighing only 3lbs and 7 oz, so early but healthy. She stayed in the NICU for over a month and my husband and I practically moved in. We brought her home on a heart monitor and watched her grow stronger every day.

Once we knew she was okay and growing well and normally reality hit again. Oh yeah, I was in medical school and I was supposed to be heading to the West coast for major surgery. When Olivia was 5 months old, I packed up with lots of supportive family behind me and headed to California. My sister stayed with her 9 month old and my 5 month old. (Angels do exist!) The surgery wasn't as bad as the previous one and within 10 days I was home and within a month was back to school.

I completed medical school in five years and in June 1994 graduated and my little family and I moved to Tucson, Arizona where I would do an internship in pathology and then transfer into the Internal Medicine program. Within 6 months of moving to Tucson my marriage fell apart and we divorced shortly thereafter. Whoa! Shake my head in disbelief. There I was in Tucson, Arizona beginning an Internal Medicine residency as a single mother of a 2 year old! I will tell you today that there is no harder job in the entire world than that of a working, single parent. Many times I would think of my Dad raising my three sisters on his own when I was hurt and my mother would be away with me. I knew my Mom was an irreplaceable saint, but my appreciation for what my Dad went through was new and utter.

Together Olivia and I did it. Sometimes not too gracefully but we did it. So many nights I would get called into the hospital and she and I both got good at just loading up the stroller and heading in. It got so the hospital staff just knew that if I was coming in so was my toddler. She is the only toddler to have ever spent every third night in the hospital on call room. Once when Olivia had spent some time in South Dakota with my parents my Dad had told her that she was just so beautiful, and when we would go in to the hospital at night the nurses would ask her how she was and she would answer, "I'm just so beautiful." And she was. As my residency went on, the schedule got lighter and life eased up a bit. As a senior resident my job changed from doing to teaching and training. My body was healthy and strong and life was good.

Sam Keen the master at putting together words like sensuality, sexuality and spirituality quotes Alice Walker in *The Color Purple* and I can come up with no more beautiful example of what he calls primal theology: "I think it pisses God off if you walk by the color purple in a field somewhere and don't notice it…Any fool living in the world can see it always trying to please us back…It always making little surprises and springing them on us when us least expect. Everything want to be loved. Us sing and dance, make faces and give flower bouquets, trying to be loved. You ever notice that trees do everything to git attention we do except walk?"[32]

True sensuality, we cannot quite define it but we know it when we see it. It is an aura, *a way of being.* It comes from someplace deep within the being. It is that "It" that some people have and others do not. And those of us that do not are once again guilty of donning the "how we think it ought to be" masks and trying to "act as if". We wrap ourselves in designer labels, dab on the most recent fragrance, style our hair just so, eat raw fish and order expensive wine, become boisterous, bold and flirtatious and then boast that we have successfully titillated each one of the senses but we fool no one.

Sensuality is not superficial, it is found in the depths. When it is present it is effortless and unmistakably genuine. It doesn't need labels. It is one of those things that cannot be willed. We can will listening but not hearing, we can will touching but not feeling, we can will looking but not seeing, we can will friendliness but not empathy. (Empathy is derived from the Greek *empatheia* and literally means 'passion' or 'in + feeling'. Like sensuality it comes from some place deeper.) The difference between listening and hearing, looking and seeing is that sensual something that makes the latter a gift while the former remains a skill. Our goal in telling our stories and reorienting our now is precisely this. Our goal is not to look and listen in this moment but rather to see and hear in this moment. The *bridge of now* will be very different if we encounter it with sensuality rather than simply sensibility.

So, how do we revive the senses? We give the *body* permission to reconnect and *fully participate* with all that makes us whole—the *spirit*, the *mind* and the *heart*. We tell our stories. We listen to other's stories and recognize that when we do we are both giving and receiving a gift. We *come to believe* in something Bigger than ourselves, we *become willing* to release all that we cannot control, we *learn to allow* feelings and we give the body permission to *fully participate*. A touch with the *body* is a handshake, a touch with the *body, heart, mind* and *spirit* is two beings recognizing their completeness in the Being, recognizing their wholeness in the Whole. The body *participates* with the senses, sight, sound, smell, taste and touch. The being, when it combines all of its parts, elevates these senses to a spiritual, sensual plain and discovers senses beyond.

How do we see, really see and not just look? We do it with intention and with all that makes up our being. To see means several things. It means to perceive with the eyes, to detect by sight, to form a mental picture of, to understand and to witness by personal experience. To see therefore means much more than just looking, it means understanding, experiencing, discovering and embracing something our eyes and our minds detect. Hearing can also mean several things beyond perceiving with the ear. We can hear an inner voice. We also hear a calling which usually involves a unique kind of knowing of where we are meant to be or what we are meant to be doing. Our challenge is to go beyond the senses we are accustomed to and resurrect the art of listening with the being, of seeing beyond reality, of sensing with the body and its natural rhythms in activity and in rest. Our challenge is to re-learn how to experience our bodies alone and with another. Although there are many ways to become "re-enchanted" with the body I have chosen these to get us on our way: fantasy, wonderment, serendipity, intuition, stillness, motion, solitude, communion and attentive sensuality.

The Sense of Fantasy

With imagination and wonderment comes *fantasy* and the opening of ourselves to all possibility. We have talked extensively about the will and mis-use of the will and it is here in these few paragraphs on fantasy that we will discuss the correct use of the will. It seems quite counter-intuitive to think of the correct use of the will in fantasy rather than in a concrete, serious discussion based in reality but go with me here and I will try to explain further. As mentioned early on in this book, psychologists today report a trend of patient's complaints and reasons for seeking professional help centering largely around their sense of emptiness or purposelessness. We are a society of persons in which many of us feel as though we have been carried away in the stream of things. As though the hustle, bustle and lightning pace of our world has swooped us up and carried us in the current leaving us as helpless unintentional tide riders. We wonder how things got to where they are now, we feel like we didn't have time to think, to imagine or to *fantasize*. Life just swept us away. We find ourselves wondering what happened to those idealistic goals and dreams, and feeling as if we are hamsters in the wheel spinning and spinning and spinning and gradually realizing that we are not going anywhere. The dreams have died. *Fantasies*, imagination, dreams and desires need to be brought back to life. The correct use of the will is to *fantasize* every fantastical possibility, to imagine how life would be with these possibilities as realities, to dare to dream of the desires that we so easily dismiss as flights of fancy and to, with the will, take action and make decisions with all possibilities present and accounted for. This is sensual lesson number one, it is time to release the *sense* of emptiness that comes from lackluster goals and tepid actions and trade up for the *sense* of possibility that comes from giving our beings permission to dream, desire, wish, *fantasize* and imagine and to make passionate, abiding decisions based on a the complete field of potentiality. Hope is threatened when decisions are made on partial possibilities. Our wills will proceed to action only when we take into account our hopes and dreams and goals. The reality is...*fantasy* matters. Whether we have always dreamed of planting a garden, writing a book, opening a business or learning to play the violin, those dreams matter, they are part of what is real in us. They are a part of our stories and they need to be revived and to live again. *Fantasies* make us rich and raucous and wretched and raw. Most of all they make us real. Without the *sense* of goals, *fantasies* and imagination we open the door for the most lethal sense of all—the *sense* of hopelessness. Perhaps God doesn't exist, but perhaps he does. Perhaps desires and dreams and wishes won't come to fruition, but perhaps, just perhaps they will. "Hope dies last." Hope must always die last.

The Sense of Wonder

Our sense of *wonder* is only present when we can set down the sense of duty long enough to give our attention to everything that is trying so desperately to "git" it. *Wonderment* starts where our own imaginations leave off. I like to think of it as awe. To me, awe is an overwhelming, spiritual feeling full of astonishment and unexpected *wonder*. Funny thing is we wander through life thinking that awe is something that comes once in a lifetime to a select few when the truth is as Alice Walker wrote, the awe is there for the taking if only it could "git our attention". The elegant allure of nature, the majesty of a thunderstorm, the sublimity and magic in Gothic architecture, the void and nothingness created in Eastern paintings, the *mysterium* of utter silence or utter darkness. All that deserves awe and *wonderment* surrounds us at every moment, at every twist and turn that we make. When we hit the ground running with a "To do" list three pages long and a little box drawn neatly beside every task just waiting to be checked off, extraordinary and ordinary can be below our noses but they will not capture our attention.

When I am alone I notice things that I, on a normal day would never have appreciated…moments of *wonderment*. I love to tell you a wonderful story of a beautiful flower pushing its way through a crack in a concrete wall refusing to be shut out by the concrete jungles of our inner cities but my story is a little more gruesome, but I found *wonderment* in it.

It was fall and the leaves on the trees were gradually making their way to the ground. My house backs up to a ravine that is surrounded by very tall old oak trees that completely block our view of any other house in the neighborhood. The cold late autumn air was blowing and we had already fired up the furnace and the fireplace was burning away. Suddenly I hear a screech from the kitchen and my 16 and 11 year old daughters are standing on the kitchen island. *"A mouse! A mouse!" They screeched. My eight year old son rolled his eyes and acted irritated that he interrupted his computer game for this. I re-assured the girls that I would get some mouse traps and then the mouse would be gone. My idea was met in chorus, "No mom you can't kill him. We don't want you to kill him we just want him out of the house." "Well, he is gone for now, get off the counter and we will figure something out." I said trying to figure out how I was going to catch this mouse in a trap and dispose of it before the kids realized that I killed the mouse.*

As luck would have it, Sam my 8 year old son and I were up late that night and low and behold, our cute little grey mouse decided to pay us a visit. Despite his lack of fear of the mouse, he was completely on board with his sisters with the idea that the mouse was to be captured and not killed. We spent 2 hours chasing this mouse. All the while I am thinking, if we do catch this thing I am driving it two miles away before I release it so it doesn't just come back in. Bless his little heart, he finally did get it trapped under a piece of furniture and just as his little hand was about to grab him he slipped into a tiny crack in the wall and was gone.

Months past and remnants of the mouse made it obvious that he was still living with us though we never saw him again. I did set covert traps but apparently he was also a bright little fellow because he was having nothing to do with my traps laced with cheese and peanut butter. Well, winter turned to spring and the days were warm and sunny and it had been some time since I had seen evidence of our little house mate. One morning at about 5 am I was out on the back patio reading and writing and watching my kids maneuver on the "ripsticks" that I thought they would never master. I spent every early morning on my back patio, sometimes alone on rare occasions I would be joined by children. Nevertheless it is my quiet time and I treasure it. Recently I had grown fond of watching a large grey owl who would sit high upon one of the oaks that was now re-covered with fresh spring leaves. On one particular morning when my two youngest kids were zigging and zagging on their ripsticks and I was sweeping the patio in the wee hours our beautiful owl spread its amazing wings and made a nose dive into our back yard and grabbed something in his beak. We all jumped in shock and fear and then as quickly as he flew downward he flew back up to his perch high on the tree. Except now dangling out the side of his mouth was a little grey tail. And I knew my mouse drama had just come to a natural God driven end. No one cried or became upset because the mouse had died. It was as if even the littlest ones recognized the divinity on the great circle of life.

The Sense of Serendipity

Serendipity has been called one of the most difficult English derived words to translate. Best defined as, it is the effect by which one accidentally discovers something fortunate, especially while looking for something else entirely.[33] I have a Russian friend who speaks English fluently as a second language and when preparing to write this chapter I asked her what *serendipity* meant to her. She replied, "seren..what? I do not know of this word." When I explained it to her she said, "In Russia we say that every stroke of good fortune is caused by a misfortune in the past. This is as close as I can get to your seren.. word." Most authors who have studied *serendipity* in science, both in a historical, as well as in an epistemological point of view, agree that a prepared and open mind is required on the part of the scientist or inventor to detect the importance of information revealed accidentally. The French scientist Louis Pasteur famously said: "In the fields of observation chance favors only the prepared mind." This is often rendered as "Chance favors the prepared mind."[34] Is this a sense of serendipity? I think no. *Serendipity* is what we call it when our open mind recognizes something that occurs that seems *beyond* chance. We have a *sense* of the uncanny, *sense* that something *beyond* mere chance has just happened to us. Pasteur does, however, wisely counsel that an open mind is the essential component. *Serendipity,* or unexpected good fortune, happens all the time it is just that it is quite infrequently that our minds are open to recognize, appreciate and experience it. In our Post-modern rational mind set we call it good luck, or worse yet, hard work. When we open our minds and embrace it with all of our senses, sight, sound, smell, taste and touch and experience it with the totality of our beings, our *spirits,* our *minds,* our *hearts* and our *bodies*....well then we know with a sense that comes from deep within that we've been touched by the Spirit. If you skip along singing, "Oh what a lucky girl am I!" Then my only recommendation would be to go back to chapter 6 and take a closer look at what you have *come to believe.* To miss the divine love taps that are there for us every day is indeed a sacred cataclysm.

The Sense of Intuition

Another sense that we can chose or not chose to listen to is that sense of *intuition.* It is that sense that there is something, though we do not know what, telling us the correct answer. French Philosopher Henri Bergson (1859-1941) spent much of his philosophic career on the idea of intuition. In layman's terms we call it that "inner voice". The dictionary defines it as, direct perception of truth or fact independent of any reasoning process; immediate apprehension.[35] Bergson said, it can be seen then that the sense *intuition* is a method that aims at getting back to and knowing the things themselves, in all their uniqueness and ineffable originality. The one thing, it is certain, one can grasp from within through *sympathy* is the *self.* Intuition cannot be shared, it cannot be gotten, it cannot be willed. It is a God given *sense* that we all carry deep within that spiritual core of our beings. It is a purer, more absolute way of knowing. We live in a world of: collect all of the data, divide it into groups, analyze the shit out of it and decide what is most true about it. And then say to ourselves, "Boy you accomplished the hell out of that!" *Intuition* just is. It is indefinable, awe inspiring and above all indivisible. Just as "duration is a never ending spance of time in which each moment cannot be held motionless in time and analyzed without destroying the next moment," so it is with *intuition,* it is a never ending, rarely tapped reservoir of God given absolute wisdom that once, in a very great while, slithers into our conscious. If we stop to analyze it or go digging for more we destroy it. This is another one of those things that we just don't need to know. We don't know why we know it. We just need to know we can trust it and that it comes from something much, much Bigger than us. We need to embrace the fact that it is correct and that it is to be heeded. *Intuition* is a sense, and it is a sense beyond our everyday senses.

True *intuition* does not mislead us; wishful thinking mistaken for *intuition* misleads us. The eye sees only what the body is prepared to comprehend. The *intuition* sees what data, facts and reason do not tell us...The Absolute. "An Absolute can only be given in an *intuition*, while all the rest has to do with analysis." It takes something deeper than the intellect to truly apprehend reality. It is here, I believe Kant and his followers failed. They believed that the highest source of the freewill was pragmatic faith. No chance, no serendipity, no *intuition*, no freewill.......a sad calculated (no pun intended!!) existence!

A wee tale on intuition...

I sat not too long ago having coffee with my ex-husband, the father of my children and one of my best friends in the whole wide world. I said. "So when are you getting married?" "What?" he replied, "I am not getting married. Whatever gave you that idea?" I sat back and I sighed and finally I said, "This told me." And I pointed to my gut. "I just know. My intuition doesn't whisper, it screams, rattles and rolls. And I won't tell a sole but I know that you are getting married this summer. Congrats. I am so happy for you." His replied, "There is no possible way that you can know that, with the certainty with which you claim to know it." "I feel my intuition as though it were the actual breath of God...I hear it, I feel it, I touch it, I taste it, I see it and most of all I believe it. I know it like a mother knows the scent of her own child." He shook his head, smiled and later that summer re-married.

I am sure there are as many hypotheses about intuition as there are authors who have addressed the sense and why it seems to be a trait that shows itself stronger in women than in men. Here comes mine and I have no doubt that it is far from original. I think women innately have an easier time trusting. Especially trusting things that they cannot see. I think it comes from the experience of child bearing, from that instant that the menstrual period fails to come one month and the God given trust that there is a brand new human life growing within her. She can't see it, or feel it, or taste it, or touch it or hear it. But she knows with all of her being, with everything that makes her real that she is now two human beings growing off one body. Men can build and create and discover and explain. They can send men to the moon they can beam data around the world faster than a heartbeat. They can even create a human life in a test tube but they will never, ever, ever know that kind of Knowing.

The Sense of Stillness
&
The Sense of Motion

Ah yes *stillness and motion*…if you are expecting me to jump into a dialectic on prayer, meditation and physical fitness you will be sadly disappointed. Those are things that the outside forces tell us to do with our bodies to *redeem* them, *relax* them or *reform* them into things that these outside authorities think would be "a good idea" or should I say "a good ideal". *Stillness* is a sense, that when experienced somehow tells us that we are not alone. The gift of being able to quiet the hustle bustle around us and just be is one of most untapped gifts. It sounds as if it should be so simple. Just go into a quiet place and be still. The art is quieting the mind, completely. In absolute *stillness* all that we should feel is our heart beats and our breathing. But, let's get real, very few of us are skilled in the ancient arts of emptying the mind and achieving the transcendence of the desert fathers and other famous aesthetics. Quite frankly, most of us don't want to be. What we can do and what is one of the greatest benefits of experiencing the sense of *stillness* is to turn our minds into a sacred relay station that allows all thoughts run in and run out. There is no waiting room, no place for thoughts to hang around and interrupt our visits with ourselves. They only get to flow in and flow out. We sit very *still* and rather than taking the most recent thought or problem or concern and chewing on it like we so often do in everyday life, we let each and every thought flow in and then flow out. We sit as an outside observer and view the personality that has developed through the years. We watch the thoughts go in and out and see which things have hurt us, which things have left us with guilt and shame, which things have comforted us. We get to note when we felt superior or judgmental, when our personas were hurt and we felt small and vulnerable. We get, for probably the first time, to view our personalities from afar. We get to see that, despite the chaos both present and past, it is the personality (our biggest addiction) that sends us spinning into a world of insanity. In absolute *stillness,* with thoughts floating in and floating out we find the self. We realize that all that occurs "out there" is simply the ego, the personality. The self is protected deep within and remains constant and true. The self stripped of the defensive mechanisms, the hurts, the pains and the agonies of being human. We find the self that at long last gets to speak and it tells us that under all that the personality, the familial influences, the society pressures—"I remain". It says, "I remain waiting for the superficial to be stripped away and to show you how to connect, to feel complete, to find wholeness, to experience the gifts of freedom, gratitude, humility, tolerance and compassion. I am a quiet, even keeled, loving, calm source of strength that despite the absurdity and madness of the thoughts that the personality bombards me with continually remains solid, sound, sane and steadfast. I am docile, loving and open to and longing for connection with every other self in the infinite Self." We find what is real and pure in us and we find that the self is not alone. It is connected in the web of humanity longing to be whole and Whole. The self says, "Come back and visit me often and we will become stronger and we will find meaning and we will see the purpose in it all." In our moments of utter silence, when thoughts are merely passersby we imagine that we can hear every heartbeat in the world and we never forget that we are part of something much Bigger.

Whereas *stillness* observes the thoughts from afar as they float in and the out of our minds, *motion* plays with them. *Motion* of the body brings the mind to life and lets us play with all of our thoughts. *Motion* stimulates the mind into dreaming, fantasizing or even into "thinking" more clearly about everyday things. Now, I am not talking about the kind of *motion* that strives to turn the body into the perfect Herculean specimen but rather any kind of *motion*. *Motion* aimed at being just that—*motion*. Way too often we moderns think of physical activity as a way to get into shape, to flatten the belly, cut the pects, pump up the pipes, chisel a six pack. What I am talking about is the kind of *motion,* any *motion* that gets the blood flowing. A walk, a hike, planting a garden, cleaning the garage, hanging Christmas lights. My kids and I have a favorite, we turn the music up loud and all three kids and Mom just dance. Some on the coffee tables, some bounce off the couch, some join hands and country swing. They all 3 come up with moves that are absolutely frightening. I think to myself, "Where did they learn that? Too much TV, Youtube?" Either way, we all move and we all move together and there is a familial spirituality that floats in the air. Not to mention the fact that we are making memories that we will cherish forever.

Stillness quiets us. *Motion* wakes us. One thing that both *stillness* and *motion* should make us feel, really feel, is our breathing. It suddenly turns from something automatic to something we notice, feel and experience. The stressed out breathing of anxiety goes like this; we take a breath in and our chests go out, we exhale and our chests go in. This is called a sigh, a sign of stress and angst. When we are breathing whole and pure; we take a breath in and our chests go in, we exhale and our chests go out and our bodies have been cleansed and refreshed and filled with the breath of life. (Seriously, try it!) It moves every part of us, our spirits, our minds, our hearts and our bodies to a higher plain, to somewhere higher than it was before we allowed the breath of life to move us. Many of the troubles of the modern mind, in my opinion, come from the sedentary status quo of the modern body. For crying out loud, we need to get out there and mow our own damn yards. Outdoor jobs involving movement of the body are now considered "blue collar" and somehow less than. Hmmm? Since when did tables, chairs, fax machines, printers, computers, cubicles and iridescent lighting become the panacea of healthy, wholesome living. Strange thing is that the more time we spend in these manmade corporate monsters the stronger their hold is upon us. They suck and suck and suck until there is no part of the bodily energy left to, "mow our own damn yards".

Look, I have no illusion that my little rant is going to change the world we live in but let's agree to do this one thing…lets never get so into being part of this "culture" that we live in that we cease to remember that first and foremost we are part of the earth and that nothing that man can make could ever possibly top that. Our bodies are part of what was created along with this earth. They are not manmade machines so let's appreciate them, move them, allow them to move us and allow them to bring life and vitality to our whole, to the whole of everyone else who shares our cosmos and to the Whole.

The Sense of Solitude

Next comes the sense of *solitude*. The key point here is that solitude is very different from isolation or loneliness. Synonyms of loneliness are desolation, alienation and even heartache. Synonyms for isolation are hiding, withdrawal and alienation. Man, none of those sound like anything that we should try in the name of spiritual growth. *Solitude* on the other hand means privacy, detachment and silence. What we need to recognize, is that there is a vast abyss between loneliness and *solitude*. One can be lonely in a crowd. One can experience loneliness in a room full of friends. Loneliness is the *sense* that something is missing. Very similar to the *longing* that we started with in chapter one. The biggest difference has to do with choice. We choose *solitude* or alonetime. We don't choose loneliness or isolation. But choose it we must.

Now, more than ever, we need our solitude. Life's creative passions require alonetime. People will inspire us, information can teach us and practice makes perfect, but we need quiet time to figure things out, to emerge with new revelations, to spark original observations. The natural creativity in all of us, the slow insights, the sudden bursts and gentle clarifications of imagination, are found in alonetime. Passion grows in aloneness. Both creativity and curiosity grow through contemplation. Solitude teaches us boldness and braveness, and the ability to satisfy our own needs. A restorer of energy, the peacefulness of alone experiences provide us with much-needed rest. The need for *solitude*, for alone time can be a definite "tugger" on relationships. Aloneness and attachment are not either/or conditions. Remember, we are both/and beings. We must come together and go apart and come together and go apart, and trust the healthy rhythm of it all. It is time to emancipate aloneness from thought of "I don't want to be with you" and learn to treasure and cherish it as that solemn *solitude* that empowers thoughts to flow freely, recharges lovers to be more passionate, titillates dreams to be more expansive, more playful. *Solitude* of the body brings forth in all, our longing to explore, our curiosity about the unknown, our will to be individual, our hopes for freedom. *Solitude* is fuel for life.

The Sense of Communion

Ah connection! We are over connected and disconnected all at once! The problem is that "Reach out and touch someone" means make a phone call and not literally touch someone. We must remember that although touch is one of the original five senses, there are many ways to touch someone beyond the physical touch. We can touch someone with a smile, with a look, with a kind word or a friendly handshake. The one thing all of these "touches" have in common is that they all require us to be in the presence of another. We need to be connected with living breathing human beings and not solely with words on a screen. Modern technology is fabulous at connecting us with others. It simply cannot and must not be used as a replacement for the flesh. *Communion* is defined as, a joining together of minds or spirits. And any connection we make with another is *communion*. But being connected, truly connected to another human being implies a binding together of the spirit, the mind, the heart and sometimes the body. *Communion* with other human beings requires effort. Remember, love is a verb. It is an action word. When we tell our stories to other human beings and listen to their stories we are connected. Although we always need to watch for the us/them separations, this is where joining is vital for us. Join a church, join a group, join a club, just get connected with others. Make a conscious effort to meet up with a friend. For crying out loud call your mother! The key, do it! Connection to and *communion* with others is basic and crucial. It is with others that we create meaning beyond our own lives. It is in the collective and connective spirit that we create a team that is part of something larger than ourselves. Viktor Frankyl called it "ultimate meaning". Others may call it connection to a greater Whole, to a collective good, to God, to love or to a universal consciousness. Regardless, of what we call it, being and doing together fulfills and transforms us. A grand belly laugh requires company. Pain can be lifted with nothing more than a touch. The spirit of a connected group is much more powerful than the sum of the individual spirits. Team spirit is sometimes all that is necessary to accomplish a goal. A tear shed in solitude is called feeling ones feelings; a tear shed in front of another is *communion* and connection that lifts us to a higher dimension.

One thing that I have started doing is communicating with what I call, "Top Secret Friends" more fondly referred to as TSFs...

The idea came from my ponderings about sharing my struggles in an intimate relationship. What I found was that my closest dearest friends really cared about me. They really wanted what was best for me. Problem was that they all thought they knew what was best for me. "Get rid of the guy." "You are too good for him." "He can't treat you that way!" Besides being over protective of me they also had an interest in what I did next. My relationship had pulled me away to some extent from friendship time. They were also the ones left to pick up the pieces every time that I had a struggle. They were the ones who had to ride with me in the ups and downs of the relationship. They got me when things were bad and when things were good I was off to the races again.

I sat one evening realizing that they were all against this guy because I had shared with them everything that went wrong. They were not there for everything that went good. I had made them dislike the man that I loved and now I found myself struggling to have a relationship with someone that all of those close to me had serious misgivings about. Aaaaahhhh! I sat and thought, "I should have just gone to a bar and spilled my guts to the bartender." After all they have heard it all right? Then the idea hit and the unconscious wisdom, of sharing with someone who will listen but does not really give a rip about what I ultimately decide to do, struck me between the eyes.

Ah the bartender and the beautician. They are the soles that hear it all. Not sure why but men belly up to the bar and spill it all and women hop into that stylists chair and it all starts pouring out. I don't think we do the pause, put your hands in your pockets thing. I think we subconsciously just sense the safety and then start dumping. God Bless these people!

I have decided to take the wisdom to heart and now I have 4 Top Secret Friends that I text back and forth to and we help each other think and feel things through. We don't have an interest in what each other ultimately does in their respective lives we just listen and share and trust and remain Top Secret. Several times a week I get a message that simply says, "Hi TSF, hope you are well." If I don't respond, believe me sirens will start going off across the country. If I was absent my TSFs would search until they found me.

Attentive Sensuality

This is what is called being in the now, being entirely and utterly present in the moment. Many of us have this mastered in the work place. When I pick up a scalpel, I am entirely present and attentive to the moment. Attentive sensuality is the art of being aware and immersed in our interactions with others and with ourselves. Thoughts of the past and of the future are absent and we are regardful only to the person or thing that we are interacting with. In other words, we are out of the self and into what we are focused on, whether it be a person, a project, a flower or a thought. Again, children do it naturally and do it well. It is called play. For adults it takes practice and a conscious effort. But we can learn to play again. We can learn to let go of all that concerns us and immerse ourselves fully into the moment, and when we do this sensuality blossoms. We look and we see, we listen and we hear, we touch and we feel, smell and we discover, we taste and we savor, we reach out a hand from the depths of our beings, this is sensuality. And when we apply attentive sensuality in our most important relationships, our most intimate relationships, they will grow and flourish. And the story we will be able to tell tomorrow will have become one that we have authored by our *choice* to be present right here, right now. Right here, right now will be the story that we get to look back on by and by.

Leslie Masters, MD

11

The Tribe

We are born into a community of family and friends and as we grow and evolve and venture out into the life that we have been given our communities change. What remains the same is our universal need for other people. "Others" and our relationships with them just are and always will be. So often we view our relationships with others as necessary but a "hassle-ridden". Life cannot exist in a vacuum. As many of the great thinkers emphasize again and again, there is no me if there is no you, without "others" I am a being floating and there is no reason to call myself me because in saying "me" I am implying there is a "you". If *who we are* is our stories, a compilation of events and people and choices and actions, then *who we are* is made up of thousands of interactions with "others". From the breast that nursed me, to the hands that held the bike steady as I learned to peddle, to the lips that first kissed mine, to the voice that taught me that $E=mc^2$, to the patients I held and attempted to comfort as I told them they were dying, to the children who looked and listened for my voice on the sidelines, to the voices of authority that sent trembles through my body as my fate rested in their hands, to the hand of a stranger squeezing mine in prayer and desperation as we battled a common demon, to the lover who stole my heart and then broke it.......my story, my life is made up of "others" who helped, hurt, shaped, molded, influenced, manipulated and inspired me into what I have become.

Love them or not, "others" are us. "Others" see us in a way we could never see ourselves, they hear us in a way we could never hear ourselves. That said, we are the "others" to everyone we meet. We see things in them they are totally unaware of; we see them in a way that they could never see themselves. Each of us sees and hears something unique in any given "other". As we line up rank and file and follow the social norms, as we strive to live up to the expectations that mom and dad laid out, as we join the right clubs and drive the right cars, as we stand for the causes that are currently en vogue, we must admit that we are shaped by and defined by "others". As we have trudged through our stories, faced our fears and resentments, tackled our character flaws, come to believe in some sort of Keeper of the stars, become willing to allow this Keeper to work in our lives, allowed ourselves to experience authentic feelings and began to fully participate with our entire beings, we have gradually come closer and closer to the "self" that each of us are beneath all that has been layered upon us as we have tumbled, stumbled and rolled through our lives. Thus is the great paradox, the closer and closer we get to the "being" we are, the more and more aware we become of the undeniable truth that not one of us is able to exist as an "I" alone...there must be "Thou's". In reality we are surrounded by "Thou's" and the "Thou's" are necessary for us to truly be "I's". "Thou's" or "others" make our worlds go round and in these "others" we will find a wholeness and we will find that infinite, unfathomable connection that brings "Wholeness". It is in our stories that we find the web that connects us all. As we recollect we see all of the "others" that have played a part in our stories and likewise, we have played a part in their stories. As I open myself to you and tell you my story I am inviting a new connection. As you open yourself to me, I get the pleasure of becoming part of your story. As your story changes me so it changes all of those that I connect with. We can talk of the tangible 'degrees of separation', we can speak of how we know intuitively that we are all connected by our humanness, but if we were to speak quite literally of the ways in which we have touched one another's lives the connections would be incomprehensible. We are each a thread in the tapestry and our threads weave in and out, up and down and connect us all. The final picture is indeed dependent on the delicate, masterful intertwining…an intertwining beyond our understanding but within our grasp.

Isolation and Loneliness

Isolation and loneliness suck the miracle of life from our very souls. There is a reason that we use solitary confinement as a punishment. It is because it is painful, raw and agonizing. "Others" are the delight in life. A touch, a smile, a glance in a crowd, a familiar face…these comfort, warm and en-courage us. Unfortunately the community those of us living in this time were born into is one of increasing depersonalization. We have gradually traded face to face conversations for telephonic conversation for emails and text messages. A full day's work can be done without seeing or talking to a live human being. More power, prestige, money have somehow slithered into our psyches and, without our permission, become the goal as opposed to deeper, richer connections with other people. We continue to be more concerned with how we "look" to other people and what they can offer us than we are with experiencing them as people in our lives. Social gatherings are now considered a way of networking rather than a way of connecting with those around us. Today, "How are you?" rarely wants an answer. It is merely a rote greeting not interested in the actual response. We have lost and forgotten the necessity of reaching out to touch someone…their hand, their life, their heart and their soul.

Love thy neighbor as thyself…what if we did? What if our twitters and facebooks and texts and emails were not so much about letting people know what "I" am doing but a way of reaching out and climbing inside another, of sharing in their hopes and dreams and hurts and pains and secret sagas, of connecting with another and becoming part of their ongoing story. What if our tweets and all were used to not say "look at me" but rather to say this is my story, this is where I have been, what happened and where I am today and join me as my story plays out. How lovely it would be if our technology were used to connect us all at the heart, at the soul in an ever more intricate web that grows stronger every time another life story is shared, every time a fear is owned and disclosed with another and every time a voice from around the world answers, "Me too, that scares me too." And yet another voice chimes in and says, "That use to be me and this is what I did…". How much healing would take place if we could say, "I did this and I am so ashamed…I don't see how I can ever repair the damage I've done." … because without a doubt a voice of experience and hope would answer and a hopeless soul would see a glimmer of light and a possibility where none existed before.

———————————————

Jack's story…
Renee's story…

His name was Jack J_____ski and I first met him when he came to visit me in the Hematology/Oncology clinic at the Tucson VA hospital. He was a scruffy almost disheveled looking guy with a smile that was infectious. He was articulate and just one of those generally happy people that made those around him feel happy too, for no particular reason. I don't remember his exact age but he was somewhere in his late thirties. His presenting complaint was that he just didn't feel well. He was tired, short of breath and couldn't hold a job because he fatigued so quickly. Typically he worked in construction but had been unable to do that type of work in over a month. He had been working near Lake Havasu, Arizona and had hitched his way to Tucson because there was a VA Hospital and he was a Veteran. He had no appointment so had just appeared one evening in the emergency room and was given an appointment the next day to be seen by me in the heme/onc clinic. (It meant blood disorders or cancer.) He didn't even know what heme/onc meant only that this is where he was told to come.

A quick glance at his blood work from the emergency room told me what was wrong and explained why they had overbooked him into my already packed clinic. For some reason his body wasn't making blood cells. His red blood cells, white blood cells and platelets were all extremely low, dangerously low. Which meant one of three things, his bone marrow wasn't making them, his body was destroying them or his body was hiding them somewhere. Further review of his blood studies told me that in all likelihood there was something wrong with his bone marrow. I proceeded on that very day to perform a bone marrow biopsy and to admit him to the hospital for red blood cell and platelet transfusions. Before I sent him up to the medicine floor I told him that what I was looking for was not good. I was looking for leukemia, lymphoma or something called aplastic anemia, none of which were good. Two days later I saw him back in my clinic to review the results with him.

A review of Jack's bone marrow had revealed no malignancy, but rather evidence that his bone marrow had just quit making blood cells all together, aplastic anemia. You can't live without blood cells. I explained to Jack that the only option for survival was a bone marrow transplant and for that we would have to find someone that was a match to him. I asked him if he had brothers or sisters that would be willing to be tested. This is the first time I saw that smile leave his face. He said yes that he had four siblings but went on to explain that he had not spoken to any of them in nearly twenty years and that he didn't even have any idea where they were. He suspected that they were spread around the country and stated that he was quite sure that he could not find them nor was he willing to try. There had been a falling out, that he didn't explain to me, and to his knowledge, none of the siblings were in touch with or speaking to each other. When he finished he asked if there were ways to find other options for donors. It took one look at his last name for me to know that he would be a difficult match, J_____ski. I talked with Jack for over an hour that day, but was unable to persuade him to search for his siblings. They had been raised in Milwaukee, Wisconsin, but he was quite sure that no one was still there. Our conversation ended, I told Jack that he would, from here on out be dependent on the transfusion of blood products to live and that I would start the search of the bone marrow registry but that I wasn't optimistic. He smiled that smile and said thank you.

It was already 6 pm and I sat alone in the oncology clinic writing my notes from a busy oncology clinic day. As I got to Jack's note I thought, what the heck it can't hurt to try. I picked up the phone and dialed directory assistance for Milwaukee, Wisconsin and asked for any and all listings for J_____ski. I doubted there would be any. There was one listing, R. J_____ski. I called the

VA operator and ask to be connected with the number. The phone rang and then a recorded voice telling me only that I had reached this certain number came on and asked me to leave a message. I said the following: "Hello, my name is Dr. Leslie Sibley. I am calling from the Tucson VA Medical Center. Please disregard this message if I have reached the wrong person, but I am looking for someone who may know Jack J_____ski. If this is a correct number I want to assure you that he is okay but I do need to speak with you if you know him." I left my VA pager number and my home phone number and hung up. A shot in the dark but at least it is a shot, I thought as I grabbed my bags and headed home.

It was after 10 pm when my home phone rang that same day. It was a ladies voice and she was crying. She kept saying, "Oh my God we found Jack. We found Jack." She went on to explain that she was his oldest sister and that while she had married and changed her name, she had chosen to keep a listing in directory just in case Jack ever came looking for her. And here we were nearly twenty years later and her maiden name in directory assistance had paid off. She continued to cry throughout our 30 minute conversation. I started to explain to her that Jack had been diagnosed with a rare blood disorder and she immediately interrupted me and said, "Aplastic anemia?" I was shocked. She went on to explain that their sister, Renee, who now lived in Louisiana, had been diagnosed with the same thing and had been told she had a rare genetic disorder. She told me that all the siblings had already been typed for bone marrow transplant. Renee had been found to be a match with their oldest brother who lived in Phoenix, Arizona but that he was now refusing to donate the necessary bone marrow for her to receive the life saving transplant. Renee had been living on transfusions for over a year now. She went on to provide me with the name and number of Renee's doctor so I could get access to the bone marrow typing and see if Jack had a match. "Tell Jack I love him." She said between sobs as we said our goodbyes.

Jack's eyes welled up and tears flowed down his cheeks as I gave him the news. I again called the VA operator and asked to be connected to the number I had found in directory assistance. I cried too as I watched two siblings that hadn't spoke in twenty years reunite. Jack cried through the entire conversation and his cries turned to sobs and thank yous when he hung up the phone.

I contacted Renee's doctor and obtained the necessary records to see if Jack had a match in his sibling's pool of bone marrow typing. Jack and I celebrated as we received the news that his brother in California was a match and I sat at his bedside as he called him and asked him to give the life saving gift of a bone marrow donation. Things moved quickly after that. Jack was transferred to the University Hospital and into the care of oncologists that specialized in bone marrow transplantation. His brother flew in from California and, at least for Jack, the prospects of a new life were looking up.

I couldn't sleep. I couldn't get Renee out of my mind. Though I had many of my colleagues tell me to leave it alone, I could not. Renee had a match and that match was only two hours away from me. I talked many times to the sister in Milwaukee and she told me I was welcome to try but that she was quite sure it was a lost cause. The oldest of five siblings had made it clear that he was not willing to donate the bone marrow necessary to save Renee's life. She gave me her brother's phone number in Phoenix and we hung up the phone. With my husband's encouragement I muster the courage to make the call and make one final appeal on Renee's behalf. Again I got an answering machine. I identified myself and asked for a return call that never came. A week passed and I was still restless. I could not swallow the idea that anyone, let alone a sibling, would just stand by and watch another die when they and they alone could save them. My husband, also a physician, would be in Phoenix for the upcoming weekend and after much conversation agreed to step into what had become my own personal drama and to attempt to pay a personal visit to the eldest brother.

My husband found him. Made his appeal and tried his hardest to make the oldest brother understand that Renee would really die without his help. Andrew left his house, having had completed my agenda, but without a feeling one way or another whether the visit had done any good. He did leave my pager and our home phone number and we were in a wait and see mode. Nothing. The prayed for phone call never came. My heart ached for this family that was so overjoyed to be re-united and yet so devastated with Renee's rapidly worsening status and their brother's refusal to help. Again, I picked up the phone and dialed the Phoenix number. This time a person answered. It was a woman who identified herself as the brother's girlfriend. I talked with her for 20 minutes and tried as hard as I could to explain the disease of aplastic anemia and why a bone marrow transplant is the only chance these patients have for survival. I explained that her boyfriend was Renee's only chance. I explained that Renee had been on transfusion support for over a year and that she couldn't wait much longer. The conversation ended with the woman promising me that she would communicate my words to her boyfriend, Renee's brother and only bone marrow match. I gave her all of my contact information and told her to call day or night.

Three days later I received a phone call from this same woman. I never knew her name. She said that her boyfriend had said that he would do it if he could donate in Tucson and I handled the procedure. Goosebumps went up my back and down my arms and tears welled in my eyes. I ran as fast as I could to the bone marrow transplant unit to tell Jack and his other brother, who had stayed by Jack's side throughout his bone marrow transplant ordeal. Tears flowed and they were overwhelmed with pure, honest joy.

Before I could call the sister in Milwaukee, she called me. Renee had just died. Renee had just died waiting on a bone marrow transplant from her brother. I called the woman in Phoenix and that was all I said to her. I said, "Renee has just died. Renee has just died waiting on a bone marrow donation from her brother."

Renee was gone. Jack did well, however, and had recently been discharged from the hospital after a 4 week stay while he waited for his brother's bone marrow to grow inside him and re-populate his blood cells. Several months past by before I saw Jack again. He was a great letter writer though and I loved my letters from Jack. I always pictured that sweet little happy smile as I read them. I also received many cards and letters from the rest of Jack's family including two from Renee's husband.

One afternoon, several months later, I arrived at the VA hospital oncology clinic to a beautiful surprise. Jack, Jack J_____

ski. He looked so wonderful and so happy. In front of the entire oncology clinic he presented me with a letter from the Chief of the VA hospital commending my actions to help Jack and Renee. He also gave me a plaque that still hangs in my office, it reads:

To
Leslie Ann Sibley, M.D.
On This Date
August 10th, 2000
Is Awarded The
Oncologist
Of The Century Award
On Behalf of the entire
J_____ski Family. Not only for the
Care and Kindness you gave to Jack,
But also for going Above and Beyond
The Call of Duty of a Doctor
On Behalf of Renee
And the rest of our Family.
As of this date
You and Your Family shall always be
Honorary J_____ski's.

All I did was make a single phone call to directory assistance, but that was all it took to make a difference.

Just do it. Just say it. If you care, say something, do something, anything...

Let's take it a step further and honestly look at what people are in our lives. Our interactions with others are purposeful, but the purposes, intentional or not, conscious or not, are seldom pure. Seldom do we have interactions that are pure and for the purpose of letting someone know us and seeking to know them, of letting them into the story we are writing with our lives and reaching out to become a small part of their story. It is time to get rigorously honest and look closely at our relationships and at our interactions with others and see, maybe for the first time, what truly motivates and drives them. Are we users? Are we suckers? Are we parasites? Are we stranglers? Are we collectors? Are we rescuers? Are we whores? Are we snipers? Are we gloaters? Are we maleficent? The answer is a resounding yes to all. You want rigorously honest? People our relationships are a mess!!!

Somewhere, at some point, we have lost the art of connecting with "others". Our relationships with "others" have become pragmatic, utilitarian, a means to an end. Our relationships today are frankly, openly and matter-of-factly useful. Our connections with "others" have become purely and plainly and disgustingly self-serving. We use people to get something we want....power, status, a step up the ladder, affection, a ticket in the door, love, sex, stuff, attention, self-esteem, chutzpah, hubris, pride, comfort, security, control..... our connections with people serve a purpose. They are people we encounter and are friendly to because they make us feel privileged, entitled. We smile, shake hands, toss an extra buck their way and gloat privately to ourselves or openly to those we are seeking to impress. And those we are seeking to impress have something we want as well. A promotion, a raise, connections to "others" who also have something we want, a sexual encounter or whatever. More often than not the "what we want" is a stroke of some kind for that ever fragile ego and its constant companion insatiable pride.

The new Deity has quite simply become the ever-present, ever-cunning cowardly ego. We have sacrificed loving, connections on a me, me, me altar, we have burned compassion at the stake. And when what we wanted proves to not to be what we needed, when what we wanted quits working, we are left desolate, isolated and disconnected... alone in our angst, alone in our anguish, alone in the facticity of our failure, alone in the facticity of our aloneness, our individualness. This aloneness has a yearning attached to it, a wish, a want, a hunger, a desire, an urge, a thirst for a connection with something, someone. This aloneness is sad, dark and unsettling. This aloneness is an uncomfortable, self-conscious feeling, a feeling that there is something missing, something absent. This aloneness wants something, anything, anybody, somebody to fix the *fisher king wound,* the torn-to pieces-hood. This aloneness wants something to fill the hole, something to make us whole. "Others" make us whole and connect us to the whole of humanity and to the Ultimate Whole. "Others" make the pain of our individual aloneness tolerable. Ultimately I think it comes down to the one thing that sums up all of the frailties of mankind: fear. The "Seven Deadlies", envy, lust, sloth, gluttony, greed, anger and pride, can be summed up in this one word.

Fear, fear that we will lose something that we have or won't get something we want. Grrrr! Fear screws up our relationships in a major league way It all goes back to the first law of economics "sufficient allocation of a scarce resource for unlimited wants". We all want the good stuff and we are full of fear that we will lose it or not get it. The absolute uncanny fact in all of this is that the good stuff we claim to want isn't even the good stuff. It is merely that stuff that will keep us from having to face our deepest most basic fears And we continue to go along with the socially sanctioned "good stuff" idea because it is less scary and less painful than owning our truth...we are scared. So we cling to the "good stuff" that we know is nothing more than a vaporous mass that we will never be able to grab onto and hold. And we will continue to allow ourselves to be herded with the masses until the pain of the circumstances we find ourselves in hurts more than the pain of facing our fears. And when that circumstance presents itself we will find our own way into ourselves (we will write our stories) and find our way back out (we tell our stories). It is there that we will find the courage to change the only thing we can change...ourselves.

Enough barking about our darker nature, the real question is what are we actually afraid of? When we take everyday human fear, that fear that is experienced by the common man on a daily basis, that fear that Viktor Frankyl would call the fear of the "man on the street" and break it down what do we find? Usually basic human fears like fear of abandonment, fear that we won't be accepted, fear of not being good enough, fear of being alone, fear of humiliation, fear of being exposed for who we really are deep down inside, fear of financial insecurity.

Outside & Insides

We all have two beings, the one that is subjective, private and intuitive, the inner self known only to the self and the objective, outside, intentional self. The self we "put on" for "others" to see, the self we are willing to expose to the outside world, the person that we pretend to be for them, the person that still puts on masks to protect what is real. It is this outside person that has learned to cope, to handle life's problems, to fight the fight. Somewhere this outside self took on the role of protector, he (pardon the gender) assimilated all of the roles given to us by our families and society, learned the lessons that our instincts had to teach, memorized all of the should and should nots, remembered all of the danger signals and has perfected the behaviors and protected us and he has now put on the armor necessary to forge out into this cruel, cruel world weapons in hands. At some point he recognized that life was hard and became the defender of the self safely buried far down inside our beings. A noble task indeed! But just as a child that is smothered and coddled and over protected becomes unable to step out as a responsible adult, the subjective self becomes meek, quiet, hidden and impotent. The inner self becomes disoriented and conditioned and eventually cannot tell the true from the false. So often we will hear someone say, "I don't even know who I am anymore." This is why.

The honest and true self has been shut off for so long that we have to dig down, find it and become reacquainted with it. That is exactly what we have been doing in the dissecting of our stories and the trudging through to the *bottom of our daemons*. We've been getting to know that inner self that has been extinguished by the ego who has been dealing with the pressures of life in "survival mode". This self however cannot come to be in a vacuum. It has to interact with "others" and at the same time stand strong as a first person singular. As we proceed to the telling of our stories and address our fears, resentments, sexuality and feelings we start the process of making our outsides match our insides. We begin to mend the "Fisher King wound". Thus is the art and the lesson of storytelling. We come to know the self and then we reconcile all that has developed to cover the self. As we stand on the bridge of now, and see this place for the first time, we will strive moment by present moment to match our outsides with our insides. We heal.

Connecting

The self, that we all are beneath it all, needs to connect with "others" as they are integral to our lives in the real world and they are integral to our continuing to become. When I find my self in another's story or another finds part of their self in my story we not only connect but we connect in love. We connect in love not because of our strengths and our mutual wonderfulness, we connect in love because of our weaknesses, our flaws, our imperfections...our humanness. We can be admired for our beauty but we are respected for our realness. By telling our stories to one another we do not find that we are these glorious beings "worthy" of love but rather, we find that we are these wretched beings that are indeed lovable. If we are to be measured by our deeds or the pureness of our hearts none of us are worthy of love. It is in Divine Perfection then that love is so deeply ingrained in our very essence as human beings that we are capable of loving ourselves and others despite our inadequacies. We love significant others because of what is lovable in them and if we can do this then surely we are capable of finding a love strong enough and broad enough to find something loveable in each "other". There is something lovely and indeed glorious in every face we meet.

When we find in our cores the capacity to love in this way then our need for "others" persists, but now the aid they give to us does not come in the form of something we want from them but rather in what we can learn from them and what we can experience as lovable in them. Our eyes need to simply pivot from a life of demanding to be satisfied, a life seeking the enchantment of admiration, a life running about in efforts to shower ourselves in the glee of getting. The eyes of the self are charged with the duty of re-focusing on that which has value, that which endures, that which gives back the richest and most cherished of treasures. Eyes that have pivoted enough to alas apprehend that the good stuff is not good stuff at all...for "it cannot feel when you are near". The connections we make need to become fluid interactions of "you tell me your story and I will tell you mine". They must become more than connection, this connection must indeed turn into community. Into a community that exists where there is now "us" and there is not them because the community is one of humanity...it is a whole community and a community of the Whole. In other words, we learn from each "others" experience, strength and hope. When the inner self surfaces, Love thy neighbor as thyself becomes manifest and becomes the Ultimate ideal.

What would our "community" look like?

If you could fit the entire population of the world into a village consisting of 100 people, maintaining the proportions of all the people living on Earth, that village would consist of:

> *57 Asians*
> *21 Europeans*
> *14 Americans(North, Central and South)*
> *8 Africans*

There would be:

> *52 women and 48 men*
> *30 Caucasians and 70 non-caucasians*
> *30 Christians and 70 no-Christians*
> *89 heterosexuals and 11 homosexuals*
> *6 people would possess 59% of the wealth (all from the USA)*
> *80 would live in poverty*
> *70 would be illiterate*
> *50 would suffer from hunger and malnutrition*
> *1 would be dying*
> *1 would be being born*
> *1 would own a computer*
> *1 (yes, only one) would have a college degree*

If we looked at the world in this way, the need for acceptance and understanding would be obvious. But consider again the following:

If you woke up this morning in good health, you have more luck than one million people who won't live through the week.

If you have never experienced the horror of war, the solitude of prison, the pain of torture, were not close to death from starvation, then you are better off than 500 million people.

If you can go to your place of worship without fear that someone will assault or kill you, then you are luckier than 3 billion (that's right) people.

If you have a full fridge, clothes on your back, a roof over your head and a place to sleep, you are wealthier than 75% of the world's population.

If you currently have money in the bank, in your wallet and a few coins in your purse, you are one of the 8 privileged few amongst the 100 people in the world.

If you are reading this you are extremely lucky because you don't comprise one of those 2 billion people who can't read.[36]

Although never reachable, this ideal remains pure and relationships become give and take and give again. "Others" become a source of nourishment to us and us to them. Being connected in an intricate web of "others" allows my self to break through and remain. My self on the surface is what will en-courage "others" to allow their self to rise up. "Others", in other words, are what help me remain real. The forces that drove the self down and that the persona vigorously protected remain, family, society, employers, churches, government, intimates… They all tempt the persona to jump in and react in the traditional expected ways. Like-minded "others" teach us to pause, to act rather than react, to own our center and to possess our values. In simple language, like-minded "others", that we have invited into our stories and whose stories that we have entered, call us on our slip ups, our lapses in rational, real, true, centered behavior. They call us on our idiocies, irrationalities, inconsistencies, ridiculousness, senselessness, silliness and stupidity; and they love us in spite of these.

Trusted "others" refuse to co-sign our bullshit. They point out the "red flags", the warning signs that we are about to screw up with old behaviors, that do a disservice to the honest, true and pure self. All that we have learned to this point is for naught without "others" to help us. Escaping expected roles, thwarting social norms and expected behaviors, addressing instincts that attempt to run rampant, coming to believe, becoming willing, allowing feelings…blah, blah, blah… is great in theory but cannot become a "way of life" without the assistance of "others". "Others" make the self possible and the self made possible will change the way we connect to "others".

A "red flag" story---

There is this guy I now that I know that is what I call a TSF (top secret friend). He is one of those "Others" that is invited to call me on my bullshit and I am in turn am invited to call him on his. He is recently out of a long term relationship and determined to proceed with his life in a healthy, self-aware fashion. He is back in the market looking for a healthy gal to have a relationship with and the search goes something like this...

Guy: "Hey I met a really cute gal at work today. She is short and thin and perky with dark brown hair and big blue eyes. She is married though."
Response: "Red Flag"
Guy: "I went to dinner with a really nice lady last night. She doesn't drink or do drugs. She is new in recovery from pills. She sent me a text saying, 'I like the way that you are sexy without being cocky'.
Response: "Red Flag"
Guy: "I had coffee with a younger woman yesterday. She knows my daughter. She kinda talks in the same lingo that my daughter does."
Response: "Red Flag"
Guy: "I've been thinking that maybe I need to stop sleeping with married women"
Response: "Red Flag""Red Flag" "Red Flag""Dude we need to talk"
Guy: "She just showed up at my front door one night."
Response: "Red Flag"

What he hears from me is not always much saner...

Response: "Remember my crazy nanny? She was really helpful, I was thinking maybe she'd be okay if she didn't live with us?"
Guy: "Red Flag"
Response: "Had football practice yesterday, my S.O. said I was 'socializing too much'. "
Guy: "Red Flag"
Response: "He wants to get married but not live together."
Guy: "Red Flag"
Response: "Yeah, I told him I had work this weekend, and he said, 'That is self-centered' you can't even give me half the weekend'."
Guy: "Red Flag"

Trusting

When it comes right down to it, to love someone is to deep down inside desire someone. To love someone is to desire to be loved in return. Soren Kierkegaard writes in *The Works of Love* "How *deeply* the need for love is grounded in the nature of Man!" He then goes on to describe this as the very first observation, the observation made by God when He stated, "It is not good that man be alone." "The woman was taken from man's side and given to him for community—for love and companionship first take something from a man before they give."

This is indeed a tough nut to swallow in this day and age of "what have you done for me lately". Maybe that is why God gave us desire. He knew that we were just selfish enough and just skeptical enough to never want to give first, to give on the gamble that we might not get something in return. Desire to be closer to another, either as a lover or a friend, gets us started.

As we have rolled through this life we have learned that when we give love, compassion and caring we usually get it back. Unfortunately, we have also learned that we risk getting burned, we risk getting bit, we risk getting heart broke. In a nutshell, we risk getting hurt. So many of us are snake bit in love that the idea of even reaching out in friendship and brotherly love comes with apprehension, distrust, hesitancy, leeriness and reluctance. This is why the whole idea of burrowing down in to the depths of our stories, facing our daemons, righting, as much as we could, our wrongs, patching up the wreckage of the past, addressing our short comings and coming to believe and trust is so difficult. What we have learned, however, is that despite the noble gesture by the ego to protect the inner self from the ravages of reality, the self is the voice that will not be silenced. What is real and right within us will demand our attention. This is the longing, the torn-to-pieces-hood, the hole that hungers.

To take this new found self and reach out to another is a frightening move, however, the pain of not doing so is worse. The *choice* to not trust enough to take that step leaves us in a make believe world, where we put on costumes and play the part and allow our stories to be written by the rush of the passing days. This passive gesture to not trust allows the world to author the remainder of our stories. We consent to continue living in a state of fancy or pretend and ultimately we find that this masquerading is just a way to perpetuate the lie.

So in uncovering the self, by digging to the *bottom of our daemons* and coming to the awareness that belief in something, anything, Bigger than ourselves, we come to the undeniable, incontrovertible, binding truth that the solution to the hole, to the *fisher king wound*, is self forgetting. To fill the emptiness, to find purpose, to discover meaning comes by getting right with my self, getting right with my God and getting right with "others".

Before we can find the connection, the community, that before we were ever even a twinkling, God saw as necessary for humankind to exist and perpetuate, we are directed to do these three things. Get right with our selfs, our God and our "others". In the preceding chapters we have sought to uncover the self and to uncover a faith in something Larger than the self, now we must get right with "others" from the past, from the present and to remodel our approach to "others" going forward into the future.

The "Glitter Ball" metaphor...

I have a friend who describes this damage done to relationships over time in a metaphor that I like. It goes something like this...

Each relationship is an elegant crystal ball covered exquisitely in glitter that spins above the relationship for eternity. And our goal as members of the human race, as individual selfs and as partners in this relationship is to take care of this ball and keep it as pristine as the day it was hung above this new found union. However, every time there is turbulence in the relationship a little bit of glitter falls off the ball. When there are major outs in the relationship a lot of glitter falls off the ball. The key here is that this is a magic ball. It is a magic crystal that when filled with love can pull the glitter from the ground below it, suspend it in air and draw it back when amends are made, wrongs are righted and the relationship is repaired. This pull of the glitter from the floor below can at times be so powerful, so fueled by brotherly love that more glitter is pulled back than what actually fell leaving the relationship stronger than it was before. Thus is the power in amends. Thus is the fragility of relationships. The choice is always ours to step forth in brotherly love and attempt to replace the glitter or to let the glitter continue to fall and to leave the glitter on the floor and watch the ball, that will always be there even when the relationship has completely dissolved, grow barren and tarnished.

Before stepping forward into developing and growing and fostering better relationships it is best to repair the existing ones and, in straight forward good old fashion American lingo this is how you do it: make a list of the people that you have a resentment toward, decipher what it was that each particular instant threatened for you and then determine what in this interaction was your part. Oh yeah, we did this before… chapter 7. Hang with me…just for a quick two paragraph review!

Relationships and resentments have one thing in common— they both take two people and we, as adults, always have a part. I must add that children and victims of crime do not share in this always having a part and some of us have resentments and bitterness that will have to be resolved between us and our Higher

Power. However, in typical everyday human disputes both parties play a part. For me, my part in many of my resentments was that I allowed it to happen. There was never a consequence for hurting Leslie so treating her poorly was easy and without issue and that was my part. There was no aftermath for hurting Leslie but Leslie was the one left with the resentment and Leslie was the one who needed to look at herself with brutal honesty and decide why, decide what was threatened in me. Usually it was my fear of insecurity, fear of being abandoned if I had an opinion or fear of feeling stupid, humiliation that left me silent. Every resentment has this sort of a triad. What happened, what did it threaten (yep, we are back at one of those basic fears again) and what was my part.

Relationships are hard, but people remain and they remain essential and as we will come to see it is in them that we experience our part in the Greater Whole. Next, share our list with God and another human being. Choose a trusted confidant, a mentor, a member of the clergy...oh heck send me an anonymous email...just share it with someone. Finally, make amends wherever possible. And by wherever possible I mean unless this would cause harm to you or someone else. For example, if you slept with a married man and are resentful because he didn't tell you he was married or that he didn't leave his wife for you, it is unwise to try to make amends by telling his wife that you are sorry you slept with her husband. That would cause harm and you have no business approaching either one. First of all do no harm. Amends means saying I'm sorry, saying where I was wrong and leaving it alone. It doesn't mean that your honest attempt to reconcile a wrong will be accepted or met with reciprocity. It just means that you have done what you can to clean up your side of the street. Amends are made for ourselves. They are made to acknowledge our wrongs so that they are simply part of our story and are not baggage that we carry with us. The wrong and the amends both become part of our story. And we move on carrying a load that is a little bit lighter than it was before. Doesn't sound fun does it? Just do it. It is not easy but it is simple and it is what allows us to march on to a new way of life, a new way of interacting with "others" and to that spot that repairs the torn-to-pieces-hood that defines we humans that build up baggage throughout our lives and then die under a heap of rubbish that we chose not to clean up. Just do it, put the glitter back on the ball, it promises you a life of possibilities beyond your wildest dreams. Wow, two paragraphs full of tough, callous but unalterable demands. Unless one chooses to become a monk on a mountain or to find a cave and endure alone, relationships are life. The damage must be repaired before the connection can grow into something better.

Loving

So where do we go from here? We have worked to get right with our selfs, our God and our "others" and it is time to proceed on to something new and better and that means we are going to talk about love. Pure, unadulterated brotherly love. Again I quote Soren Kierkegaard, "So deeply is love grounded in the nature of man, so essentially does it belong to man...".

When I think of love I am attempted to call it a "gift" like humility and forgiveness, I am tempted to treat it as something vaporous and ethereal that we are given when we are ready much like the above and I guess I would include serenity and gratitude on the list. But love is more than this, it precedes these. As Kierkegaard says we are grounded in it. Is it an instinct? No, I think not, I think it was there before our instincts. It preceded them as well. It is something that is at the very core of mankind and for me Frankyl came the closest when he described the spiritual core of man, a spiritual core that is made up of moral conscience, love and artistic creativity.[37] It is these three that come from the intuitive spiritual core of mankind. They come with the very essence of man and differ from the instincts in that they are different and unique to each being. The instincts are constant across the human race whereas the spiritual intuitions are unique to each person. We love different things, with value different things, what one person sees as right might be wrong to another and artistically we all create differently. When the true artist does create however it is an intuitive process, that is, it comes from the spiritual core.

Yikes! Let's dumb it down and say that love is woven into our very fiber just as conscience is woven into our very fiber, and from those, who we are and who we are to become is built. What we have done up to this point is clear the foundation of the debris so as we go forward we can complete the story of our lives consciously and conscientiously, sweeping up the rubble we create (and we will) as we go, owning what we value, trusting in a Power greater than ourselves, feeling our emotions, allowing our entire being to participate in life and yes loving, not only those that we find lovable, but rather loving in a way that finds something lovable in every face we meet.

We all love with the desire to be loved back. The beloved that is the object of our affection, is loved with the deep rooted longing to be loved in return. I suppose the love a parent has for a child is the closest we human beings can get to loving unconditionally, but even there when we dig deep, we fall short. We want our children to love us in return. Only that Supreme Being can truly love unconditionally. That is why the *'as thyself'* at the end of the second commandment is such a tall order. Even so, we need to consider the fact of our desire to be loved closely and to take to heart that "others" have this desire as well. We all do. The Gospel of John demonstrates that even Jesus, The Holy One manifest in flesh and blood and living as a human being had the yearning to hear that he was loved when he asks, "Simon, son of John, do you love me?"

There is indeed nothing more sustaining than the renewed assurance that we are loved in return. In other words, if you love, if you care, if you feel sorrow for, if you ache with, if share in their joy, if you are proud of, if you understand the "other"....communicate it. Whisper it, shout it, proclaim it, explain it, mention it, show it. With a word, with a gesture, with a nod, with a touch, with a look...Aaaahhhh! Just say it!! Lord almighty, tell them!!! Say it in whatever manner you chose, just let it be manifest in your being. Let it be known.

Love communicated never stops at the "other", it sprouts and grows and breeds and pervades beyond itself. There is no greater travesty than, when love in which ever form it is experienced, is not shared. When we communicate our love in one way or another we are touching the soul of another and we are giving them an ineffable, enduring gift. We are creating a community with another that is fertilized and ready to grow. We are saying that together we are, in point of fact, more whole and indubitably part of the greater Whole.

12

The Story

So what is the point to all of this? I think the point was made best by Viktor E. Frankyl, a survivor of the Nazi death camps, when he said, and I paraphrase, that the most human of all human phenomena is the "will to meaning" That is to say, that deep down, at the bottom of our daemons, in the depths of our beings and the heights of our spirits we human beings have built in a need for meaning and purpose in our lives. And we spend our lives searching for that meaning. Studies of college student in the 21st century reveal over and over again that young adults list a need for meaning as their primary objective in their future careers. 60% of US college students report having an "abyss experience". And that "abyss experience" was related with the desire to find meaning in life. Frankyl goes on to describe what he calls the "existential vacuum", a feeling of emptiness, a sense of meaninglessness…a spiritual distress.[38] This is a Fisher King wound. So how do we proceed with the tools we have learned and build a life with meaning? Number one we realize that the past is behind us and simply is. It is not changeable, it is not negotiable and it is without potential or possibility. If I were to die today, at this instant, my past would, in a twinkling, become the sum of what I was here on earth. My story would be concluded, my destiny set in stone, my past would be me.

Leslie Masters, MD

My past is me…

I am dead. There are no further future possibilities. There is no more story to write. My past is me.

For me the unsettling thing about my past being me is that as I look back over it I feel as if it happened to me. I sort of don't remember choosing. I feel like so often I fell into the rank and file, I ran with the herd, I did what good girls did, I over achieved because someone called that good, I married when it seemed like the time to get married, I became the 21ˢᵗ century woman and did the mad, insane, preposterous thing of becoming a wife, a mother, a doctor and pretended to have it all together because it was the "in" thing to do, I buried myself in my duties (or more accurately my duties buried me) and just shuffled along doing what I was supposed to do, when life became utterly meaningless I turned to pills to take all of the sharp edges off the world around me. If everything was dulled a bit it was more tolerable. I became wrapped by a world of expectations and I didn't even know who exactly was doing the expecting. I just knew that I kept doing what someone expected of me until I was left with the choice of going mad or dulling my world. I had pain, I had children, I had dying patients, I had bosses, I had a husband, I had an ex-husband holding my daughter hostage and all of the "I hads" made the pain that I had so much worse. I whirled and raced and spun and took pills and the pain got worse and worse and worse and I was in a fog and there was no way out. It felt as if any bump in the routine and it would all fall apart. If I got sick or hurt all of these balls that I was juggling would come tumbling down to certain disaster. As life would have it, and the truth people, is that very often life does have its way with us, I was given a second chance (and if I am being completely honest, it was more accurately my ten thousandth chance). Life came to a screeching halt at The Betty Ford Center but that was only the screeching halt. I had a long way to go before I could see sunlight again. For me, that sunlight came in the faces of hundreds of alcoholics and addicts, some skid-row others far from it. My sunlight found its way shining through smoke-filled rooms, filled with stale coffee, hard chairs and big blue books. It is there that

250

I connected with people who showed me how to get right with my self, my God and my "others". It was there I learned to let go and not have to run the world, where I learned that the only thing I controlled was my actions and my reactions, where I learned that other people had a right to make their own decisions and that my acrimony was just that, mine. It was there that I dared to take that sometimes modest and sometimes not so modest leap of Faith in to the arms of an unperceivable God that I believed in down to the depths of my being but had not trusted in a long, long time. It was there that I learned to pause just long enough to become the author of my story again.

Freedom

Well, I am not dead nor am I helpless nor am I all powerful. I am the self uncovered from digging down to the bottom of my daemons. What I do have is what we all, as members of the human race, have freedom. No matter what the circumstance, we have a *choice* of how we are going to handle it. Now this is far from saying that we have unlimited choices, it is simply stating the fact that we are free. Even in the most dire of situations we have a *choice*. The tortured can chose to scream out or remain silent, the torturer can choose whether to inflict pain or to abstain. In every deed we perform, word we say, movement we make, in every action we take or don't take we make a *choice*. We and we alone make that *choice* and ultimately we make that *choice* alone. Sartre calls it being 'condemned to freedom'. The only thing we do not have a *choice* in is in choosing whether or not to be free. In this we have no *choice*, we are 'condemned to be free'. And herein lays the major difference between the past and the future. God made man to travel in fast-forward only, we cannot go backward and be free and make *choices*. The past is without possibilities. It is. We as humans, along with our inalienable freedom, are free only in the moments that lie ahead of us. The past has been lived and is, the present is that shadowy fraction of a fraction of a fraction of an instant between what was and what might be and the future is each moment just before it passes into the shadow of an instant. Freedom, *choice*, possibility and ultimately meaning are in front of us.

The quite uncanny thing is this, from the moment when we are able to make cognizant *choices* (and I am going to leave the "when" of that statement alone as I can smell one of those "when does life begin" debates coming) we struggle and strive to give away the freedom that we cannot escape. How do we give away our freedom? We give it away little by little as we go through life and add layer upon layer to the persona that we display to the outside world. Over time we succumb to the shoulds and oughts that family, intimates, society and the times we live in put on us. We give it away when instincts go awry and we become runners, fighters or hiders. We give it away when we begin to "use" things to make ourselves feel better be that money, sex, power, prestige, gambling, spending, drugs or even eating. We give it away every time we put on a mask and assume a role contrary to the self. We give it away when we cease Believing and become slave to our fears. We give it away when we begin feeling too much or too little, we give it away when we quit listening to the voices of intuition and the sounds of serendipity. We give it away when we become the hostages of "others" because of resentments that we cannot let go. We give it away every time we withhold love in a "what is in it for me" mentality. A look back at the story that I don't think I authored tells me that I have for most of my story, attempted to give away my freedom.

For some of us giving away freedom is more like an abdication of power and we bow to the wants and needs of other people or things and gradually allow them to become our Higher Power whether it be a lover, a career, a parent, an image, a boss, a spouse or an alliance with a particular party or social (not necessarily socially acceptable) group. And, obviously, there are those who are only too happy to pick up that power, that freedom and have their every want and need bowed too. Ah yes, the controllers, they too give away freedom. Is not the opposite of free, control? And indeed it is. Taken a step further, the opposite of freedom is fear which is what controllers live in...the fear that if people, places and things are not just so they will lose something they have or not get something they want. For some this can be as elemental as if my house is not just so I will lose my peace of mind. Controllers are more like traders than abdicators, they have traded their freedom for fear and the controlling is simply a last ditch, frantic attempt to abate the fear. The biggest danger comes when they are so in need of answer to the question, "what is going to happen" that they quit trying. Then at least they have my answer. Sadly their need to control has extinguished the possibility that rests in freedom. Controllers are not free, they are prisoners of their fears.

So why all this talk about freedom? Because it is there that after we have told our stories, after we have sorted through all that we have become as a result of the roles that we have assumed and the lives we have lived thus far that the self emerges. The self emerges not in the fact of freedom but rather in the consciousness of freedom. And here we must distinguish freedom from power. We are free to make or not make a *choice* in every situation, but we do not have the power to pick every situation. We only have the freedom to *choose* in the situations before us. But that is a huge freedom. The scary part about freedom comes in another fact that we as humans cannot escape, the fact that we are also responsible for our decisions. Freedom is liberating. (Which is a lot like saying 2=2, but I am going to leave it.) The consciousness of the fact that we are indeed free within our given circumstance is an emancipation of sorts. This whole responsibility thing sort of puts the kabosh on the liberation however, and herein lays the angst and the anguish of the human condition. We are free to make decisions and each person has, in the first person singular, the freedom to *choose* how they will act or react but each person also, in the first person singular is responsible for their decisions. The weight of this responsibility is why we continually (and we all do it) give away our freedom. We give it away to escape the responsibility that comes with that freedom. Argh!!!

Change

Change is hard and the kind of change we are talking about here does not come without action. The change begins with telling another human being our stories, and I mean our whole stories not just the biographical high points. What we each need to do to bring about a transformation from incompleteness to wholeness to Wholeness is to begin by telling another human being our stories, our dauntless, searching and uncompromisingly honest stories. It is there that we come face to face with our instincts gone awry, where we catch a glimpse of how our fears have directed our lives and harnessed our choices. In our stories we find and sort through all that has occurred in our time here on earth and how it has gradually enveloped the self and turned us in to our personas, how we have gently, and usually unconsciously become our outsides keeping the self protected and keeping the self unknown not only to "others" but also to ourselves. And there, at the bottom of our stories is where we find our freedom, our freedom to chose what we believe in, what we value, what we stand for, what we are passionate about and what we will not tolerate. It is there that we discover that we are part of something much Bigger, and where we each, as first person singular individuals, come to believe in a Power greater than ourselves. Having found a new freedom and a person we had lost and a Being that is bigger than we, we become willing to step forward in faith and trust and into a world owning our own spirituality, our own feelings, our own bodies, our own sensuality and our own sexuality… our own beings. Knowing that this newly revealed self is fragile but strong we begin the process of cleaning up our side of the street. We continue to face our freshly exposed fears, we begin to believe in our intuitions and to trust serendipity, we begin to place confidence in the voice from within and to place value in the power of trusted "others". We shed our resentments by recognizing our part in every interaction and by making amends wherever possible. We step forward confessing the fact that we cannot will the world to our standards, confessing that we cannot change "others", accepting that we are responsible in our freedom to change the things we can and that a Strength larger than us will be there to give us the wisdom to discern the difference.

In the end there holds a truth, "we are not free to cease being free". At the bottom of our daemons is where we find the self, the spiritual core, the stuff that is a part of our very essence. There we are given love, a conscience and artistic intuition. It is there in the unique spiritual core of each person, that one finds what one values. And therein lies the question that each of us must ask ourselves. What do I value, what is important to me, in what lays my passion, for me, what really matters, in what can I find meaning? How do I want my story to play out? What kind or person do I want to be? How can I make a difference? What would I like to leave behind? How do I want my story to read? Each of us has a "good", a way being that we aspire to, whether we value sincerity, generosity, charity or whatever. Now I am not talking about a way of "acting" because we think that will make us "good" but rather a way of being because it is a value woven into our every fiber. It may be something that in our lives before now we have never emulated but it has remained deep within as a way, that to us as first person singulars, holds great esteem as a mode of being, as a thread that makes up the tapestry of the self that continues to be a being becoming.

As we live moment by moment, day by day the tapestry of our lives continues to be woven and our freedom and our *choices* directs each thread in what direction we want it to go and guides the weaving of the picture that will become, in the very end, our lives as we chose to live them on this earth. As the weaving proceeds, our self is manifest as we, each of us alone in this world, would have it be. We take our hits in life and the world continues to turn and although we are *selfs* with our bodies, we are also bodies within this world and in this world we must live and interact and partake. And so we come full circle...

It may be hard for an egg to turn into a bird: it would be a jolly sight harder for it to learn to fly while remaining an egg. We are like eggs at present. And you cannot go on indefinitely being just an ordinary, decent egg. We must be hatched or go bad.

C. S. Lewis

Authoring The Story

It is time people that we hatch and go out into this beautiful world. No matter what the past holds the possibility in the future is greater. No matter how severe the wreckage, no matter the situation we find ourselves in now, no matter the pain, the hurt, the injuries or the scars that we bare, we can soar. The possibility is there. Broken wings can heal, clipped wings can grow again, stifled eggs can hatch and when they do, it is this world, this time and this situation that they must live in. As life goes on (and it will) we step forward and are faced daily with life, but the face that life sees has changed. It sees a new being, a being that is true to its own passions and its own standards and its own beliefs. It sees a being that is comfortable in the skin that surrounds it, a being that is not more than or less than, a being that knows where it fits in the whole and in the Whole. The world sees a being becoming and a being that beams from the gifts of humility, forgiveness, a being that resonates in a place of peace and comfort knowing that it is imperfect and flawed and cracked and broken and above all forgiven, a being that is strong and steadfast but one that must face the trials of life and will make mistakes and hide from freedom and carry burdens that are not theirs to carry. And in all of its brokenness this being will be growing and evolving and falling and getting up and making messes of life and cleaning them up and reaching out to "others" to help and for help all the while becoming something better than it was the day before. We find a being that no longer whirls with the dervishes but steps aside a lets them whirl. The craziness and chaos goes on but the joining in is now optional. And at times we will jump in and spin but with tools laid at our feet we know how to get out rather than getting caught in. We have dropped the baggage and made reparation and although we will undoubtedly pick up that baggage from time to time, in a moment of pause, in a quiet inner space will remember once again to set it back down. We will realize that it is no longer a load we must hump with us through life. The only thing that 'is' is the past and once settlement has been made it must be filed away in the past, lessons learned, wisdom gained and regrets released, and left there as a small part of the story we call our lives. That which is ahead is our chance to get it right, to author consciously this part of our stories, to dance even if there is someone else watching, but to know that if indeed someone is watching our dance will change them.

A Call To Action...

> *"Mom, please come. I feel like I'm dying," I wept into the phone*

at my bedside. "They don't know what is wrong with me and I have lost so much weight and I can't eat. I feel like I'm dying." "I'm on my way Baby. I will be there tomorrow." She would need to fly from across the country, but she was on her way and at that moment, that was all I needed to know. I knew she would be traveling on her birthday and that she was probably, at this very moment, cancelling plans that she had made for her day. But I also knew that she knew that I wouldn't ask if I were not in real trouble. I had been sick for about a month and despite my best efforts and those of my doctors I was only getting worse.

I was initially quite certain that the problem was with the pain pump implanted in my abdomen but now I was not even sure about that. I had a tremendous amount of agitation and those closest to me began to think that this was some sort of mental break. In response to their concerns I had started seeing a psychologist, who knew me well, again just in case they were right. He was convinced that I was fine and that this was something physical. All that was for certain was that I had been unable to take solid food for over two weeks and was living off the Ensure nutrition drinks that I forced down daily. I had a tremor and horrible sweats and had lost an easy 10 pounds off my 115 pound frame. I was a single mother of three kids and a business owner and a physician and I was unable to attend to any of the above. My youngest two children were being cared for to a large degree by their dad, also a physician. He was as perplexed as the rest as to what was wrong with me. My eldest, then 16, was left to fend for herself. I needed help. I knew I needed help but I didn't know where to turn and I was on the brink of no longer being able to care for even myself.

My Mom arrived the next day as promised to me trembling, sweating and weak. She spent the next two days talking to everyone that knew me well. And by the end of the second day I was certain that she had decided that it must be mental and she voiced her desire for me to enter into in-patient treatment. "Just until they know what is going on," she said to pacify me. All I knew was that I wanted to feel better and if that meant checking into a psyche hospital then that was fine, although my psychologist was still yelling no to that idea.

The very next day that my Mom went into my clinic to try to get things organized for my indeterminate absence. I had driven to my office but couldn't even face the idea of going in and so I sat for a long time in my car outside of my clinic and did nothing but think. It was suddenly clear to me what was going on. I called my pump doctor and made him re-calculate the doses of medications in my pain pump. Over the past several months we had needed to increase my pain medication and it suddenly dawned on me that there were two medications in my pump and that every time we increased the dose of one the dose of the other went up as well. I cried into the phone, out of frustration, out of joy, out of fear. I don't really know but it had suddenly occurred to me that I was toxic on a medication called Clonidine. I don't know why or how that came to me and I have often wondered if I were not a physician how long would it have taken to figure this out. I didn't have the strength to go into my clinic to tell my Mom that I thought that I had figured it out so I called her and told her to come out to me. She drove me to my pain doctor's clinic where they put a long needle into my pump and withdrew the medication and replaced it with a new mixture. It would be 16 hours before I would start to receive the new medications and would therefore continue on the toxic dose until then. To me, this felt like an eternity. I had done the calculations and I knew that it would be another 16 hours after that before the toxic doses would start to breakdown in my body and I would gradually and hopefully, start returning to normal.

And I did. And this was the problem. It took a full six weeks of nothing but Ensure before I ate my first solid meal. Friends and lover nursed me back to health and without them I am certain I would be in a locked unit by now. It is the same friends and lover that stood at my bedside in the Neuro ICU one year later as I battled an infection in my spinal column and a cerebral spinal fluid leak after having the pump removed from my body once and for all.

The pump was in my body for 6 years. It took me 4 years to come to grips with my fear of pain. And after I did, I struggled for another two years of repeated failed efforts to come off of the pump. Finally I came to accept the pump and just reconciled myself to the fact that I would always have this bulge in my abdomen and that I would for the rest of my life be dependent on it to protect me from the pain that I had become inconsolably afraid of. What I remember is this, one winter while faithfully watching the Detroit Red Wings make their way to a second Stanley Cup playoffs final round in a row, I was uncomfortable. I hurt more than usual and, on occasion, I felt "twitchy" and restless. I guess the playoffs were a good distraction because when I finally consulted my pain doctor with a concern that something was wrong with the pump again I was stupefied to learn that the catheter that delivered the medication to my spinal cord had become entirely crystallized. In other words, I was receiving no medication at all. I was off the pump.

My pain doctor's first words were, "I could probably clear the crystals through." "No, I shouted. Don't re-start it. I want it out." I was scared but I knew the hard part had already occurred. My opinion? This was God doing for me what I could not do for myself. If He was willing to do that much of it for me then I was brave enough to do the rest. And I did. I didn't anticipate the complications, but I guess it was only fitting that I said good bye to the pump, my protector with a bang. I am without a pump and I hurt often, but I am not afraid of it and it doesn't send me into a panic like it used to.

So today I stand before you, my story has been told. My daemons are out there for the world to see. The pump is no longer there to cover my pain, and funny thing is, my hair is about an inch long. Again, I am naked, bare, without cover, without camouflage. Vulnerable but true. Pure, plain and palpable. Earthy, raw, sensual and real. Scarred, marred, scratched, dented and perfectly imperfect.

And so I ask of you to do the same. Tell your story. To a trusted friend, to a mentor, to a pastor, to a priest…to me. I have talked critically at times about our over-connected world. But here is the truth…it is here and it is here to stay…our duty, our obligation, our province to use it for good. What if we could make it in to a divinely connected world? It starts with you telling your story to another and that person telling their story to yet another and the web begins to be spun…until one day…someone comes up to you and says, "Can I tell you my story?" It starts with a hand and a

**heart outstretched to another human being in love and acceptance
of their sovereignty as an individual. It starts with an appreciation
of the millions of rudimentary strokes in the painting that are each
imperfect but together create a masterpiece.**

I want to know your story: masteryourstory.com

Our lives affect "others" and our effect on "others" reverberates far
beyond the small part of the world that we inhabit. We have a *choice*
to touch the world with love. We have a *choice* to lift up or push down.
We have a responsibility to act as we would wish every person in the
entire world to act. Often we won't but it is okay to stop, step back and
try again. Responsibility to love *'as thyself'* and to *'do unto others...'* is
surely a load to bare unto itself, but it is not a load that we have to or
that we will bare perfectly. We will as members of the human race bare
it imperfectly.

We will never become and live to see it. We can only be becoming
until we are gone and our story has concluded. Our stories will be left
here for another to see. And will they be able to find meaning in it, in
the lives lived before theirs? I don't know. Each of us must find our
own meaning. Meaning is a powerful, personal and deep-down-inside
deal. I can't tell you what the meaning is for you and you cannot tell
me what the meaning is for me. What I can do, however, is tell you
where I have found meaning...

**I guess first and foremost and ultimately I found meaning in
Awe, in the Awe of the universe and the Ultimate Being that I
personally believe is responsible for it all. I would like to say that
"I know" that there is a something Bigger, but the truth is that
nobody knows that is why we call it faith. It is a belief in something
we cannot see. But to myself I know and it is not just because of the
blue and purple space that rescued me from pain. As I have grown
and matured I have explored all sorts of religions and theological
teachings. I have read most of the great philosophers and thinkers
and I have concluded that nobody knows. I can theorize all I want,**

and I love to click my brain into that existential gear, but nobody knows. What I do know is that nobody knows. It is a leap of faith, trusting in something we cannot see and touch. I believe that no one religion can work for everyone and I have grown quite intolerant of the "mine is right and yours is wrong mentality". My philosophy is just Believe. I think that religion will survive and endure but that it will evolve into something more personalized. For me, spirituality fits better than religion into what gives me meaning. It is a profoundly intimate, inner connection with everything and everybody. I think the 'everybody' part is the most important, but it doesn't come first. God comes first. First I have to believe utterly and then I must turn my will and my life over to the care of Him and then I have to get connected to Him each morning and I pray only for the knowledge of His will for me and the power to carry that out. This works for me and I think first and foremost spirituality has to do that…it has to be a spirituality, a belief, a God that works in each person's life. Each person is unique and so is the way that they experience spirituality. I think we are not sinners in a fellowship trying to get perfect but rather cracked, flawed, wounded beings that make up what we call the human race and are merely trying to heal…much as the sick try to get healthy.

I have had enough pain and suffering and seen enough pain and suffering to know that God comes in through the wound. And by this I don't mean that when things are bad that it is, then and only then, that we go looking for God. What I mean is that we are all wounded and imperfect and hurting in one way or another and we have an innate need to believe that there is some rhyme or reason to it all. For me the peace comes from accepting the mystery in life, from accepting that I cannot and will not ever understand the "why" of many things. I trust this Power, that I call God, to let me understand what He wants me to understand and to let me handle what He wants me to handle. As for all of the things that I do not understand, as for all of the "whys" that go unanswered, as for the unknowns that tomorrow will bring, all of that requires that "leap of faith", trust, acceptance, absolute belief that there is a God and I am not it and a conscious "letting go" in faith that "God has it".

I have to accept the fact that I will do all of this imperfectly and *that I have to re-new my efforts every day, sometimes every minute. Often I will let go of what I cannot control and feel a peace and serenity and then I will do the all-to-human thing and take it back and pretend that my fussing and worrying will somehow "fix" my angst and then I will let it go again in faith that "God has it" and low and behold the peace returns. I practice every day, not because practice makes perfect, but because practice is a process that I need to trust. I practice life and life is a process of learning and growing and teaching and growing, and I find peace and contentment only when I trust this process as opposed to trying to direct it. I expect of myself progress, not perfection.*

I give myself permission to be human and imperfect, accepting that I am powerless over much in this world, always careful to not use my humanness as an excuse for bad decisions. My humanness and imperfection and powerlessness is not an excuse. It is a reason. It is the reason I need God. It is the reason I need "others". Here on earth our needs are provided for largely through "others" and their needs are provided for by us. We need each other. Together we make a whole. A hand stretched out in love and support, to me, is God. A smile or pleasant patience in the check-out line can change someone's day and when that person has a good day they change the day for those around them and so on. Love is infectious, and that is God.

I remind myself daily that love is not a belief, love is something you do, love is a verb, an action word, not merely something one holds to be true. An act of love, whether it be companionship, sympathy, charity, compassion, empathy, sexual unity, a shared cause or a kind word or gesture, spreads and intercalates into the very fiber of our wholeness with each other and our Wholeness with each other and our Creator. The "Happy, joyous and free" that my father professed is indeed a lofty goal. It is not, however a goal that I attain by seeking it, but rather something I receive by giving. When I give love to this world, when I create a web of interconnectedness and spread love throughout it by reaching out to "others" and by giving my self to the passion of extending my hand in love and kindness the "happy, joyous and free" will come rest upon me as a precious gift. It is a priceless gift that must never be mistaken as mine to keep for myself. I must give it away in order to keep it. When I am "happy, joyous and free" I help "others" and when I help "others" I am "happy, joyous and free". "Happy, joyous and free" falls into that category of things that I cannot will. I can only open my self up to the idea of "happy, joyous and free" and I open my self up to "happy, joyous and free" by opening my self up to "others".

And full circle we have come… for I open my *self* up to "others" by telling my story. It is in telling my story that I find my *self* and I must first find my *self* and come to know my *self* if I am to share my *self* with you. Unless I find and come to know my *self* and share my *self* with "others", the "happy, joyous, and free", the kind of "happy, joyous and free" that one feels deep down in his soul, the kind of "happy, joyous and free" that remains regardless of the situation I find myself in, will remain remote. To receive I must give. I must give of my *self.* You give me a gift when you tell me your story and I give you a gift when I tell you mine. Likewise, you give me a gift when you listen to my story and I give you a gift when I listen to yours. We heal by telling, we learn by listening.

When we deny our stories we deny ourselves. And with this most tragic of all human mistakes comes Zerrissenheit, torn-to-pieces-hood, an inner hole, a sense of incompleteness, an existential vacuum, a noogenic neurosis, a sense of meaninglessness and emptiness, a woundedness, a not-quite-rightness…*a fisher king wound.* As each of us is born and matures we grow more and more separated from our mothers, for many of us, as life proceeds and the trails behind us get longer we become more and more separated from our Maker. At the bottom of our daemons, at the depths of our beings, in the abyss of our woundedness and at the wretched image of our imperfection is our God. He is personal, He is intimate and He cannot be given to us. He must be found. And find Him we will as we find there at our very core, at our spiritual core, a being that has been covered, masked, denied, smothered, disguised, concealed and hidden. As we uncover, de-mask and discover this being we find freedom, freedom to shed all that has shaped us before and freedom to repair our wreckage, freedom to address our shortcomings, freedom to connect with "others", freedom to share our fears and freedom to move forward making *choices* of our own, that we are responsible for and that will become part of the stories we are now writing. We find a being that is indeed free, free to have a conscience and values of his own, free to love and be loved and who is worthy of love and free to feel passion and to create a story like no other, a story that has never before been told.

Spirituality begins with doubt, it begins with the Unknown God and it begins with *choice*. Although the spiritual core may be present in each of us, we, as free beings, must first *choose* to trust in something Bigger than ourselves. We must *choose* to head out on the unchartered adventure of discovering the sacred in the events of our lives. We must *choose* to tell the unique stories of our lives thus far and to own those stories as part of the tapestry we have begun to weave. And as we share our stories with each other we realize that our tapestries are connected and woven together by the common thread of humanity. We learn that, that modest leap of faith and that trembling gesture to become honest, open and willing lands us in a community of "others" with experience, strength and hope that we can borrow when we have none. As we step forward in faith we come to accept, as Saint John of The Cross said, "If a man wishes to be sure of the road he treads on, he must close his eyes and walk in the dark." We will never know enough to be certain. We must *choose* to trust or not to trust. God either is or He isn't. One thing is, however, certain. The mystery of what tomorrow holds will always remain until it is no longer tomorrow but has become yesterday, part of our past... part of our story.

One last story...

I love it when my children say, "Mama tell us a story." And what my children mean is tell us a true story. They mean tell us when this happened or when that happened. One of their favorite stories, and one that I have told them a thousand times, is from when I was six years old and I had an accident that cut off my finger. Although they have heard it time and time again, they don't seem to ever tire of the little tale.

Not too long ago I had a friend from my childhood come to visit.

My children had never met her and it had been almost twenty years since I had last seen her. Her name is Marcia and she had heard that I lived in Tulsa. Like every 21ˢᵗ century would do, she had "Googled away" and found me.

She arrived with her 17 year old daughter and we spent the weekend catching up and telling stories of the years we had spent growing up together. We grew up in a little town in South Dakota and Marcia lived 5 houses down from me. We started kindergarten together and were rarely seen without one another. As we laughed and remembered and exchanged the typical, "Whatever happened to..." it dawned on me for the first time that Marcia had been the friend that I was playing with when I lost my finger.

When I made this little realization out loud my kids shrieked with excitement. "Tell us the story Marcia! Tell us the story of when my mom got her finger cut off."

Marcia obliged and I watched their faces light up with excitement and then contort as Marcia included every detail she could recall. They giggled and asked questions and said plenty of, "Eeeeewwwss".

I must say that even I, who was frankly quite sick of the 'same old story', enjoyed Marcia's rendition. I had not realized that I had never really heard the story through her eyes. As her story drew to an end my children said, "Tell it again. Tell it again." Even I, who had lived the story, wanted to hear more.

Through the weekend Marcia told that story again and again and again. Told through another's eyes it was novel and original.

Despite the fact that I had just spent a year writing over three hundred pages on storytelling, I was astounded at the power of the myth.

Now are you not wishing right now that I would tell you the story of when I cut my finger off? Next book.

But perhaps you now believe...as I do...

*"God created man because He loves stories."*³⁹

This is my story...this is our song...

Index:

A

abyss 17, 24, 94, 222, 249, 263
addict 14, 127, 128, 151
addiction 70, 78, 83, 86, 110, 111, 127, 128, 150, 151, 220
adulthood 62, 68, 71, 82, 87, 184
allow xii, 5, 21, 27, 45, 50, 56, 69, 70, 72, 107, 119, 123, 140, 144, 153, 160, 162, 164, 172, 184–187, 189, 193, 197, 207, 208, 212, 222, 228, 237, 241, 244, 252
aloneness 131, 173, 222, 236, 237
alonetime 167, 222
amends 107, 108, 112, 148, 149, 245, 246, 254
anger 51, 52, 54, 91, 126, 143, 144, 178, 184, 197, 237
answers 12, 13, 19, 75, 105, 117, 118, 229
anxiety 34, 66, 163, 185, 221
Aristotle 16, 124
arrow 96–100, 162
attachments 153
author 56, 92, 137, 185, 207, 208, 244, 251, 256
awe 76, 79, 86, 90, 122, 126, 169, 184, 214, 217, 260
awry 47, 48, 50, 51, 54, 57, 59, 61, 62, 64, 70, 75, 77, 86, 95, 117, 131, 139, 252, 254

B

baby 5, 12, 31, 39, 64, 77, 109, 113, 124, 130, 210, 257
becoming 38, 70, 75, 76, 90, 99, 106, 120, 132, 140, 142, 152, 157, 183, 196, 228, 229, 241, 250, 255, 256, 260
beings xiii, 17, 20, 26, 27, 35, 38, 45, 50, 52, 55, 56, 59, 62, 70, 75–77, 81, 82, 85, 90, 91, 96, 97, 101, 106–108, 117, 119, 120, 125, 131, 159, 162, 167, 170–172, 177, 181, 183–185, 187, 208, 212, 213, 217, 219, 222, 223, 225, 228, 237–239, 248, 249, 254, 261, 263, 264
  experience of 18
  rapture of 18, 106, 131, 132, 143, 156, 162, 188
  sensual 50, 208
  sexual 159, 181
  singular 106
beliefs 11, 20, 76, 119, 121, 132, 256
believing 15, 33, 51, 54, 123, 137, 140, 152, 156, 252
Bergson 217
Bhagavad Gita 118, 119
Blaise Pascal 122, 153
Blake 185
bodies 20, 54, 100, 147, 162–164, 169, 177, 187, 208, 209, 212, 217, 219, 221, 222, 254, 255
both/and 81–83, 85, 89, 91, 222
bottom 11, 19, 58, 84, 115, 117, 120, 125, 130, 131, 133, 139, 142, 159, 167, 178, 198, 238, 244, 249, 251, 254, 263
boundaries 62, 64, 172
breathe 12, 14, 66
bridge 117, 119, 131, 132, 139, 140, 151, 159, 177, 183, 188, 197, 199, 207, 211, 238
Brown, Norman O. 16, 17
buffalos 103, 104

Citations:

1   (Salmon, Staff writer, 2008)
2   (Brown, Life Against Death, 1959)
3   (Keen, Hymns to An Unknown
    God, 1994)
4   (Kurtz & Ketchm, 1992)
5   (Peck, The Road Less Traveled,
    1978)
6   (Keen, The Passionate Life, 1983,
    p. 86)
7   (Kingsley, 1987)
8   (Keen, The Passionate Life, 1983,
    p. 119)
9   (Keen, The Passionate Life, 1983,
    p. 138)
10 (Peck, The Road Less Traveled,
    1978, p. 15)
11 (Otto, 1923, p. 53)
12 (Kurtz & Ketchm, 1992, p. 20)
13 (Buber, 1947, p. 251)
14 (Taylor, Sources of Self, 1989, p.
    33)
15 (Frankyl, 2000)
16 (Taylor, Sources of Self, 1989, pp.
    18-19; Frankyl, 2000)
17 (McCain)
18 (Wikimedia Project)
19 (Otto, 1923)
20 (Kurtz & Ketchm, 1992, pp. 279-
    280)
21 (Aeschliman, 1988, pp. 91-98)
22 (Koilpillai, 1973)
23 (Wikimedia Project)
24 (Frankyl, 2000)
25 (Staples, 1994)
26 (Keen, Hymns to An Unknown
    God, 1994)
27 (Keen, Hymns to An Unknown
    God, 1994, p. 158)

28 (Keen, Hymns to An Unknown
    God, 1994, p. 177)
29 (Brown, Life Against Death, 1959,
    p. 312)
30 (Keen, The Passionate Life, 1983,
    p. 117)
31 (Keen, The Passionate Life, 1983,
    p. 117)
32 (Keen, Hymns to An Unknown
    God, 1994, p. 130)
33 (Keen, Hymns to An Unknown
    God, 1994)
34 (Wikimedia Project)
35 (Wikimedia Project)
36 (Village12)
37 (Frankyl, 2000)
38 (Frankyl, 2000)
39 (Wiesel, 1967)

Sources:

(n.d.).

Aeschliman, M. D. (1988). Discovering the Fall. *This World 23* , 91-98.

Alcoholics Anonymous. (1981). New York: Alcoholic Anonymous World Services.

Beattie, M. (1990). *The Language of Letting Go.* United States: Hazeldon Foundation.

Brown, N. O. (1959). *Life Against Death.* Middletown: Wesleyan University Press.

Brown, N. O. (1966). *Love's Body.* Los Angeles: University of California Press.

Buber, M. (1947). Tales of the Hasidim: The Early Masters. New York: Schocken Books.

Campbell, J. (2008). *The Hero With A Thousand Faces.* Novato: New World Library.

Campbell, J. (1991). *The Power of Myth.* New York: Anchor Books.

Cumming, R. (1965). *The Philosophy of Jean-Paul Sartre.* New York: Vintage Books.

De Montaigne, M. (2003). *Apology for Raymond Sebond.* Cambridge: Hackett Publishing Company.

Dictionary of Quotes. (1992). Merriam Webster.

Farber, L. (1976). *Lying, Despair, Jealousy,Envy, Sex, Suicide, Drugs and the Good Life.* New York: Pantheon Books.

Farber, L. (2000). *The Ways of The Will.* New York: Basic Books.

Fisher, R. (1990). *The Knight with Rusty Armor.* Hollywood: Melvin Powers Wilshire Publishing Group.

Frame, D. (1943). *The Complete Essays of Montaigne.* Stanford: Stanford Press.

Frankyl, V. (2000). *Mans Search for Meaning.* New York: Basic Books.

Freud, S. (1938). *Basic Writings of Sigmund Freud.* New York: The Modern Library.

Hegel, G. (2009). *The Philosophy of History.* Scotts Valley: IAP.

Hegel, G. (2009). *The philosophy opf history.* Scotts Valley: IAP.

Hong, H. a. (2000). *The Essential Kierkegaard*. Princeton: Princeton University Press.

James, W. (1987). *Writings 1902-1910*. New York: Literary Classics of the United States.

Kaufmann, W. (1954). *The Portable Nietzsche*. New York: Penguin Books.

Kaufmann, W. (1967). *The Will to Power*. New York: Vintage Books.

Keen, S. (1991). *Fire In The Belly*. New York: Bantam Books.

Keen, S. (1994). *Hymns to An Unknown God*. New York: Bantam Books.

Keen, S. (1994). *Hymns to An Unknown God*. New York: Bantam Books.

Keen, S. (1980). *Inward Bound*. New York: Bantam Books.

Keen, S. (1999). *Learning To Fly*. New York: Broadway Books.

Keen, S. (1983). *The Passionate Life*. New York: HarperCollins Publishers.

Keen, S. (1970). *To A Dancing God*. San Francisco: Harper and Row Publishers.

Keen, S. (1997). *To Love and Be Loved*. New York: Bantam Books.

(1962). In S. Kierkegaard, *Works of Love* (p. 153). New York: HarperPerrennial Modern Thought.

Kierkegaard, S. (2008). *Fear and Trembling*. Radford: Wilder Publications.

Kingsley, E. P. (1987). Welcome to Holland.

(1973). In J. C. Koilpillai, *The Power of Negative Thinking and Other Parables from India* (p. 63). Madras, India: Orient-Longman.

Kurtz, E., & Ketchm, K. (1992). *The Spirituality of Imperfection*. New York: Bantam Books.

Leibniz, G. W. (1991). *Discourse on Metaphysics and Other Essays*. Indianapolis: Hackett Publishing Company.

Leibniz, G. W. (1985). *Theodicy*. LaSalle: Open Court Publishing Company.

Martin, R. (1991). *Bullfinch's Mythology*. New York : HarperCollins Publishers.

McCain, E. (Composer). I'll Be. [R. McIntire, Performer] USA.

McCain, E. (Composer). (1998). I'll Be; Misguided Roses. [E. McCain, Performer]

McClellan, V. (1998). *Wise Words and Quotes*. Carol Stream: Tyndale House of Publishers.

McGuire, J. (1998). *The Power of Personal Storytelling*. New York: Penguin Putnam, Inc.

Nietzsche, F. (2005). *Thus Spoke Zarathustra*. Oxford: Oxford University Press.

Otto, R. (1923). *The Idea of Holy*. Oxford: Oxford University Press.

Pattakos, A. (2004). *Prisoners of Our Thoughts*. San Francisco: Berrett-Koehler Publishers.

Peck, S. (1998). *Further Along The Roadless Traveled*. New York: Touchstone.

Peck, S. (1978). *The Road Less Traveled*. New York: Simon and Schuster.

Prabhavananda, & Isherwood. (2002). *Bhagavad-Gita. The Song of God*. New York: New American Library.

Pratney, W. (1979). *The Thomas Factor*. Old Tappan: Chosen Books.

Priest, S. S.-P. (2001). *Basic writings*. New York: routledge.

Ries, A. (1986). *Marketing Warfare*. New York: McGraw Hill.

Salmon, J. L. (2008, June 24). Most Americans Believe in Higher Power. *Washington Post* .

Salmon, J. L. (2008, june 24). Staff writer. *Washington Post* , p. a02.

Sawyer, R. (1994). *The Art of War*. New York : Barnes and Noble Books.

Sawyer, R. (1970). *The Way of The Storyteller*. New York: Penguin Group.

Simmons, A. (2001). *The Story Factor*. New York: Basic Books.

Staples, B. (1994). The End Of Solitude. *New York Times* .

Taylor, C. (1975). *Hegel*. New York: Cambridge University Press.

Taylor, C. (1988). *Hegel and Modern Society*. New York: Cambridge University Press.

Taylor, C. (1989). *Sources of Self*. Cambridge: Harvard University Press.

Taylor, C. (1991). *The Ethics of Authenticity*. Cambridge: Harvard University Press.

Tolle, E. *The Power of Now*.

Village12, G. (n.d.). *www.scribd.com*. Retrieved October 2009, from http://www.scribd.com/doc/23479898/global-village12

Vogler, C. (2007). *The Writer's Journey*. Studio City: Michael Wiese Productions.

Waldron, R. (1999). *The Hound of Heaven at My Heels*. San Francisco: Ignatius Press.

Waldron, R. (1999). *The Hound of Heaven. Poetry as Prayer.* Boston: Pauline Books and Media.

Waller, R. (1988). *Old Songs In A New Cafe.* New York: Warner Books.

Wiesel, E. (1967). *The Gates of The Forest.* New York: Holt, Rinehart and Winston.

Wikimedia Project. (n.d.). Retrieved March 10, 2010, from wikipedia. org: http://creativecommons.org/licenses/by-sa/3.0/

Wolf, P., & Justman, S. (Composers). (1981). Rage in The Cage. [J. Geils, Performer]

Yogananda, P. (1995). *God Talks With Arjuna. The Bhagavad-Gita.* Los Angeles: Self Realization Fellowship.

About the Author

Leslie Masters is a physician, an entrepreneur and a single mother of three children, Sam 9, Georgia 11 and Olivia 17. She grew up in a small town in South Dakota and lives today in Tulsa, Oklahoma.

Dr. Masters received her undergraduate degree in General Science from the University of Iowa and her Medical Degree from the University of Minnesota. She went on to receive her post-graduate training in Pathology, Internal Medicine and Medical Oncology at the University of Arizona in Tucson, Arizona.

Today she works in the area of Cosmetic Medicine in Tulsa, Oklahoma where she owns and operates her own clinic-The Masters Clinic. Dr. Masters has been featured in the Tulsa World, Oklahoma Family Magazine and on numerous TV and radio shows. Although trained initially in the areas of Internal Medicine and Medical Oncology, Dr. Masters entered the world of Medical Aesthetics in 2005. Not long after beginning her work in the area of aesthetics, Dr. Masters noted a recurring theme. The vast majority of people seeking her help presented their goal as, "I just want to feel better." This trend provided the impetus for this book. Dr. Masters life experience took it from there.

In addition to writing her first book, Dr. Masters sends out a daily "Thought Of The Day" via text message and expands further on the TOTD on her daily blog--lesliemasters.com. Dr. Masters spends her "spare time" darting between football, soccer, cheer, voice and tumbling events. When asked what is the hardest thing she has ever done she smiles and says, "I became a parent."

Breinigsville, PA USA
23 August 2010
244111BV00003B/5/P